WALLACE

Not that I much blame Duffy. Duffy was face to face with that margin of mystery where all our calculations collapse, where the stream of time dwindles into the sands of eternity, where the formula fails in the test-tube, where chaos and old night hold sway and we hear the laughter in the ether dream. But he didn't know he was. . . .

–Robert Penn Warren
ALL THE KING'S MEN

WALLACE

Marshall Frady

Meridian Books
The World Publishing Company
NEW YORK AND CLEVELAND

A MERIDIAN BOOK

Published by The World Publishing Company
2231 West 110th Street, Cleveland, Ohio 44102
Published simultaneously in Canada by
Nelson, Foster & Scott Ltd.

First Meridian Printing—1970

Reprinted by arrangement with
The New American Library, Inc.

Library of Congress Catalog Card Number: 68-31468

PRINTED IN THE UNITED STATES OF AMERICA

WORLD PUBLISHING
TIMES MIRROR

ACKNOWLEDGMENTS

First of all, I want to acknowledge the substantial and indispensable assistance of Bob Cohn, Atlanta bureau chief for Southeastern Newspapers Inc., in the research for this book. His work included, but was not limited to, participation in over half of the interviews, the acquisition on his own of relevant newspaper files and other materials, and aid in making a number of strategic contacts. To him should go a significant share of the credit for whatever worthiness this book may have as an exercise in journalism—because he eminently deserves it.

In addition, I want to thank Ray Jenkins—editor of *The Alabama Journal,* a man of deep conscience and civilized perspectives who, with a kind of quiet and stubborn outrage, still perseveres in Alabama—for all his courtesies, both personal and professional, during our eight-month encampment in Montgomery.

I am also grateful for the gracious considerations extended by the Sea Pines Company at Hilton Head Island, S.C.—and by John Smith in particular—during our stay there for the actual writing of the book. It was, after Alabama, a benign and restorative place to be to get this project finished.

In a very special way, I am indebted to Joseph B. Cumming, Jr., Atlanta bureau chief for *Newsweek* Magazine, under whom I learned that the highest journalism is informed by the insights of the poet and the artist. That is the order of journalism to which he belongs: instinctively he brings, to the hectic combustions of events, a most delicate sense of the dynamics of life, the most exquisite perceptions, a Dickensian relish for character, and a grace and vitality of language that approaches magic. His spirit has presided over every page in this book. I hope it does not dishonor him.

Finally, I owe more than I could ever record here to my wife, Gloria: not only for her encouragement and sensitively tuned criticisms during the day-to-day labor on the manuscript, but for the immeasurable patience, calmness, sweetness, understanding, and elemental courage with which she bore all the unpleasantness that attended this enterprise. It was not easy for her. And if, in this generally grim story, there is anything good or kind or beautiful, it is a reflection of her.

FOREWORD

It was sometime back in the spring of 1966, when I was covering the Alabama governor's campaign for *Newsweek,* that it occurred to me George Wallace was worth a book as the palpable, breathing articulation into flesh of Willie Stark in Robert Penn Warren's *All the King's Men.* I had wanted to write it as a kind of journalistic novel, employing all the stagework, style, and larger vision of the novelist. Not only were the parallels with Stark myriad and giddying—an uncanny instance of life imitating art—but it also seemed to me that Flem Snopes had a lot to do with George Wallace.

After that, of course, he assumed a pertinency beyond that of an intriguing character from which to fashion a novel. When I undertook this project, the prospect that he would be a presidential candidate was still rather vague. But later, as this book was being finished, it seemed quite possible, albeit still somewhat surreal, that he might actually manage to pitch the election of the next President of the United States into the House of Representatives for the first time in 144 years—which conceivably could have placed him in the position of arbitrating who our next President would be, and in the process negotiating what certain strategic domestic policies would be. That did not materialize. But he came virtually out of nowhere to intrude himself into the most vital political process of this country, at one of the most perilous moments in this country's history. For some time now—perhaps since the assassination of John Kennedy—there has been the sense of a certain beserkness in the national life; in some subtle but fundamental way things seem to have become ungeared. It has been a long season of anarchic happenings and advents—a natural time for a happening like Wallace. Whatever, he has become a special phenomenon whose significance will probably surpass that of any other maverick political figure—William Jennings Bryan, Huey Long, Henry Wallace, Teddy Roosevelt during his Bull Moose gambit—in this country's history.

Unquestionably his candidacy for the Presidency in 1968 was a rough approximation of the potential for an American fascism—which would be a strictly indigenous and unique variety, ferociously decent, quite righteous and patriotic, myopically innocent, unrecognizable to a great number of people. The outcome of his campaign is not necessarily reassuring on this count. He accomplished the formidable feat of obtaining official status on the ballot of every state in the union, and it was only in the last weeks of the campaign that his vitality began to dissipate—and that largely for oblique reasons. At the least, he cast a certain chill on the adventurousness of the issues (it's hard to imagine, if there had not been a Wallace, the kind of issues and rhetoric that existed in 1968—however illusionary the debate of presidential campaigns may be—as well as Spiro Agnew as a vice-presidential candidate). As the campaign evolved, Nixon began to assimilate that part of his support which preferred a more conventionally respectable air in their spokesman. Also, Strom Thurmond, in the closest he has ever come to any possible national relevancy, managed to sabotage Wallace in some Southern States in exchange for certain polite gestures later on from the White House (equally hard to imagine, if there had not been a Wallace, is Thurmond appearing in the escort of a party convention's presidential nominee). In addition, working men outside the South were finally persuaded to regard Wallace with suspicion—a triumph of propaganda over reality, since Wallace, if nothing else, has always identified himself fundamentally with the frustrations and impulses of the blue-collar working man. Too, the heckling that attended his rallies became progressively more cunning, spectacularly disconcerting him on several occasions, and provided rhubarbs which hinted something of what the nature of his Presidency might be. But finally, there was the ponderous debacle of selecting General Curtis LeMay as his running mate—the General being about as politically graceful as a rhino in a game of ice hockey. Wallace's instinct, no doubt, was that LeMay would lend his wildcat campaign a degree of dignity and legitimacy (he has always been peculiarly vulnerable to persons of any consequence), but he made the uncanny mistake of associating himself with a Goldwater-like figure who had all of Goldwater's political liabilities but few of Goldwater's charms. Before long, it became obvious, particularly from Wallace's hasty and strenuous defensiveness on the subject, that LeMay afforded him profound uneasiness. And significantly, it was when LeMay was announced as his running mate that his showings in the polls began to falter dramatically.

Even at that, Wallace drew some ten million votes. Actually, although his expectations in the beginning were minimal the polls later exalted them somewhat, but he finished about as he had originally and privately calculated he would. It has long been the tradition in Alabama's higher politics to first run for an office as an introduction and dress rehearsal for the more serious and meaningful second campaign—this was the pattern of Wallace's own ascent to governor of the state. Perhaps even before election night in 1968, he began priming himself for 1972. Though local political moods do not necessarily carry into presidential elections, many have begun to wonder if certain mayoral elections in 1969—startling assertions of the Wallace mentality in such cities as Los Angeles and Minneapolis—were not intimations of what one might expect in 1972.

But whatever happens to Wallace in the years ahead, the effect he has already exerted on the political life of this country has been considerable. Aside from the fact he was more or less the ghost writer for many of the issues in 1968, the dishevelment in our electoral procedures that was posed by his candidacy may accomplish, in the end, the elimination of the electoral college system. If this electoral reversal enhances the import of additional parties, it will serve to vitalize even more his American Independent Party. Most importantly, though, Wallace almost single-handedly alerted the national custodians to a massive, unsuspected, unanswered constituency, a great submerged continent of discontent; Wallace was an occurrence that social seismologists and journalists and politicians will be gauging for a long time to come.

But the man himself is the reason for this book. Oddly enough, he has remained, in the popular mind essentially a garish caricature, as flat and depthless as a figure scissored from tinfoil. Part of the reason for this is that simply as a man, apart from his political existence, Wallace is curiously substanceless. What one briefly glimpses of him on television is really all that he is every day of his life, from waking to sleeping. He is the complete democratic demagogue, the political creature carried to the ultimate—fascinating as are all pure specimens of a kind. And while this book is basically a tale of the methodical, relentless, and inexorable progression of a political Snopes, with a dauntless, limitless, and almost innocent rapacity, to the threshold of our most important political office, perhaps it also describes, in the form of Wallace, something of the nature of The Demagogue.

In a sense, Wallace is common to us all. That, finally, is his darkest portent. There is something primordially exciting and enthralling about him, and there still seems to be just enough of the wolf pack in most of us to be stirred by it and to answer to it. As long as we are creatures hung halfway between the mud and the stars, figures like Wallace can be said to pose the great dark original threat.

Marshall Frady
Atlanta, Georgia
August, 1969

Part One

On a cold, rain-flicked night in 1967 a rickety twin-engine Convair 240 began a blind and uncertain descent through low clouds, abruptly breaking out over the scattered watery lights of Concord, New Hampshire. It came in headlong, less by instruments and calculation than with a precipitous lurching optimism.

A damp huddle of greeters was waiting in the dark, and they waggled dime-store Confederate flags when he emerged from the plane—a stumpy little man with heavy black eyebrows and bright black darting eyes and a puglike bulb of a nose who looked as if he might have stepped out of an eighteenth-century London street scene by Hogarth. Wrapped in a black raincoat, he bobbed spryly down the steps as flashbulbs stammered in the rain. Someone held an umbrella over his head while he said a few words to the newsmen. Asked if he were offended because no local officials were there to welcome him, he answered jauntily, "Naw"—his voice rising just a bit—"Naw, 'cause it's the workin' folks all over this country who're gettin' fed up and are gonna turn this country around, and a whole heap of politicians are gonna get run over when they do." With that, he was bundled into a car at the head of the waiting cavalcade, and, with a swift surge, everyone—he, his entourage, the reporters, his local supporters—vanished into the night. One had the peculiar fleeting impression that a squad of commandos or guerrillas, irregulars at any rate, had just landed in the dark and was now loose in the New England countryside.

At a press conference that evening in a crammed smoke-hazed motel room on the outskirts of Concord, he seemed—peering over a thicket of microphones that came up almost to his chin, perspiring and a little haggard in the harsh glare of television lights—an improbable apparition. His baggy dark suit was buttoned tightly over his paunch, with a tab-collar shirt hugging the bulky knot of an inexpensive tie. His breast pocket was bulging with plastic-tip White Owl cigars and scraps of paper on which were scribbled random notes, addresses, telephone numbers. He looked somewhat like a traveling novelty salesman. But what this chunky little man was occupied with, what had brought him out of the night from distant Alabama all the way to this New Hampshire motel room, was the election of the next President of the United States—an event now only a year away. He carefully affected, out of deference to this unfamiliar assembly, a subdued and amiable manner, with much congenial winking, and his grammar and enunciation were studiously precise, faintly stilted. (On the flight up, he had mused, "Them New Hampshire folks, you know, they a little more restrained and genteel than Alabama folks. They gotten kind of overbred up there.") At one point, he announced, "Well, I'm mighty happy to be among all you very intelligent-lookin' folks." But later, when he interrupted a woman reporter, "What's that, honey? Could you say that again? I don't hear too good," turning his head with his hand cupped behind his ear so that he had to look at her out of the corner of his eye, he seemed solemnly impervious to the ripple of titters in the room.

Morning revealed a landscape that had the tidy miniature quality of a model train set, with a trivial city skyline under washed drab skies. It was alien country. Though the month was April, the weather was wintry—not his kind of weather—as if the South and North described not so much regions as perpetual weathers, summerland and winterland. Syracuse, into which he had ventured the week before, had had a profoundly remote look about it, cold and wan under bare bleak trees, with junkyards, power lines, and oil tanks set out in wide weedy fields and cement trucks moving through a rubble of construction. All the towns in the North where he was appearing seemed generations older than those in Alabama, and over Concord's streets there was a kind of static quiescence, a worn and antique quality. When he spoke that afternoon in the square downtown, he was regarded from the capitol lawn by an incredulously scowling statue of Daniel Webster, and his grits-and-gravy voice blared down a main street that was a turn-of-the-century tintype of stark brick buildings crested with Yankee brass eagles.

But it could have been a rally on a musky spring afternoon in Suggsville, Alabama. His finger stabbing downward, his eyes crackling, the microphone ringing under the impetuous barrage of his voice, he barked, "If one of these two national parties don't wake up and get *straight,* well, I can promise that you and me, we gonna stir something up all over this country. . . ." Afterward he greeted people along the sidewalks with an instant, easy intimacy: "Honey, I 'preciate yawl comin' on out here today in this cold, heunh? Tell yo folks hello for me, heunh?" When a small girl suddenly kissed him square on the mouth, he looked around him for a moment—at all the pleasant faces, at the moil of reporters, at the candy-green capitol lawn, the thin exquisite sunshine, the vast benign blue sky—and grinned almost blissfully.

Driving on to Dartmouth later for an evening speech, through Devil-and-Daniel Webster country—weathervanes atop white wooden farmhouses, stone fences and apple orchards, birches and dark cedars sheltering small secret ponds the color of graphite—he removed his wetly chewed cigar to remark, "This sho does look like North Alabama, don't it?"

He found the thought cheering. "Yes, sir," he murmured happily, "you go up there around Gurley, New Hope, Grays Chapel—country up there looks just like this," and he leaned back in his seat and returned his cigar to his mouth, satisfied.

Two hours later, after nightfall, over the still, shadowed campus at Dartmouth, there pulsed a dull, steady roar from the auditorium where he was speaking. Scattered groups of students were hurrying toward the sound under the dark trees, but people were already milling under the windows and around the front steps. Inside, students were standing along the walls and sitting on windowsills and in the aisles, and the noise they were making was like a single continuous howl existing independent and disembodied above their open mouths. On the stage, while a student tried to read questions submitted by the audience, he paced restlessly, exhilarated by the violence heavy in the air. Occasionally he spat into his handkerchief and then plunged it back into his hip pocket. When he pounced to the microphone to answer a question, it was as if he were deliberately lobbing incendiary pronouncements into the crowd. He would crouch, looking up, his left arm gripping the lectern and his right swinging and whipping with pointed finger, as if he were furiously cranking himself up: "I'm not against dissent now, but I believe anybody that stands up like this professor in New Jersey and says they *long* for a victory by the Vietcong over the American imperialist troops, and anybody that goes out raising *bluhd* and *money* for the Vietcong against American servicemen, they oughtta be drug by the hair of their heads before a grand jury and indicted for *treason,* 'cause that's what they guilty of, and I promise you if I—" And then he would step back and spit into his handkerchief again, shooting it back into his hip pocket as the roar rose around him.

At one point there was a charge by students down the center aisle, led by a young professor with fine-spun hair and a freshly scrubbed cherubic complexion—but his mild face was now flushed, his tie askew, his eyes manic and glaring as he tried to flail his way through campus police and plainclothesmen, bellowing with a crack in his voice, "Get out of here! Get out of here! You are an outrage!" That berserk charge—anarchic and hopeless, an abandonment of fairness, proprieties, all civilized approaches, a retreat to simple brute action—testified not only to despair and fury over the fact that this man could be speaking there at all, but to a sinking of the heart over the absurdly serious import of that figure's audacious aspirations, a dread that something sinister and implacable was afoot in the land. As he was hustled offstage during the short melee, he glanced quickly back over his shoulder at the furor with a curious, bemused, almost awed expression.

Outside, after his speech, his car was engulfed. White and Negro students kicked the fenders and hammered on the hood, and one policeman was hauled back into the maw of the crowd and disappeared into it, his crumpled cap reappearing a moment later in the hand of a student, who waved it high in the air in triumph. And it seemed as if he, too, this stubby little man, might be on the point of vanishing, consumed whole by the kind of popular violence he so savors. As the crowd seethed around his car, there were glimpses of him sitting in the back seat, his face not worried, but just empty whenever the reeling TV lights washed over it, huddling behind the rolled-up windows with his cigar, all of him as small and still and inert as a rabbit in a burrow while hounds swirl and bay in the grass around it. The car began to ease forward, slowly nosing through the mob—he still not moving, looking to neither the right nor the left—and then, rapidly, it was gone.

At the least, he is a simple primitive natural phenomenon, like weeds or heat-lightning. He is a mixture of innocence and malevolence, humor and horror. "He's simply more alive than all the others," declared a woman reporter after the Dartmouth fray. "These professors like Galbraith, Schlesinger, the politicians and bureaucrats in Washington—God knows, I've been around all of them, and they don't really know what's going on. You saw those people in that auditorium while he was speaking—you saw their eyes. He made those people feel something *real* for once in their lives. You can't help but respond to him. Me—my heart was pounding, I couldn't take my eyes off him, there were all those people screaming. You almost *love* him, though you know what a little gremlin he actually is."

Many still find it hard to regard George Corley Wallace as anything other than merely the most resourceful, durable, and unabashed of the Southern segregationist governors. But the fact is, he passed that point long ago, and has intruded himself now into the history of the nation. He has become, at the least, a dark poltergeist whose capacity for mischief in the land is formidable. The havoc he has intimated in the procedure of electing the next President of the United States has already raised substantial doubts about the system: he has materialized as the grim joker in the deck. More soberingly, the significance of his candidacy invokes certain questions about the basic health of the American society, both at this time and in the future.

To many he portends the eventual arrival of a final racist psychology into American politics. It seems certain that his candidacy can only increase the racial alienation in the country. A moderate Alabama politician declares, "What he's trying to do in the nation is what he's managed to do in Alabama. When you draw the line the way he does, the whites go with the white, and the blacks with the black, and when that happens, you're in for warfare." A former Alabama senator echoes, "It's conceivable that he could win a state like Illinois or even California when he puts the hay down where the goats can get at it. He can use all the other issues—law and order, running your own schools, protecting property rights—and never mention race. But people will know he's telling them, 'A nigger's trying to get your job, trying to move into your neighborhood.' What Wallace is doing is talking to them in a kind of shorthand, a kind of code."

At the same time, despite his public protestations that he is only an Alabama segregationist, what Wallace has been encountering in the violent demonstrations that have greeted him as he has junketed over the nation has been the same instinct he venerates in cabdrivers and dirt-farmers, "that tells you when you can trust somebody and when you can't." If a Birmingham steelworker or a country barber in Marengo County "knew Castro was a Commie just by instinct," so do Negroes and most liberals know "by instinct, just by looking at him and hearing him talk," that Wallace is a racist. Segregation is necessarily predicated on racism, and it doesn't have to be of the malevolent variety—it can be Wallace's kind of faint amicable contempt. Racism, fundamentally, is the persuasion that there is an innate, generic, permanent difference between the races in all the traits that describe humanity. Actually, Wallace himself once confided to a reporter in the lobby of a Cleveland hotel, removing his cigar for a moment to whisper behind his hand, "Let 'em call me a racist. It don't make any difference. Whole heap of folks in this country feel the same way I do. Race is what's gonna win this thing for me."

The simple prospect that his candidacy could impinge upon the system to the extent of throwing the presidential election into the House of Representatives (with giddy swiftness the outrageous becomes the possible and then the probable) can only make more acute the cornered mentality among America's disenchanted and estranged. "By God," muttered a young liberal after one of Wallace's campus appearances, "this could be the time. Just because all the others have missed before—the Know-Nothings, Joe McCarthy, Goldwater—that doesn't mean they'll keep on missing. This could be it. He might be the one with the right combination." The desperate outbursts of violence that attend his wanderings about the country leave one with the uneasy feeling that alienations, not only racial but also intellectual, have reached the point in our society where the potential for revolution is more palpable than ever before.

Actually, Wallace could be only one reflection of a general shattering of the American society, a disintegration into fragments. The American mystics—such as Norman Mailer—are unintelligible to the sturdy American Boy Scouts like Ronald Reagan and Billy Graham. Lyndon Johnson could never understand Timothy Leary or Allen Ginsberg. Stokely Carmichael could never understand Roger Blough. The efficacy of dialogue seems to be waning, and with it a sense of the American community. It's like a new Tower of Babel. Nothing seems to mean anything anymore except action. For Wallace, talk is finally not for the purpose of communication, explanation, or persuasion, but just another form of action: rhetoric. Action is all. The unsettling thing about his candidacy now is that it will tend to reduce America's disaffected, those who view him as an omen of a wider mentality, to a reliance on the same brute processes.

In this sense, Wallace represents the dark side of the moon of the American democracy—the tradition of direct popular violent action in community crises. He belongs fundamentally to the vigilante ethic, with certain apocalyptic overtones, and the potential in any social crisis for violent confrontation and climax enthralls him. One autumn evening in 1966, driving back to a Birmingham hotel after a shopping-center rally, he sat in the back seat of his car, gesturing in the glare of headlights behind him. "Nigguh comes up to a white woman down here like they do up North, tryin' all that stuff, he's gonna get shot. Yessuh. Or get his head busted. That's why we don't have any of that business down here.They know what's gonna happen to 'em. They start a riot down here, first one of 'em to pick up a brick gets a bullet in the brain, that's all. And then you walk over to the next one and say, 'All right, pick up a brick. We just want to see you pick up one of them bricks, now!' Let 'em see you shoot down a few of 'em, and you got it stopped. Bob McNair, guvnuh over there in South Carolina, he's one of them *nice* fellas, you know, he don't go for that kinda talk—like Carl Sanders over there in Georgia. Now, I like Carl, I don't know whether he likes me particularly or not, but I got nothing against him. But he's one of those nice fellas wantin' to moderate everything. But, of course, he found out you can't do that. Like ole Ivan Allen over there. Knocked him offa that car, you know, those rioters, when he was tryin' to talk to them. They oughtta done more than that. Hell, we got too much dignity in government now, what we need is some *meanness*. You elect one of those steelworkers guvnuh, you talk about a revolution—damn, there'd be shootin' and tearin' down and burnin' up and killin' and bloodlettin' sho *nuff*. Steelworker wouldn't have to think about it—he'd just go ahead and do it. Anyway, I been tellin' folks for years, you ask if I hadn't, that there'd be fightin' in the streets one day between rightists and leftists, between whites and blacks. Hell, all we'd have to do right now is march on the federal courthouse there in Montgomery, take over the post office and lock up a few of those judges, and by sunset there'd be a revolution from one corner of this nation to the other. We could turn this country right around."

It has become Wallace's conviction—more than conviction, visceral sensation—that he exists as the very incarnation of the "folks," the embodiment of the will and sensibilities and discontents of the people in the roadside diners and all-night chili cafés, the cabdrivers and waitresses and plant workers, as well as a certain harried Prufrock population of dingy-collared department-store clerks and insurance salesmen and neighborhood grocers: the great silent American Folk which have never been politically numbered as the Wallace candidacy promises to number them. His candidacy poses questions about what illusions we may have been under about the American public. There's no doubt he has sensed a subterranean political consciousness congenial to him. In *The Earl of Louisiana,* A. J. Liebling suggests that "if Hoover by some disastrous miracle had been reelected in 1932, Huey [Long] might within two years have crystallized around himself all the discontent, rational and irrational, in the country. . . ." In this time, if there is an ominous conspiracy underway in the United States, it would be the silent massive *suspicion* of a conspiracy which threatens home, job, status, the accustomed order of life. And Wallace's variation of Long's coalition of frustration is a "fusion" of the working man with the large industrialists and tycoons of Mid-America. "We got part of it already," he declares; "we got the workin' man, and now we're gonna get the other part of it—the high hoi-polloi. They gonna come around, you wait." Indeed, when he has appeared before large groups of industrialists, the receptions have been robust. At a patio party recently in New Orleans' French Quarter, an oil millionaire from Dallas allowed, "I'd vote for him in a minute, and give him all the money I could, if I just felt I could trust him—if he wouldn't wind up getting tamed by Washington like Lester Maddox over there in Georgia. I'm a Republican, but I'd love to support him, and every one of my friends—oilmen, fellows in wheat—feel the same way."

Nevertheless, the man himself seems hopelessly implausible as a national political figure. For one thing, he looks on the entire world as merely an extension of Barbour County, Alabama, where he grew up—full of chillun and folks, some of them liars and cheats and no-counts, most of them decent people minding their own business, whose interests are simple and who are polite to each other, but with a certain measure of orneriness and villainy going on, the best answers to which are Barbour County's kind of commonsense solutions. In an age of freeways and high-rise apartments, he seems a whimsical anachronism: his are essentially village sensibilities.

More than anything else, he is a consummate political and

cultural articulation of the South, where life is simply more glandular than it is in the rest of the nation. Southerners tend to belong and believe through blood and weather and common earth and common enemy and common travail, rather than belonging, believing, cerebrally. The tribal instinct is what they answer to. That is part of the reason why the most recent incarnations of the Boston Abolitionists—those gaunt, tense, electric youths from the snows of the North and the seasonless hothouse clime of California who, lank hair falling over ethereal faces, ventured into Negro neighborhoods in Alabama and Mississippi—were not only incomprehensible but also faintly repulsive to most Southerners. They were tinged with the perversion of having subjected life to ideas. Any politician like Eugene McCarthy, with his diaphanous abstractions, would be impossible in the South. The region is ruled by humid passion, and a fine old-fashioned sense of sin. There is a lingering romance of violence, a congenital love for quick and final physical showdowns. Not just the filling-station attendants, the cabdrivers and deputy sheriffs and beauticians and tabernacle evangelists, but also Rotarians, bankers, teachers, the urbanites of Atlanta and Charlotte, stockbrokers and reporters who have moved away to the cities of the North—virtually all those born in the South have about them, to a certain degree, that air of an immediate and casual familiarity with violence, a quality of loosely leashed readiness for mayhem. Even those Southerners who come from large cities—although, say, having martinis in some expensive New York restaurant, surrounded by Continental waiters and chandeliers—seem to have emerged from another dimension where the days are fevered and dreaming with honeysuckle and wisteria, from a different and more passionate play of life, a slow, sensuous, easy, lyrical, savage marriage of man and earth. They carry with them the sense of another landscape—primeval mountains, scruffy pine hills populated with mules and moonshiners, cottonland as level and limitless as the sea, fierce skies—a land where winters are only a dull and sullen hiatus with a pale ghost of the sun passing through vague chill rains.

Wallace is a direct product of this society where things—be they theories or institutions or political machines—do not count for so much as passion and people. Accordingly, he operates outside the conventional political wisdom. There has been an almost childlike naïveté about the way he has undertaken to run for President. One afternoon shortly after his wife's election as governor, he sat in his office and calculated, almost as an afterthought, the financial strategy for his whole national campaign, scribbling on the back of a memo pad with his ball-point pen: "Let's see, we got better'n $380,000 when we went into three states back in '64, three goes into fifty about seventeen times—don't it?—yes, and seventeen times $380,000 that oughtta be—that's $6,460,000. That oughtta be enough." In fact, he seems to regard formal political organization with a vague contempt, as a sign of political effeteness, an absence of vitality—as if he is already naturally blessed with what political organization exists to create. His simple directness is, at once, part of his absurdity and part of his genius.

"Power comes from the people," he declares, "and if my health holds up, I'm gonna change things in this country. Anyway, I don't have a single thing to lose, and everything to gain." Indeed, there is surrounding him an uncanny aura of limitless possibility, of adventure, of incredible prospects—a feeling that anything is possible. The sheer hope, the happy half-reckless presumption of his candidacy for the highest office in the land, gives one the sense that the demonic is still at work in human affairs, even in this age of computers and slide rules and pundits and public-relations task forces: that life and politics, after all, are simply larger than arithmetic. Accordingly, his candidacy is a reminder that anything, including the unthinkable, can happen in a democracy. In the same way that he went into the 1964 Northern presidential primaries in touch with potentials that no one else seemed to be in touch with, he has proceeded this time from absolutely nothing—not precedent, rumor, or normal political equations, polls, press, or the patronage of the American establishment—but merely from his own clear sense and vision of the democratic possibilities for himself. For him to have aspired seriously to the presidency right now, in this age—or even to have expected to figure importantly in the election—has required more originality, audacity, optimism, and dauntlessness than has ever been required of any other significant presidential candidate in this nation's history, including Huey Long.

In the final analysis, whatever becomes of him in the months ahead, it seems probable that George Wallace will be recorded as the greatest of the American demagogues—the classic of his species. That is true not only because of the magnitude of the rapport he has already invoked in the country (television having enlarged the stump to the size of the continent), but because of his own nature as a politician and a human being. He is really more elemental than Huey Long; it is quite beyond him, for instance, to take a case of whiskey up to the top floor of a hotel and come back down six weeks later with *Every Man a King*. He doesn't think about it all enough to write a book about it. He is more essential than that. Abstractions do not really exist for him. "He doesn't ever talk about purposes, causes, destinies, anything like that," says one Alabama politician. "He differs from every other politician I've ever known in that respect." Wallace himself cheerfully allows, "Naw, we don't stop and figger, we don't think about history or theories or none of that. We just go ahead. Hell, history can take care of itself." In this rude sense, he is the most existential politician in the country today. He seems empty of any private philosophy or persuasions reached in solitude and stillness. He is made up, in mind and sensibilities, of the clatter and chatter and gusting impulses of the marketplace, the town square, the barbershop. His morality is the morality of the majority. "The majority of the folks aren't gonna want to do anything that ain't right," he insists. He is the ultimate product of the democratic system.

Not only are abstract ethics alien to him, but he entertains a particular antipathy to people who live and act from them. It's something like the Dionysian principle applied to politics. "Hell, intellectuals, when they've gotten into power, have made some of the bloodiest tyrants man has ever seen," he maintains. "These here liberals and intellectual morons, they don't believe in nothing but themselves and their theories. They don't have any faith in people. Lot of 'em don't really *like* people, when you get right down to it." (His own vision of man is the old vision—man is perpetually embattled on this earth, his state fixed and imperfectible, composed of natural wickedness and natural virtue in a balance that can never really be altered, poverty and grief and injustice and conflict irrevocable parts of his lot. "Life's basically a fight," declares Wallace. "People have to go out and make a livin', have to fight snow and cold and heat and natural disasters. People enjoy fightin'. That's the way folks are. . . ." Accordingly, he operates on the most elemental assumptions about the nature of the human species, such as: "Nigguhs hate whites, and whites hate nigguhs. Everybody knows that deep down.")

His political mystique of "the common folks" reduces everyone to a simple and almost biological common denominator. While standing at the edge of a crowd waiting to speak at a 1966 rally, he declared to reporters, "When the liberals and intellectuals say the people don't have any sense, they talkin' about *us* people—they talkin' about the people here. But hell, you can get good solid information from a man drivin' a truck, you don't need to go to no college professor. The fella on the street has got a better mind and instincts than these here sissy-britches intellectual morons, like the editor of *The Birmingham News,* for instance. He's just one man, that's all he is. You take this fella here—" Without taking his eyes from the reporters, he reached out at random and pulled over an elderly man, dressed in coveralls and an old army field jacket, with a light frosting of beard on his cheeks. "—this fella here, he's one man too, just like the editor of *The Birmingham News.* He weighs just as much as the editor of *The Birmingham News*—" The man listened with a mute, bashful pleasure and an awkward little grin while Wallace held on to his elbow. "—he's got eyes and ears and a mouth just like the editor of *The Birmingham News.* He's got a mind, too—fact, he's got a better mind. And the editor of *The Birmingham News* has got just one vote, like this fella here. So who is the editor of *The Birmingham News?* Folks like this fella here know just by instinct, just by havin' lived with folks, more'n all the newspaper editors and professors up yonder at Harvard will ever know. Any truck driver'd know right off what to do at the scene of an accident, but you take a college professor, he'd just stand around lookin', with his hands in his pockets and gettin' sick."

As a private person, Wallace himself is curiously vague and weightless. He seems only marginally and incidentally aware of home and family, food and friends, the gentle comforts that bless the lives of ordinary men. One of his oldest associates declares, "Whenever he comes over here to eat, he's just not conscious of anything except the people around him. He knows where the ketchup and the milk are, but that's all. Because he's only here to keep on talking to somebody. He never knows what he's eating because he's too busy talking—it could be filet mignon he's eating, it could be hamburger, it could be the end of his tie, he don't know. Just that whatever it is, he wants to put ketchup on it."

Neither does money interest him. His one luxurious indulgence, reports a Montgomery businessman, "is having his fingers manicured downtown at the Exchange Hotel Barber Shop by Edna Taylor." What money arrangements have been necessary in past campaigns have been quietly attended to by aides, out of his sight, out of his knowledge. Finance, high or low, leaves him wretchedly bored anyway; as one observer has noted, it would seem he never got beyond decimals.

He seems to exist in a constant state of energy and ebullience that never vanishes altogether but simply flares and pales. It's as if, at the instant in his childhood when he comprehended what he was going to do, time simply ceased for him, and he began to exist in the same tense charged moment —the absolute fact of his destiny, a condition of will that was quite outside time.

"He don't have no hobbies," declares an old crony from Wallace's hometown. "He don't do any honest work. He don't drink. He ain't got but one serious appetite, and that's votes." It is the recollection of one official in Wallace's home county that since 1947 there has been only one election in which Wallace's name was not on the ballot for something. When he was a small child, remembers his grandmother, "He couldn't bear to see anything thrown away. His grandfather would drop a piece of paper in the wastebasket, and he would fetch it right back out and say, 'Well, Grandpa, this is *some* good. . . .' " And it's as if he is still collecting scraps from his grandfather's wastebasket, as if he were born with a compulsive, indiscriminate acquisitiveness. Shaking hands in a Birmingham shopping center during the 1966 governor's race, he paused in the midst of the crowd before one man, holding onto his hand, and inquired earnestly, "Yes, now, and how is Faye? Now, she was in St. Vincent's, wasn't she? I meant to write her a letter—" He released the man for a moment and plunged both hands into his coat pockets, bringing up two thick fistfuls of business cards and folded envelopes, dog-eared, a bit soiled, covered with scribbles; he shuffled furiously through them, intent and absorbed, oblivious now of the crowd and everything else around him, until he found a vacant space on the back of one relatively fresh envelope on which he promptly scribbled yet another name and address, swiftly returning both handfuls to his coat pockets and seizing the man's hand again. "Now, you tell her we gonna write her, heunh?" A lady from his hometown recalls, "I kept after him to see a friend of mine who was in the hospital, and he'd whine and grumble, 'You know, I just hate to go anywhere nowadays, so many people want to shake my hand.' But he finally agreed, and when we walked into the hospital room, a nurse made the mistake of telling him, 'Some people down the hall would like to say hello to you, Governor.' He looked at her real bright and quick and said, 'Oh, yeah? Say there are?' Before I knew it, he was right back out the door, running up and down that hall shaking hands with patients, some of them people flat on their backs who could hardly talk and probably wouldn't even live until election time." He has a way of showing up, unannounced and solemn and reverential, at funerals in remote places all over the state, slipping discreetly into a back pew of the church, and later at the graveside, after the burial, shaking hands, a commiserating singsong in his voice, with the family and friends of the deceased and the minister and the mortuary officials.

His voraciousness lends to everyone, indiscriminately, a certain dearness—invokes in him an automatic compassion and solicitude. "He don't even like for us to talk about his enemies," says one of his aides. "He'll hear you cussin' out some no-good sonuvabitch that everybody agrees is no good, and he'll say, 'Now, you wrong about that fella, he's a good ole boy, you ought not to talk about him that way.'" It's something like a miser's fanatic abhorrence of waste, and it extends even to Negro voters. During one of his campaigns he told a group of Negro educators in a secret meeting on a Negro campus, "Now, when I get out here speakin' to folks, don't pay any attention to what I say, 'cause I'm gonna have to fuss at yawl a little. But I don't mean any of it." And during the 1966 campaign, as he was riding to an afternoon rally, a newsman in the car with him mentioned that one Alabama Negro leader had suggested privately that if Wallace would only give some small sign of amicability, make some token gesture, it was still possible that the Negroes in the state could gather behind him. Even though it was already obvious that Wallace would obliterate his Republican opponent, this piece of news caused him to snatch his cigar out of his mouth and peer sharply at the newsman: "Said they could, eh? 'Cose, they realize I couldn't be meetin' with them in public or anything like that. But, uh—what kinda sign you reckon they'd want?"

In turn, it seems impossible for him to believe that anyone could just simply and naturally not like him. "It bothers him no end to think anybody living is against him," declares one of his old associates. "He'll hear about somebody didn't vote for him, he'll worry over that fella, think about him, more'n he will his friends. He finds out you aren't with him on something, he takes that to mean you're against him altogether. He'll sometimes call you around eleven at night and wheedle, wheedle, argue, argue." When finally reduced to accept the mysterious finality of someone's hostility, he and his people attribute it to some psychological defect in the person, to some peculiar and esoteric long-smoldering grudge, or to simple mental affliction—it's a sad sign that the individual concerned has deserted the company of normal and decent folks, has forsaken the human race.

It was about 1964 that his passion began to embrace the entire nation. When he places long-distance calls, he is given to chatting with the operator first: "Honey, this is George Wallace—uh, guv'n'Alabama—yes, well, you know I've gotten a lot of support from you communications workers. I want to thank yawl, you folks been mighty good to me. You know, when I was up there in Wisconsin—" talking on until the operator finally, gently, suggests that perhaps she should put his call on through. "Well, thank you, honey. Now, you tell yo family hello for me, heunh?" Trying once to reach a political contact in Denver, he was connected by mistake with an anonymous bar somewhere in the outer reaches of Colorado, and he immediately engaged the bartender in a long and cozy conversation. An old but now disaffected comrade says, "You sit in his office, and he's sifting through his mail all the time—you know, scooping it up with both hands, letting it spill through his fingers back on the desk, over and over again. He'll pick up one letter, right in the middle of a conversation about something else, and say, 'Look ahere, here's a letter I got all the way from I-dee-ho. . . .' "

In Alabama Wallace has managed to pass the point of being just the most popular politician in the memory of the state. He has become a Folk Hero. Alabama, along with the rest of the South, has been changing into something more like the rest of the nation, and in the process, a particular devastation is being worked among its people. In his transition from the gentle earth to the city—the filling stations, the power lines, the merciless asphalt, the neon Jumboburger drive-ins—the Southern yeoman has acquired a quality of metallic ferocity. At the same time, the central fact about the South continues to be its defeat in the Civil War. There lingers a kind of mortal irreconcilability, an incapacity to forget—embarking on a kind of folk crusade a century ago, throwing everything into it, making a total commitment of honor and valor and hope and pride, it could not afford to lose: but it did. The malaise of spirit that disaster left behind has not been dispelled by the South's transmogrification into an imitation of the North, and has only been deepened by its recent ten years of racial anguish. What Wallace has done in Alabama is assume the legacy of defeat, the burden of his state's embarrassment before the rest of the nation, its lurking sense of guilt and pettiness, dread and futility. "They think he's the greatest thing that's ever come along," snorts one Alabama judge. "He keeps tellin' 'em, 'You the children of Israel, you gonna lead this country out of the wilderness!' Well, goddamn. We at the bottom of everything you can find to be at the bottom of, and yet we gonna save the country. We lead the country in illiteracy and syphilis, and yet we gonna lead the damn country out of the wilderness. . . ."

"I don't have no inferiority complex about runnin' for President," Wallace announced in town squares all over Alabama during his wife's campaign for governor. "I want you to know, when I go to the guvnuhs' conferences, I don't sit on the third row or the fourth row or even the second row. I sit on the front row, because I represent just as good and refined and cultured people as anybody else there. They talk like you and me hadn't got enough sense to turn around. They say you voted ignorantly when you voted for me four years ago. But I want to let yawl in on a little secret. These here national politicians like Humphrey and Johnson and Nixon, they don't hang their britches on the wall and then do a flyin' jump into 'em every mornin', they put 'em on one britches leg at a time, just like the folks here in Chilton County. Earl Warren on the Supreme Court, he's one of them big Republicans, and he's done more against you'n'me than anybody else in this country. He hadn't got enough brains in his whole head to try a chicken thief in Chilton County. I promise you, we gonna stir sump'n up all over this country, from Maine to California. We not powerful personally, it's all you good people here in Chilton County. Why, when you go to Lima-Peru or Berlin-Germany or Geneva-Switzerland or even"—one waits, suspended, to see if it will come, and it does— "Paris-France, they've all heard about Alabama. This is the first time in yo history so many big politicos been worried about us. They say we gonna hurt 'em, and I'll tell you sump'n: I *wanta* hurt 'em, 'cause they've hurt us long enough, and I'm tired of it. The Republicans now, they havin' to meet in banks tryin' to figger out what they gonna do about us down here. I'm not talkin' about the good banks of Chilton County or Alabama, I'm talking about the Chase National and the Wall Street crowd. You know, they used to meet in little biddy banks to talk about us, but this time, we got 'em meetin' in the *biggest bank in the world* talkin' about you'n'me and what they gonna do about Guvnuh Wallace down here in Alabama. . . ."

The fact is, the rest of the nation has probably never been quite so real to Alabamians as it is right now. His forays into the North and the West, answering what most Alabamians had come to consider a sudden inexplicable conspiracy by the nation to torment them after leaving them in peace for nearly one hundred years, have caused them to rediscover America. There is an almost palpable sense of excitement and national involvement abroad in the state, even if it tends to be edged with belligerence. This has been one of Wallace's accidental gifts to his people; he has, in this sense, enlarged their lives. Former governor John Patterson allows, "When Wallace was elected governor, the people in Alabama didn't know the difference between a preferential primary and the real thing. What he's done is educate 'em." One of Wallace's old boxing coaches asked a pair of newsmen: "Now, okay, I wish you'd answer a question for me. He's running for President here. Everybody says he's got to win something. Now, exactly, how can it happen? I mean, I'd really like to know." It's the same kind of wonder and dazed titillation the Hebrews probably felt on the shore of the Red Sea just after they learned it was going to open for them and then engulf their enemies. In cities and towns all over Alabama, people in restaurants during lunch hour are counting electoral votes, neglecting their desserts to make urgent calculations on wet napkins with ballpoint pens. One of Wallace's aides admits, "All these little farmhouses stuck way out in the woods, they all got a TV set now, you know. When those folks see Wallace on there standin' up to these big-city slick-hair boys, that's not just *him* talkin'. That's *them* on there. . . ."

In turn, Wallace's own identification with "the folks" is almost sensuous, almost mystic. They are his only reality. He feels that without them he is nothing, and with them he is everything and cannot be intimidated. In fact, what makes Wallace the ultimate demagogue is that, behind his indefatigable scrambling, his ferocious concentration, his inexhaustible ambition, there seems to lurk a secret, desperate suspicion that facing him, aside from and beyond his political existence, is nothingness—an empty, terrible white blank. It's as if, when the time finally arrives for him to cease to be a politician, he will simply cease to be. His terror of being alienated from "the folks" is like the terror of not being able to breathe. Probably the most traumatic period of his life was the interval between the Alabama Senate's startling refusal to permit him to succeed himself (late fall, 1965) and the spring primary that nominated his wife. The state Senate's blunt defiance was the first serious political repudiation he had suffered since becoming governor, and through the long winter of doubt that followed, there was a vast silence from the people—a silence in which there occurred repeated little ominous intimations that he might be falling, might indeed have already fallen. The worst part of it was, he couldn't really know—there was no final way to find out until the spring primary.

That harrowing winter even affected him physically. Seen lunching one February afternoon in the state capitol's bleak basement cafeteria, he had the look of a small rodent that was slowly starving: the skin over his cheekbones and narrow forehead was taut, glazed, and yellowish, his ink-black hair was combed back long and thin and scraggly to the nape of his neck, there were hollows behind his ears like empty sockets, and in his eyes was a ragged despair. He waited fretfully for the others at the table to finish eating, tearing off shreds of paper napkin with his gnawed rusty fingers and wadding them into tiny moist pills which he arrayed along the rim of his plate. He kept working almost viciously at his teeth with a toothpick, his lips curled back in an unconscious snarl.

But when, in the spring, the decision was finally made to run his wife, he seemed restored, whole, even peaceful again. In a packed café one afternoon shortly after the start of the campaign, after exchanging hugs and kisses and ardent double-fisted handshakes—oddly suggestive of secret fraternity grips—with the sun-scorched ginghamed and khakied folk filing past his table, he turned back to his plate and speculated with some glee, savagely hammering out ketchup onto his hamburger with the heel of his hand, about what "those Anglo-Saxons" in the several counties in which Negroes were running for sheriff would do to any Negro who might be elected. "The Black Panthers talkin' all the time about rev-o-lu-tion if one of their boys wins. A nigguh sheriff—the folks over there just ain't gonna stand for any kind of stuff such as that. When those Anglo-Saxon people get stirred up, boy, they don't mess around. Wouldn't one of them nigguhs last thirty minutes if he was to have the misfortune of gettin' elected." He went on to express the hope that John Doar, frequent Justice Department emissary into Alabama, would be shot between the eyes before too very long. Later, after his hamburger and buttermilk, as he stood outside in his shirt-sleeves in the warm May sunshine waiting for his wife to finish her short introductory speech, he seemed possessed of the high vivid exhilaration of someone who had just emerged from a long and dangerous illness.

Lurleen won the spring primary dizzyingly, drawing more votes than her nine opponents combined. The general election campaign began in the late fall, and though Lurleen technically was the candidate, it was more like a long celebration by Wallace of the reaffirmation of his existence. As one veteran Alabama reporter has noted, "He's never quite so alive as when he's out on the road again running for something. Each time, it's like his own little personal Easter."

The last week of that campaign began in soft October weather. The mornings were fine and bright and watery, just warm enough to produce a light dew of sweat on the upper lip. In the exhausted drab little towns where most of the rallies were held, the crowd would be gathered in a parking lot beside a brick store with a dimming inscription:

LEHMAN FURN. CO.
WARM MORNING HEATER
Drink
Royal Crown
Cola

and the hillbilly band on the flatbed trailer—pale youths, luxuriously coiffured, wearing twinkly, sequined black-and-gold suits with gold valentines running up their pants legs from black boots—would still be conjuring people out of the countryside with the lickety-split, devilish fiddle music, sawing them on out of the stores: farmers, filling-station workers, slippered women with their hair pinched up in curlers. The band would alternate spry gospel music with abject love ballads—forlorn, inconsolable, stricken, yelping, tragic, full of death, loss, violence, insanity, tears, night—which, with the arrival of the Wallace cars, would abruptly switch to rapid wheedling music while a large bell, carried from rally to rally in the back of a truck, would begin clangoring.

Wallace, in his faintly iridescent beetle-black suit, spurted out of his car, coming up on the first handshake with a slight dip, bending his knees, and then swooping upward, a flourish of body jazz, and then moved along the edge of the throng while the band kept playing, he fidgeting with his cuffs and scuffing at the pavement with the toes of his shoes, like a fighter shuffling about in his corner before the opening gong. While Lurleen spoke, he huddled with the local candidates behind the platform, and people passing behind him gave him light pats on the shoulder, which he accepted, not even turning around. (At one stop, a small pack of young razorbacks stood near him and loudly observed, "He's a rough-lookin' little devil, ain't he?" Wallace went over to them and, grinning, shook hands all around. "Glad to see you fellas out here today, heunh? Yawl doin' all right?")

When Lurleen stepped back to a spatter of applause, he would skip snappily up on the platform, take off his three-vent coat, and briskly roll up his shirtsleeves, once, twice, leaving bulky cuffs high on his biceps. Behind the microphone, his hipwork was fancy, vigorous, and vaguely obscene, with one blunt little paw constantly stroking the microphone stand: "These unidentified flyin' objects people are seein' outta airplane windows, they not flyin' saucers, they these intellectual morons and national politicians havin' runnin' humanitarian fits about my wife's candidacy down here. . . ."

(Lurleen's principal function in the campaign, besides her brief overture speeches, was to supply Wallace with a clipping or magazine from the pack she kept in her lap whenever he thrust his hand toward her— "See here, they got a picture of yo guvnuh in this magazine that goes all over this nation"— he flourishing the item and then swiftly returning it to her as he went on, she placing it back neatly in the battered packet in her lap and getting the next clipping ready and then sitting primly with her hands folded over it as she waited.) "The national press now, anything's that bad about yo guvnuh, oh yes, they gonna run that. But anything good— why, you know, one national magazine had an article by a lady out in California during one of the guvnuhs' conferences, called us Dogpatch folks down here 'cause of the way we dressed. Well, I want to tell you something, the woman that wrote that article, I wisht you had seen what *she* was wearin'." Jubilant whoops from the crowd. "The *Life* magazine—yeah, I think they out here with us today, and the *Newsweek* and the *Time,* they all here—they wrote an article criticizin' my wife for not goin' to the guvnuhs' meetings when we were out there in California. Well, of course, she wasn't guvnuh then, and they had a program for the guvnuhs' wives and they had conferences for the guvnuhs. But for the benefit of the *Life* magazine—and there's some of 'em with us today—I just want to say that next year, after she's elected guvnuh, she'll go to the guvnuhs' conferences, and I'll go out with the guvnuhs' wives." There was another roar of guffaws, and one old-timer chortled to his friend, "Damn little rascal, he would too. He'd cut up a time with 'em."

His addresses everywhere were extended monologues rather than speeches, a hectic one-man argument without any real beginning, progression, or end. He added to and took from his sack of notions sparingly, line by line. The total effect was like that of an orchestra perpetually tuning up—a cacophony of peeves and exasperations. His points were scattershot, his climaxes came hurly-burly. At one stop, in the middle of his address, he was abruptly silenced by the deafening hoot and clatter of a freight train barging interminably past behind him, and he finally adlibbed in a loud voice, "I'm glad to see our railroad folks go by, 'cause they've endorsed my wife too, and I hope we can always keep them runnin'. Yessuh." He manages to exploit any interruption, assimilate any distraction.

His head tilting to one side, one hand plunged in his pants pocket and the other chopping and stabbing the air, his hips pumping and scooping furiously, he told the crowds, "You get a bayonet in yo back with the national Democrats, and you get a bayonet in yo back with the national Republicans. This Richard Milhouse 'Tricky Dick' Nixon, he hadn't got the sense of a Chilton County mule. He comes down here to talk about Alabama politics like it was some kind of his business. Sure, I went over to Mississippi to make a speech awhile back, but it was just a philosophy speech over there at the state fair. But I'll tell you, if I had said as much and done as much against the state of Mississippi as 'Tricky Dick' Nixon has said and done against the state of Alabama, I wouldn't have the brass to go within a *hunnert* miles of Mississippi, I'd just go around it or over it or something. And this Romney, singin' all those songs about overcomin' evuhthing—and Bobby Kennedy: he's the one that wants to give blood to the Communists all the time. Now, he's gone to South Africa tellin' them what to do in South Africa. Maybe he'll stay there this time. And now they wantin' to transfer yo chillun ten miles over in another county so they can conduct *social experiments* on 'em. And if you get a book sayin' Robert E. Lee was a good man, and the Confederate flag was a symbol of honor, they can put in books sayin' Robert E. Lee was a bad, vulgar man, and the Confederate flag was a symbol of dishonor. But I'll tell you, the mommas and poppas all over this country are mighty mad about them movin' their little chillun around like this. Emanuel Celler, he called yo guvnuh a devil, but then he found out they were gonna transfer his chillun too all the way across New York City, so now he's sayin' he's gonna have to look into all this guideline mess. But I tell you, if they don't all wake up, I'm gonna go all over this country tellin' those folks in Washington, 'You better mind about our chillun. You triflin' with our chillun now, and you better watch out.' . . ."

Afterward, he would lean from the platform to shake the hands of the people filing past below him—when there was a gap in the line, his hand would grope about in the air until someone stepped up to take it. Finally, stepping down from the platform and submerging himself in the crowd, he would keep a tight clasp on someone—sometimes two at once—as he turned to talk to still another over his shoulder, and in pursuit of unshaken hands he would sometimes drag people along with him, through shrubbery and rain puddles, as if reluctant to release them until he had fastened himself to the next hand. There would slowly come over the faces of the people caught in Wallace's grasp the expression of faintly amused embarrassment. At times he would unexpectedly break through the crowd into empty space, and propelled by sheer momentum, walk in aimless circles, trailed by his bodyguards, until he found the edge of the throng again, pulling himself back into their midst with double-handed clutches, his face fixed in a cozy little nose-wrinkling, teeth-gritting grin of gratification: "Yes, yes, I know yo uncle, he works down at H. L. Green's. Tell him hello for us, heunh? He sho is our friend. I saw yawl up the road, I believe, I sho 'preciate yawl bein' with us today, heunh? I 'preciate yawl's suppote, you know Hollis Jackson died. Honey, thank you very much, heunh? Glad to see you—yes, how is yo daughter now? Well, you tell her I been thinkin' about her. Hi, sweetie pie, honey, thank you. Yes, you know, I still miss Mr. Roy. I heard, I understand she was goin' to the junior high. 'Cose, her daddy got killed, you know. I sho will. I be glad to shake hands with her. She in the car? Yeah, all right, I'll be over there in a minute. . . ." He seemed somehow to be caressing, fondling, stroking, kneading the masses between his hands, and he would sometimes draw an out-of-state reporter close to him and inquire, sotto voce, "How you like these Alabama folks, hunh? They all right, ain't they?" and bob off without waiting for an answer. At several places he was approached by local young businessmen who asked him with poignant anxiety if it were possible to bring a factory of some kind into their community—a desperation to be found in every town in Alabama, no matter how small. Wallace would rub his hands together and tell them, "Now, you just keep tryin', and you know it'll all come about," and the young men would nod—"Yes. Well, thank you, Guvnuh. Anything you could do would be appreciated"—and wander away, somewhat dispirited. But Wallace was obviously buoyant when making his way through the crowds. He would pluck fistfuls of black snap-on Wallace ties from the hawkers and distribute them himself. "Here, here you go. Here's you one. And you, too."

Inevitably there would be a flock of elderly ladies sitting in plastic lawn chairs or cane-bottom rockers under a tree or on the courthouse porch, patiently waiting for him, and when he finally approached them, they would all chorus, reaching for him with heavy wattled arms, "Good ole boy. We all pray for you. . . ." "Sleep tight, honey, you gonna make it. . . ." "I love you. I just love you. . . ." "I always said, if I ever caught you, I was gonna hug yo neck. . . ." "God bless you. You're God's man for us. . . ." As the crowd began thinning away, he would bounce on back to his car—a suggestion in his spry, ebullient haste of a schoolboy skipping and hopping—sometimes stopping to smooth out a drooping Wallace sticker on a car bumper, personally tidying up, sprucing up, putting the finishing touches on a good situation. Before leaving, though, his party would usually have to wait a few minutes while he retreated to a men's room. Finding one for Wallace—or, as his bodyguards put it, "giving him a chance to do what he wants to do"—was an unusually persistent problem all through the campaign, coming up virtually at every stop. At one gathering in a community Democratic headquarters, Wallace, while ecstatically shaking hands all around, began standing briefly on his tiptoes to glance furtively over the tops of partitions in the room, and finally, after an urgent hurried conference outside between the bodyguards and some local party officials, Wallace was conducted to the rear of a closed filling station next door.

Eating seemed to him a tedious distraction, an interruption best gotten out of the way fast in order to return to more interesting matters. When his party stopped at a school cafeteria for lunch, Wallace shook hands all the way to the feed counter. After he had settled himself at a table with his tray, a teacher came over and stood beside him for a full fifteen minutes confiding to him such pieces of news as, "Fifteen boys the other day broke into a farmhouse over yonder and tore things up pretty bad. We caught 'em and got it straightened out now. There was one colored boy with 'em." It was like a local village elder making a report to a touring tribal chief. Wallace listened, grasping a huge glass of tea with his stubby fingers and taking quick little sips, pushing food on his fork with a roll, looking up at the man only when he turned to leave, lunging to give him a fleeting pat on the back. "Well, awfully good to see you again, heunh? Tell yo folks hello for me." He managed to keep his mouth full for the duration of the meal, despite frequent pauses to turn and shake the hands of passing students. "Yes, yes, yawl in the ginnin' business, I know yo folks. You tell Charlie hello for me, heunh?" Once he turned automatically, his hand already in midair, only to discover three young Negro girls passing him with their trays, their faces serenely averted as they floated on past him. He quickly returned his attention to his plate without so much as a blink.

Toward the middle of the week the weather turned abruptly cold, and there was a flavor of woodsmoke in the November afternoons. Finally, one night, it snowed. The next morning the air was lyrically icy. Entering the little town of New Hope, Wallace's cavalcade pulled up behind a cotton gin, with a cold wind shivering puddles of melted snow beneath wagonloads of cotton, and smoke blowing through the bare pecan trees overhead. The band now looked a bit frozen and bleak in their sequins, but they were gamely whunking on for the crowd. At the edges of the gathering stood the inevitable old men, their faces and necks like those of turkeys, standing mute and alone, isolated even from each other, hands shoved deep in their coveralls, khaki shirts buttoned up all the way to their Adam's apples, their old mouse-gray felt hats yanked low over their eyes. Wallace and his bodyguards were now wearing overcoats, and Wallace spoke with his coat collar turned up against the wind. Later, down in the crowd, he would pause among the hands to dab his lips swiftly with Chapstick.

Back in his car, he put on dark glasses and lighted an oversized cigar as the party pulled away. He looked, huddling against the door, as diminutive as a dwarf; he had, indeed, something of a dwarf's quick, nimble, nervous alacrity, as well as that peculiar suggestion of danger: undersized, stumpy, brisk, he inevitably strikes one as vaguely dangerous, or at least as one secretly and suspiciously busy, in a room full of women taller than he. Yet, despite his size, he seemed in this small enclosure pent and cramped. After just coming from the crowd, where his presence dominated all the out-of-doors, his energy and urgency overwhelmed everyone riding with him now. Looking out the window, he mused, "New Hope, Alabama. Yessuh, I carried New Hope in 1962. . . ." And he recited the voting figures from New Hope in the 1958 and 1962 races for governor. There seems to be at work inside him some swift tabulation, as if, in privacy, whenever he stopped talking to remove or to receive his cigar, there might escape from inside him, briefly, a smooth, furious clicking and jingling, like an office full of adding machines all going at once.

As the car plunged on along a country road, Wallace observed, "This is some of the prettiest land you ever saw, ain't it? You know, we just about in Tennessee up here." Wallace asked someone about a local family—"They got a farm over there in the holler, don't they?"—and as the car grew steadily warmer, he began rummaging up other names, families: "Now, Bladon's wife, her name was Lila Mann, you know. There's all those Manns. . . . And Dewey, Dewey's still around, ain't he? He had that heart attack not long ago, you know." It seemed he had converted the entire state into his personal neighborhood, that every community was as familiar and intimate to him as his own flesh. Noticing an accident at an intersection ahead of them, Wallace abruptly broke off his monologue, snapped up straight in the seat, and peered at the scene through his dark glasses, turning his head as the car carried him past it, as if he had homed in on it with radar. "You reckon they all right?" he demanded. "Duhdn't anybody look hurt, do they? Reckon we oughtta stop? Reckon they called an ambulance yet?" He was reassured that things already seemed to be well in hand, and he leaned back in the seat and reinserted his cigar in his mouth. Then, going through a small town, he noticed a Negro in a pickup truck immediately behind. He turned in the crowded seat to wave out the back window, muttering, "Hi. Hi, there, fella." The Negro's face behind the truck's windshield looked down on him with a stolid impassivity. Wallace redoubled the vigor of his waves. "He must not recognize me," he explained. His men, with some uneasiness, began talking about something else. Wallace ignored them, though, even when they tried to fetch him away from the back window with cheerful calls, "Ain't that right, guvnuh?" He kept twisting around for another flurry of waves, in deep and remote concentration now. "He don't see me, see?" he murmured, more to himself than to anyone else, his face meanwhile grimacing in faintly grotesque expressions of amiability. At last, as the car turned a corner and lost the truck, he faced front again and declared in triumph, "You see that? He saluted, just at the last minute."

Now he began reminiscing about his expeditions into the North during 1963 and 1964. "Hell, some of these places, they was breakin' glass and knockin' heads and I don't know what all." He smiled slyly. "The police up there, you know, they hate those pickets—they'd wade into them with those big nightsticks of theirs, and you could hear heads cracking all over the place. Actually, a professor, I'm tellin' you, came out and tried to let the air outta our tires. That's right. The sheriff up there kicked him straight up in the air, said, 'What the *hell* do you think you're doin'?' Yessuh. Kicked him six feet straight up in the air. One place we went to, the professors were all wearin' black armbands. Goddamn, idn't that silly? I went in this room full of professors, and every one of 'em had on a black armband. I just stood there a minute and looked around and said, 'Who died?' Yeah, I looked around. 'Somebody die around here? Hunh? Who dead? Somebody dead?' " The car filled with laughter, but Wallace remained deadpan. "Up there on them Northern campuses, they just don't seem to have any manners. I don't know what's wrong with them up there. Damn uncultured, ignorant intellectuals."

He fell to talking about his opponent, Republican James Martin, a former congressman. "He gets up there, he sounds like a senator, you know. He sounds just like a nigguh preacher or senator. He gets up there and starts out, 'Naaoww, brethrenn. Ah—' " Here, Wallace sat forward in the seat, pulled back his coat, puffed out his chest, and delivered himself of a few deep mimicking phrases, his right hand, still holding the cigar, making scooping motions like an opera singer ladling out notes. His companions were guffawing, but his face remained solemn. He did it again. "Yeah, he sounds like that. Kind of pompous, you know. Well, you can't have that insincere ring, you got to talk to the folks. Martin oughtta run for senator, he sounds so much like one. But that's the way he is. He goes to church every Sunday. I go to church too, but I always slip in the back of the pew so nobody'll notice. But Martin, do you know he'll walk slap down there to the front row every Sunday morning? That's right. He's like Strom Thurmond. They got to heckling him one time when he was speaking to a Yankee audience, and he stood up there and"—his voice sank to a deep stentorian bray —" 'Well, I'm a U-nited States senatuh, Ah don't have to take such as this,' got all huffy and walked off, you know. That just don't get it." He sank back, crossed his legs cozily, and took a few rapid chugs on his cigar as he gazed for a moment out the window at the snow. Abruptly he observed, "Look at that snow. Lots of it, ain't there? You know what ole Jim Folsom said, 'It's all them atom bums.' " Guffaws erupted around him again, but Wallace only smiled, continued gazing out the window, and kept teasing the line, a favorite habit of his. "Yeah, all them atom *bums*. Big Jim said it was all them atom *bums* goin' off everywhere causin' the funny weather. Yeah. Atom *bums*." He leaned back, smiling, comfortable, tasting the end of his cigar, still looking out the window. Then, abruptly, he said, "Yeah, I don't believe in usin' religion in my campaigns like he does." In conversation he is given to making sudden blind swerves which set off hectic mental scrambles in his listeners to reassemble, reinvoke the context to which he has already secretly, by himself, returned. One thinks, "Like *he* does. He. Oh. Oh, yes. Martin. He has picked up after Martin walks slap down to the front of the church every Sunday morning. . . ." It's as if he keeps several themes running simultaneously, because one alone would be inadequate to his energies and concentration. He is like a ringmaster reclining serenely in the middle of the rapt attention of trained animals, watching, with a kind of remote lazy relish, the furious, desperate, scurrying adjustment that breaks out around him each time he blows a different whistle. "They all the time tryin' to get me to preach a lay sermon in pulpits over the state. But I don't believe in usin' no pulpit. I mean, I don't believe in anybody gettin' up there in a pulpit unless they an ordained preacher. I mean, we all got our faults. We all weak, you know."

All the while, he was keeping an ever-vigilant eye out for

Wallace stickers, frequently interrupting his monologue to murmur happily, "Lookathere, there's one." Finally he leaned forward, placing his hands together on the back of the front seat, to notify one of his aides, "We oughtta got better glue. The glue wasn't too good on our stickers this year, I seen a lot of 'em kind of hangin' off. Don't know what the matter is. 'Course, these nigguhs been tearin' a lot of 'em off at the car washes, they tell me."

As they approached the town of the next rally, the driver informed Wallace, "About twenty minutes early, Guvnuh." Wallace mumbled through his cigar, "Well, we don't want to be gettin' down there no twenty minutes early, it wouldn't look right. Just drive around town a little bit, let's look at the folks here."

When they finally began heading for the rally, Wallace, as usual, started fretting about what the size of the crowd was likely to be, inventing an exhaustive and ingenious variety of reasons why it wouldn't be large. He worried about the cold—to him, the deadliest enemy of political rallies, North or South. When someone in the car offered, "A lot of people came out here to hear you last spring in the rain," he snapped, "That don't mean anything. It was warm, a warm rain. A little summer rain on their shirtsleeves, that's all right. But folks don't like much to come out in cold like this." When the site came into view—a spot on the edge of town, along the highway—Wallace lunged forward, thrusting his head alongside that of his aide in the front seat, his forehead actually bumping the window. "Yeah, there's some folks," he declared. "I see some folks." And leaving his wetly chewed cigar in the ashtray, he scrambled out into music, excitement, extended hands.

When the last rally of the day was finished, there would emerge among the Wallace party, Lurleen excepted, a private holiday air, a festival or party exuberance, a spirit of happy release, with jubilant calls and the energetic slamming of car doors filling the dusk. Wallace would usually take aside whatever reporter happened still to be on hand and inquire one last time, his voice low and almost conspiratorial, "Well, what you think? We gonna get any votes up here?"

Among the last to leave all of Wallace's rallies were two women—a young girl, dowdily dressed, with pale skin and bad teeth and a cringing twangy voice and moist mournful woebegone eyes, and her mother, a smaller and more sprightly woman who nevertheless had the same air of besieged endurance. The two of them were entertainers of a sort. In summers, they packed their belongings into an ancient black Cadillac and journeyed down to Miami Beach, where they played a succession of dumpy little hotels, the daughter manning an organ and the mother briskly accompanying her on a set of drums. "We play *Dixie* real good and loud and clear for those Yank-kees down there," the daughter likes to declare, with the shy brave pride of a Salvation Army maid reporting on her missionary efforts with a cornet outside a corner saloon. Now free-lance members of Wallace's entourage, they peddled campaign records on the fringe of the crowd at each stop, holding samples high in the air and soundlessly waggling them to catch people's attention—having not a lot of success, since most people were facing the other way. But they showed up at each rally, that shattered expression in their eyes, smiling abjectly, with an air of having gamely and even gaily borne unspeakable suffering, which they could never for a moment be able to describe or forget, but which they would not allow to get them down, either—that embattled but plucky air which women have when left, the last functioning survivors of their family, with nothing in this world to rely on but each other. At the end of each rally, Wallace would call to them before he got into his car, as if it were the first time he had noticed they had joined him, "Mighty glad to see yawl out here with us today, heunh?"

Toward the close of the campaign, a day was spent in the state's largest city, Birmingham. It is, in Alabama, the closest thing to alien turf for Wallace, not only because of its relative sophistication, but because the Republican party is particularly robust there. "You know, I ain't really their type here," Wallace remarked, driving into town. "They got a lot of genteel folks here." But the first rallies that morning were held in a fairly congenial section of the city: the mill villages, with their close streets of little brick and frame houses ranked endlessly under pecan and chinaberry trees, where one passes 1949 Dodge coupes with rubber buzzards dangling from the rear-view mirrors or plastic figurines of Jesus set on the dashboards. At each stop that morning there were unusually large delegations of minor politicians on hand, and they collected around Wallace like a cloud of pilot fish.

Around noon, driving to a Birmingham hotel, Wallace declared as the car passed a bank, "We stopped in there for a minute this morning, and all the girls in there were for us. Real genteel girls. You could tell they was college girls, you know. You have to have a college education to work in a bank. Yeah, they were for us." He then mused, "My grandmother lives here, gonna be celebrating her ninety-ninth birthday tomorrow." Someone in the car suggested he visit her with photographers for the occasion, but he dismissed that: "It'd look like I was using her politically, to campaign with. A fella just can't use his ninety-nine-year-old grandmother. . . ." He paused. "Can he?"

At the hotel he led a charge down winding marble steps to the men's room, his cigar in his hand, and then went back upstairs, pausing only a moment to refire his cigar, to the sunny dining room, where a waitress greeted him cordially with one quick grind of the twist, which Wallace, just barely, just perceptibly under his suit coat, reciprocated. When he was seated, the waitress told him he could quit his newspaper ads, he was already too far ahead for anything to happen to him. Tickled, he grabbed her hand by the fingertips and gave it a fond little shake. "Honey, you say we don't need to run 'em anymore?" He looked at the other people at the table expectantly, in delight. "Say we don't need any more ads, hunh? Say we already got it?" He finally released her hand when she began to take the order. She recommended tapioca pudding for dessert, and Wallace inquired, "Tapioca—now what would that be like?" She told him what was in it, and he said, "Well, honey, I think I'll just have me a little bowl of banana pudding." When she left, Wallace informed the people at his table, "You know, her daughter was in an automobile accident not long ago up on the mountain. It killed her dead." Toward the end of the meal, a crony came over and sat at the table, a heavy pie-faced fellow whose name, caught fleetingly, seemed to be Jimmie Moon. Moon began telling Wallace about the recent misfortunes of a local patriarch. "Yeah, he's got cancer of the rectum, all his garbage is coming out here—" Moon demonstrated, his hands forming a large circle in the vicinity of his watch pocket. "Twelve months is gonna get him, but he don't know it yet." Wallace meditated a moment over his banana pudding. "Well, send a telegram, 'Sorry to hear you're under the weather, but glad to hear you're feeling better.' "

He then fell to chatting about the rally to be held that afternoon in the Birmingham suburb of Vestavia. "This here's gonna be a silk-stocking district. I don't really know why I'm going out there. They got one of the most elegant clubs in the United States up there on the side of that mountain, with the most beautiful view you ever saw. They call it The Club." One arm hitched over the back of his chair, his legs crossed, he dislodged a speck of food with his toothpick and chewed it ruminatively for a moment. " 'Cose, I ain't no The Club type myself. These folks where we goin', they got it all, they don't want to give it to nobody. You go put a nigguh in their school, it ain't like it is with a poor workin' man over there on the other side of town—the rich folks can send their chillun to a private school. They ain't the ones gettin' run over and trampled, it's the steelworkers and metalworkers here."

With some relish he recalled the time Birmingham had been dropped from the itinerary of the touring New York Metropolitan Opera because all the local hotels refused to accommodate the integrated company. "There was some soprano couldn't stand not to stay with the nigguhs in the bunch. So I told 'em to take their fa-sal-las and re-ti-does somewhere else. We could do without 'em. Only opera anybody around here cares about anyway is the Grand Ole Opry. The folks down home in Barbour County got real upset with me when they heard the opera wasn't coming to Birmingham—they thought it was gonna be the Grand Ole Opry. There's more real culture in that anyway, than in all this European singin'. Those are real folk songs right from the earth, right from life. Those are real people in the Grand Ole Opry."

But driving to Vestavia, he continued to fret: "This here's gonna be Martin country, now. Got-rocks country—that's what ole Jim Folsom used to say. These the got-rocks folks." He sat forward once and declared, "There's a fella in a big car got a Wallace sticker. We got a few doctors with us, I guess." Sitting back again, he murmured, "I'm gonna give 'em a speech out here, anyway."

But it was listless, distracted, and vaguely pathetic. The shopping center was filled, in the gathering dusk, with women in slacks and knit sweaters holding poodles, small boys with John-John haircuts, and small girls in Winnie-the-Pooh dresses, an expensive and well-preened assembly of suburbanites who were chattering as much to each other as they were listening to Wallace's voice blaring electronically from the amplifiers on the flatbed trailer. A good many of them simply sat in their cars waiting for someone to come back from one of the stores. Wallace's monologue, his repertoire of phrases, was plainly unsuited to them. He seemed aware of it, and peculiarly deferential and eager to be friendly anyway. Referring to a recount of votes during the Maryland primary race he entered, he said, "What they did was recapitulate on us—you folks may know what that means, but I don't," and changed one of his references to "all these folks in their air-conditioned country clubs" to "some people in their air-conditioned offices, they may not understand. . . ."

The party returned to the hotel before going on to the last rally, at Roebuck, a somewhat homier section of Birmingham. Wallace, after Vestavia, was eager to be back on more familiar ground. On the way to Roebuck, Wallace suddenly demanded of a local politician in the car, "I don't spose we gonna carry Vestavia, are we?" The politician made the mistake of agreeing that things indeed did not look sunny in Vestavia, and Wallace quickly barked, "Well, you say that, but you know we didn't do too bad out there in the spring, I recall. . . ." The politician rode the rest of the way in chastened silence.

There was a huge crowd waiting in the shopping-center parking lot where the rally was scheduled. The wind was black and sharp and wicked now, and as Wallace passed through the crowd, platform-bound, there were frequent whiffs of bourbon. He was welcomed lustily. One small snugly bundled lady tugged at the sleeve of a Wallace bodyguard and told him, "Now, you take good care of that boy, you hear?" After his speech, back down in the crowd, he was heartily hugged and bussed. "God bless you, Guvnuh Wallace. . . . I believe we got the most Christian guvnuh in the United States. . . ." As they pressed about him, he chattered jubilantly, "Yawl get cold out here? Hope we didn't keep yawl too long. Watch out there, don't mash the baby. . . ." He was engulfed for a full twenty minutes. A Negro, a young schoolteacher, surfaced briefly and announced, with only the slightest flutter of his eyelashes, "I pledge to you my support," and then promptly sank back out of sight. Finally, before Wallace returned to his car, there was one last picture for a group of college students. "I hope that turns out good, heunh?" Wallace said. "Yawl want to take another one just to make sure?" Back in his car at last, he declared, after lighting up a fresh cigar, "Now, that's the way I like to end the day." Vestavia had been more than neutralized.

With the rallies of the last day, he drifted closer and closer to Barbour County, his home, so that now it seemed as if he had been circling the whole week, drawing nearer and nearer to his origins. When he arrived in Abbeville, a little town some forty miles from the Barbour County seat of Clayton, he was in another clime, warmer, mellower, easier—southeastern Alabama's flat peanut country. A large crowd was already gathered under the pecan trees on the town square. Drugstore and dime-store neons glimmered around them in the blue twilight, and in the air there was the faint smell of fresh soap. When Wallace finished his address and stepped down into the crowd, he seemed to pull the people close around him, like a bird finally folding and preening his wings. There was only one more rally left, in Clayton. By now Lurleen looked weary and strangely frightened, as if it had come to her at last that the next day she was going to be elected the governor of a state. At moments through the campaign, she had seemed almost to crumple. Wallace, after he had finished shaking hands and started back to his car, would see her sitting in the car behind his, and, his door opened and one foot already inside, he would gesture irritably to her, arching his hand as if he were flinging seed over the town at large, and mutter, so that she could not possibly have heard him, "C'mon, honey, you got to go into the stores and things, you got to *see* 'em, you got to *speak* to 'em now. . . ." And there had been brief furtive arguments. Once, at the end of a day's campaigning in central Alabama, the two of them talked for a moment while the rest of the party stood aside waiting, Wallace leaning in the door of her car and she sitting across the seat from him against the other door, listening to him with a faint frown of harried, hopeless exasperation. A light rain began falling, ending the argument, Wallace abruptly shutting her door and getting into his own car, and as the caravan pulled away, she sat with her chin still in her hand, gazing out into the dusk.

The car now carried him the final miles to Clayton. It was only seventeen miles from Clio, the village where he had grown up and to which he had returned after the war to commence his political life. Not long after that, he had moved on up to Clayton, and since then, it has served as what home he could be said to have. He huddled in the back seat against the door, as small and self-absorbed as a twelve-year-old boy, abstractedly fingering the door lever and window latch as he peered out at the night.

At last, he said, his voice low now and a little thick and hoarse, "I like to touch people. It does something good to you, to see how people like you. A lot of places, people have passed little children up to me, saying, 'Let him touch them!' " He demonstrated, raising his short arms. "There even been folks standing out there in the rain lots of places. It really makes you feel humble." For a while he was quiet again, looking out the window. As the car approached a small litter of weakly lit stores, he leaned forward. "This here's Blue Springs, where we used to go swimming all the time. It's got a natural spring comes out of the ground. Old Confederate veterans used to like to have their reunions here back during the teens and the twenties. It used to be a real popular resort community, but you can see it's pretty run down now. But we're fixin' it up with a big picnic area, gonna turn it into a place like all them other resort areas with natural springs." He said to his driver, "Jemison, reckon we could stop and take a look at it? Ain't we got a little time yet?" Jemison wheeled off the highway and charged down into a grassy area, followed by the caravan. "This here's good, you can stop," said Wallace. "Keep your lights on it, now, so I can see it." He scrambled out and walked in the glare of the car's lights toward a black shine of water ahead of him, stepping a little high in the wet grass, his bodyguards and the rest of his party trailing after him. The night was cool, hushed, sweet with dew, filled with the myriad stitch of crickets. Wallace stopped abruptly and gestured with his cigar over the vague dark expanse of water. "We used to take running jumps off the bank here when we were boys. We gonna brick all this in here, see, where there's just mud now. We got picnic and camping areas over yonder. It's gonna be a real nice park." He tromped on around the water, eager, aimless, as if trying to find some spot where he would be able to see it all and enclose its shape once more in his mind, all the while talking and flourishing his cigar, his entourage tumbling after him and the waiting headlights of the other cars flaring in the night. "Yeah," he said, "you can't see it so good now, but all this has been built on during my administration. We fixin' it up real nice." (But in daylight the recreation area has a scraped and denuded look. Ancient trees once shaded the water, but they have vanished, bulled down and replaced with scraggly knee-high seedlings spaced with arithmetic regularity around concrete tables and benches, geometrically abstract picnic shelters painted in pastels, and blacktop driveways with raw new concrete gullies. There is even, beside the swimming hole with its natural spring, a wire-fenced pool with diving boards. The place is usually absolutely deserted. A native of Blue Springs once protested to Wallace, "It just don't seem to look like it used to." Wallace assured him, "Well, now, we still got lots of work to do out there. We gonna get it back lookin' the same. You can tell all the folks out there not to worry, we gonna fix it." But he seemed to sense that something had gone grievously wrong with this project. It made him profoundly uncomfortable.)

Back on the highway to Clayton, Wallace became increasingly chatty. The car whined over a short bridge, and he said, "Sikes Creek. Ole Sikes Creek. We used to go swimming there some—fish, set out hooks, catch catfish—kill snakes. Used to go out in the river hunting moccasins that'd be hanging around in the trees." He leaned forward, close to the ear of Oscar Harper, one of his aides in the front seat. "You ever do that, Oscar? Go out looking for them moccasins hanging up in them trees?" Before Harper could answer, Wallace leaned back again and mused, "You know, I haven't seen a snake on this road this whole year, I don't believe. Used to see them all the time. Back when I was driving this road a lot by myself, I used to run over them all the time—hit 'em, and then back up over 'em, and then get out and whup 'em with a stick. But you just don't see 'em anymore. I don't know what the matter is. . . ."

The nostalgic sites were coming to him thicker and faster out of the night, surfacing for a moment in the fleeting glare of the car lights and then sucked back into the sightless dark. "That's Bonny Smith's, where we used to shell oysters. . . . And there's Ben Bell's house. He's had a Wallace for Governor sign in his yard there since 1958, said he was gonna keep that sign nailed to that tree until I was elected governor. Now, he says he's gonna keep it up there until I'm elected President. And there's that old cotton gin, and the church I used to go to."

Clio was only a brief flicker of feeble street lights outside the windows, and then the car was on the Billy Watson Highway—a skinny graveled road that Wallace had named for the old Barbour County political impresario who had been one of his original patrons. Watson, in fact, had been probably the single most important person in Wallace's life, the relation between them like that between manager and fighter. Now seventy, Watson was spending his declining diabetic years in Clayton watching with a private high amusement the progress of the protégé he had helped loose on the public. Oscar Harper—a thin, quick man with a sharp face and pale eyes and almost white hair, and a mouth always adorned with a cigar just like Wallace's—chuckled from the front seat, "Billy says not enough signs on his highway tellin' folks who it belongs to. He says he wants one at least every fifteen miles." Wallace gave a hint of a snicker. "Yeah? Well, I don't know how many votes this thing's lost for us already. You know, I got a letter the other day sayin' this road was in pretty bad shape, full of chuckholes and things. Why can't we blacktop this someday soon?" Harper replied, "Billy ain't interested in improvin' the pavement particularly. He just wants some more signs up." Wallace snickered again. "That damn Watson. He ain't satisfied I named a highway for him, he wants his name on signs all over the place. I might just take the durn thing back again, he ain't satisfied with it." After a pause Wallace inquired, "You reckon he's gonna be able to make it out tonight for the rally? He's been awful sick here lately and all. . . ." Harper said, "Hell, Billy'd have to be dead before he'd miss bein' where there was a crowd and excitement goin' on." Wallace gazed out the window for a moment and then idly observed, "Well, they got the grass cut down mighty nice along here."

Suddenly the car was slowing into the outskirts of Clayton. "This is a pretty little town," observed Wallace. "All little towns are pretty." The car eased around the square, where that night's rally was to be held, turned a corner, went a short distance down a quiet street in deep shadows, and then pulled into the back yard of an old white frame house sheltered by large and generous trees. Wallace and Lurleen had lived there before he became governor, when it was an apartment house, and they had wound up buying it as Wallace's fortunes rose; but it was still only a token and tentative settling place, occupied now by Wallace's paternal grandmother. Called Momma Mae, she was a frail little lady with soft white luminous hair like spun glass, as thin as a bamboo slat, with a sparrowlike face and small round eyes behind rimless glasses. She greeted Wallace at the screened back door with a dry brief kiss on the cheek, as he murmured, "Hi, Momma Mae, how you feelin'?" and bolted on into the house. Harper and the bodyguards drove off to eat supper somewhere else, leaving Wallace and Lurleen there.

Wallace now was hurrying from room to room, furiously smoking his cigar, looking as if he were being propelled from one quick discharge of smoke to the next, and leaving behind him a thin trail of ash. His coat still buttoned, he paused in each room only long enough for a swift embracing glance—the spacious front parlor with clay-colored rug and green draperies and an old burnt-umber velour couch, a lot of chill air hanging between the furniture and the high ceiling this autumn evening; the back bedroom, with green floral wallpaper and thickets of family photographs on dresser and chest of drawers; the small cold dining room, with an arrangement of white chrysanthemums placed in the precise middle of a table on a white doily. Here Wallace squatted on his heels to rummage through shelves below a wall cabinet. Lurleen presently entered the room and asked, "What are you digging for, George?" He mumbled, "Scrapbook I just wanted to find." She told him, "It's not there, George. I moved it with some other things up yonder to Montgomery." He continued shuffling through the shelves until she repeated, her voice higher, "George, honest, it's not *there*."

He retreated to the pine-paneled den and watched television while waiting for supper, slouched low and deep on the sofa, his tiny heels crossed on the coffee table. Lurleen looked in, and he asked her, "How you like that Abbeville crowd, honey?" "It was all right," she said. "That was a good crowd," he informed her. Then he said, "What you gonna tell 'em tonight?" and she replied, with a touch of a smile, "I'm gonna say howdy." Wallace merely looked back at the TV—he didn't think her remark very funny.

Supper—served in the large kitchen, with its formica breakfast table and, on one of the damp yellow walls, a display of undersized plastic fruit—consisted of coffee, homemade chicken salad, pimento cheese, and more coffee. The talk around the table was of the town's Republicans, a conversation conducted mostly by the women in the shrill and slightly incredulous tones of outrage and scandal, Wallace listening to them with small sniggers. Presently a neighbor—an elderly effusive woman—walked into the kitchen without knocking and cried, "Oh, George!" Wallace now was like a small boy basking in the adoration of fond womenfolk. When he rose to leave with Lurleen, Momma Mae followed him out to the back porch, telling him, "Now, you can stay here whenever you want. That's your bedroom back there, George, that's your bathroom."

There was a huge throng at the square in front of the

courthouse, with the combined country high-school bands bleating lustily. The air was warmish, with an almost spring-like flush and promise of rain, but Wallace, when he pitched out of the car, asked the first people who approached him, "Yawl cold? It's not too cold, is it?" A woman came up and squeezed his hand and said softly, "How you, George?" her eyes twinkling with tears. "I sho am glad to be back home," he declared. The music, with a few stray squawks and honks, abruptly dwindled into silence, and the local Methodist minister opened the rally with a prayer: "Tonight, our Father, we thank Thee for Lurleen and George. We pray that Thou will use them. . . ." It did seem a special and beautiful night, limpid and sweet and filled with love and the tender thrill of homecoming. Wallace whispered to an aide, "Watson out here tonight?" and he was told, "No, Guvnuh, I ain't seen him yet."

Lurleen gave her talk, her voice ringing over the hushed crowd. Waiting for her to finish, Wallace stood by his car in a small, momentarily empty circle, his head ducked, pulling thoughtfully at his jowls, hearing finally the spatter of clapping as Lurleen turned from the mike. Then, with his own hillbilly band breaking into a spry mischievous, hot-diggety-dog *Dixie,* he was on.

Afterward he leaned down from the flatbed trailer, his bodyguards having to catch him by the coattails to keep him from tumbling into the surge of faces below him. "Hi, Josephine. Martha, honey, glad to see you. Listen, now, yawl be careful goin' home, heunh? Birdy, honey—Mr. Charlie, how are you? Don't yawl stay up too late, now, honey." An old lady, when he took her hand, fairly wriggled with fondness and wrinkled up her face. "Bless you heart, we need you so much!" A young mother lifted up her little girl for a handshake, a blessing. An old man in a corduroy coat strained up to him on his tiptoes to mutter the message he had been waiting all evening to deliver: "We got a little sumpum over yonder now to pick you up if you want—it's what we got it here for, now." When Wallace declined, the old man announced, "Well, I think I'm gonna have me a little. But I'm keepin' it for you, in case you decide later on." Wallace clung to a pretty girl's hand. "Aw, Lucille, honey, I didn't recognize you"—burst of happy laughter under him—"I got sinus trouble, you know, and it's kind of hard to see sometimes."

It was over now. Dismounting from the platform, Wallace found the youths who had traveled through the campaign distributing bumper stickers ahead of his rallies, and he told them, "Boys, we'll wind up in California someplace. . . ." He then wandered over to the Dixie Academy fried-chicken stand, a booth that had been set up on the square for the evening to raise funds for a private school in the county—a hasty assembly of raw planks now dappled with puddles of melted ice in the bleak glare of a string of light bulbs. He told the townsmen who were closing it, "I'll see all yawl in the mornin'. I'll be around with you boys tomorrow for the votin', heunh?" The square now was nearly deserted, with paper blowing in a light, damp, late night wind and a few people still lingering under the street lights, quietly talking. From somewhere came a high hoot of mountain laughter. Wallace made for his car, giving an unlit cigar two swift licks and then popping it into his mouth still unlit. Then he noticed, heading toward him like a pair of pale specters, the two women who had been following him all over the state in their aged black Cadillac. The girl, her damp dark eyes still stricken and full of suffering, whined to him with a brave little smile, "We done recorded a victory song." He instantly swerved to avoid them, calling to them over his shoulder, "Well, I 'preciate yawl bein' with us. Good-bye, sweetie. We'll see yawl, heunh?"

He could have spent the night there in Clayton, where he was to vote the next day, but, too energized, he decided to drive back to Montgomery. Lurleen went on ahead of him in another car. Before following her, he dropped by his brother's house, a few blocks from the square. There was a yardful of cars, and as Wallace got out, he exclaimed, not unhappily, "Godamightydamn, look at them people. I'll never get away." The den of his brother's home was paneled in the same bright yellow pine as Momma Mae's, but with the addition of a large brick fireplace. As soon as he entered, he asked, "Don't guess Watson made it out tonight, did he?" and someone answered, "Didn't see him, George."

A few members of the national press were waiting for him; they were a trifle uneasy, laughing a bit too quickly and loudly at the banter going on around them among the assembled townfolk. Cokes were served, the bottoms of the bottles wrapped in paper napkins. Wallace settled himself on a sofa with a jaunty, "Well, what yawl wanna distort tonight?" The newspeople from New York and Washington and Chicago all laughed heartily, but their eyes were quite blank. It was a short session.

After they left, Wallace was informed that Watson had "passed out" at the supper table that evening before the rally. "It was just the excitement, probably," someone said, "and he'd probably had a couple too. You know Billy." A moment later, someone phoned to say Watson had suffered an insulin shock but was coming out of it. "Well," snorted Wallace, "don't let him know we been askin' about him. He might get the idea we worryin' about him or something." But he seemed vaguely troubled.

On the way back to Montgomery, he talked for a while about Martin, the Republican candidate: "He's dead now. He's finished. He might could of been senator, but he ain't gonna be nothing now. He fixed himself, we didn't do it. People say we used to be close, me'n'him, but it wasn't like that—he tried to get close to me, but I was never close to him." He finally subsided into silence. As the car hummed on through the night on the long drive back to Montgomery, he periodically leaned forward to peer out the window at passing cars and trucks, still checking for Wallace stickers.

Part Two

I

The Pea River Church, on a country road between Clayton and Clio, is a stark brick building with opaque milky windows and a bleak cemetery, scantily tufted with weeds, spread under a few antique gray oaks. The oldest tombstones, many of them broken and toppled, have the small simple shape of Moses' tablet and bear the names of Baxters, McRaes, McInnesses, McCormicks, Rosses, Murdochs, and McKnights—descendants of those gaunt fierce Calvinist Celts and Anglo-Saxons who came from cold moors and misty heaths into sensual heat and honeysuckle, unaware to the last of the decadence with which they casually contracted, remaining in the midst of slavery as plain and harsh as the churchyard into which the generations of them have been commonly absorbed, the final sum of each of them a single dimming inscription on a mottled slab: ANGUS MCLEAN ASLEEP IN JESUS BLESSED THOUGHT. . . . BELOVED WIFE SHE WAS TOO GOOD, TOO GENTLE AND TOO FAIR TO DWELL IN THIS COLD WORLD OF CARE. . . . Like most Southern cemeteries, the churchyard is also dense with tombstones from all the crusades: that first great, grave, gray crusade more than a century ago; then the crusade in France; and then the one in Europe and the Pacific twenty years later.

The countryside is flat and grassy and only thinly inhabited. The narrow highways on bright empty Sunday afternoons are roamed by spidery, grimy youths with flowing hair who explode out of the stillness on motorcycles, bent forward over the chromium handlebars in a rigid furious lean of eternal anticipation, like the figures on the prows of wooden ships, sometimes with famished-looking yellow-haired girls clinging to their humped backs, vanishing with a blattering roar back into calm and timeless space. The land abounds with palmists and fortune-tellers who live in trailers and tiny pink concrete-block houses under pecan trees. Carnivals come with the fall, appearing overnight in some pasture a few miles out of town, shabby and raucous and sourceless, like wicked gaudy beggars, and for the span of their uncertain and not quite real tenancy in each field the soft cool nights are filled with calliope music and the high slow twirl of a ferris wheel and a dense, crazy cacophony among the gaming booths and the secret illicit tents.

This, the southeast corner of Alabama, has always been an amiably violent county. "We aren't particularly mean here," says one native, "we just have a lot of murders." Its past crackles with shootings, explosions, angry burnings, deputies with shotguns trampling through autumn woods behind baying bloodhounds. "I can remember," says a resident of Clayton, "when folks during the Depression would blow up their houses and stores because they didn't have the money to pay taxes. It mostly happened on Thursday nights for some reason. Got to where the boys and girls would make their dates by saying, 'I'll see you at the fire Thursday night.' Got to be a kind of habit. One fella trying to burn up his store got blowed all the way across the street, and they found him by following the blood where he had crawled away." In one of Wallace's first cases as a lawyer, he defended a husband who had planted eight sticks of dynamite under his wife's bed "and then went off dancin' with another woman to wait for his wife to blow up. He was right in the middle of dancin' when the sky lit up"; the plea was insanity. Not long ago, reports another Barbour County native, "we had a banker who had him two Caddies, an airplane, a fine home with a swimming pool. He was storing peanuts for the government, and he came up about one hundred thousand dollars short on the amount of peanuts he was supposed to have in his warehouses. So one night he goes out by himself and gets into his plane and takes off, circles over town about three times, and then dives. The next morning, we find him up in trees all over the place."

The stories would make a plump volume: *Tales of Barbour County*. Wallace's youngest brother, Jack, who is now a circuit judge in Clayton, recalls, "We had a fella here once who blamed his daddy for the loss of his leg—seems like his daddy had gone up to Montgomery and gotten drunk and had called down to Clayton for his son to come get him. On the way up, the boy had an accident and lost a leg. He just never got over it. I knew him pretty well. I used to take him over to Blue Springs swimming a lot, but he really wasn't a very pleasant fella to be around after he lost that leg. He had a terrific temper. He asked his daddy one time if he could use the car, and his daddy told him no, so he took his walking stick and bashed out a windshield. Anyway, one day around noon his daddy was coming home from work for lunch, he was going up the front walk with two bags of groceries under his arms, when his boy steps out from behind some bushes where he'd been waiting with a shotgun. He didn't say a word. He just blew his daddy to pieces right there. Wasn't but a few hours later that I heard about it. I was kinda scared to go over there—I'd been trying to avoid the fella lately, I'd told him several times I couldn't take him to Blue Springs and he'd gotten right mad. I didn't know what he'd do now if he saw me. But I heard they had him upstairs in the house in his room, fixing to leave with him, so I went on over. I went on into the house and walked upstairs. When I opened the door to his room, there were some policemen standing around him, and he was packing his bag on the bed. He looked up at me and kind of smiled, real calm, almost like he had been expecting me. 'Well,' he said, 'I don't guess we'll be going to Blue Springs anytime soon, will we?' "

Clio, a humble settlement of a few hundred souls, is seventeen miles from Clayton. The square in Clayton really serves as the town square for all the other little villages around it. Dry-goods, drug, and grocery stores drowse in the sun around that inevitable obelisk, the Confederate monument, planted in the center of the community's consciousness and conscience like an altar to some half-forgotten religion. Clayton's Confederate soldier, set atop a granite shaft on a meager patch of faded grass, has about him a faintly neglected and extraneous look. But still he leans on his rifle atop his pedestal with a kind of heroic Greek slant-hipped languor (a pose which Wallace, canting his hips as he speaks before crowds, seems unconsciously to be imitating), a curiously puny figure, a bit less than life-size, his steady, unblinking, blind scowl fixed forever on the North in complete changeless granite-bound concentration. The legend beneath him reads:

In Proud and Loving Memory
of the Confederate
Private Soldier
He bore the brunt of the great war
His privations and sufferings
Were surpassed only by
His manhood and his courage
He was of our home and blood
And we love his name
And memory with a feeling
That is beyond the reach of pride
Or the power of misfortune
COMRADES
TO OUR
CONFEDERATE
DEAD

Behind him, across the street, is the courthouse—actually, Barbour County has two courthouses, the other maintained in the larger town of Eufala, some eighteen miles to the east. This odd extravagance owes to the fact that, despite its being barely populous enough to justify even one courthouse, Barbour is probably the most virulently political county in the state: one courthouse simply wasn't enough to satisfy its appetite and energies for politicking. It's as if the fury of its politics works in inverse ratio to the scantiness of its population. It has produced an inordinate number of aggressive state politicians, and the number of governors it has sent to Montgomery is wildly out of proportion to its size. Growing politicians has been its chief industry and its major pastime. One of Wallace's current cronies was elected mayor of his town when he was only twenty-one, and Wallace himself was campaigning door-to-door for the local candidate for secretary of state at the precocious age of thirteen.

Beyond his grandparents, all that is known of Wallace's progenitors is that there was a Methodist preacher once, and a great-grandfather who was wounded at Chattanooga in the Battle of Lookout Mountain—the family still has the pocket Bible he carried through the war, in which the event of his wound is recorded in faint spidery ink, and the worn tablespoon which he used to peel potatoes. Behind him there is only a vague glimpse of Wallaces filtering down into Alabama out of the mountains of North Carolina sometime in the early 1860's. Then they are lost, there is no memory of them, they disappear somewhere into the teeming faceless tides of immigration from Scotland and Northern Ireland during the late eighteenth century.

The most recent Wallaces are buried in the Pea River cemetery, and among their tombstones is a plain chaste tablet marking the remains of a member of the family who is usually recalled as "Uncle Edwin, the holy terror." He perished at twenty-four, leaving behind him only a few rather gaudy memories. "Uncle Edwin was married once, but it didn't last long," says one of Wallace's brothers. "I remember him coming by the house late one raining night—we were all in bed when he knocked, and Daddy got up and went to the door. His yellow LaSalle convertible was parked outside, and there was a gal in it waiting on him, and he told Daddy he was on his way somewhere from Miami and needed a little money to frolic on. Daddy just slammed the door in his face—the power company had just cut off our own lights. Yeah, Uncle Edwin. He was up in Washington, D.C., on an excursion boat on the Fourth of July around 1935, and he fell off and died."

Also resting in the Pea River cemetery is Wallace's grandfather. He was a sturdy and austere country doctor in rimless glasses who kept one drawer of his office desk brimming with "Hambone's Meditations," which he clipped out of local newspapers. Most of the pecan trees now flourishing around Clio were planted by his hand. And in a sense, he provided many of the voters necessary to start his grandson's career. "People are sprinkled all over this county who were delivered by my grandfather," says Wallace's brother Jack. "A lot of them are named for him—Wallace Mozelle, Wallace Tillman, Wallace Carpenter. . . ."

It was the doctor's hope that George would become a minister. A relentlessly pious man, he rehearsed his grandsons in Bible verses to recite before each meal at his table, and he himself read through the scriptures over and over again, from Genesis to Revelation; his frequent passages through the book are marked with neat rows of dark pencil notches in the margins. His disposition was generally unbudging. In 1928 he was elected probate judge, served out his six-year term, opening every session with a prayer, and then went back to his practice because he had promised when he ran that he would not seek reelection. His passion against alcohol was obsessive. "He was the biggest whiskey-hater in this part of the country," a Claytonian recalls. "He was all the time totin' around temperance petitions, which to him wasn't for temperance but outright annihilation. We had a candidate for governor once whose name happened to be Boozer, and Dr. Wallace announced one morning to a bunch of us downtown, "The name alone would cause me to be against him.' "

The doctor's one indulgence was fine horses. Momma Mae, whom he brought back from Kentucky as his second wife not long after the death of his first, remembers, "Dr. Wallace purchased a mare which he had been led to believe by certain interested parties had been bred to a Tennessee Walking Horse. I don't believe I ever saw him so excited in all the time I knew him. It was all he could talk about while he waited for the mare to foal—he was going to have himself a Tennessee Walking Horse. After the mare foaled, Dr. Wallace would go out every evening when he was through with his duties just to look at it for a while, and then come back in the house and talk all through supper about how he couldn't wait for his Tennessee Walking Horse to get grown—he was already riding it, you might say, cantering around the square and all over the countryside. Even after a few people began to remark how the colt's ears seemed to be growing unusually fast, seemed to be awfully long already, he kept on talking like that. In fact, he started talking a little more and a little faster about it. Finally one evening a close friend of his came by to take a look at the thing. They went out back together, and shortly returned to the house. His friend told him, 'Doctor, I don't believe I've ever seen a Tennessee Walking Horse with ears quite like that,' and Dr. Wallace said, real quiet, 'No.' His friend said, 'Doctor, I believe that is actually a mule out there,' and Dr. Wallace said, 'Yes, I suppose it is.' After his friend left, Dr. Wallace didn't say anything all evening. He had finally admitted it, and he was sick for months afterward. It was hard to get him even to eat."

It seems that Wallace was closer to his grandfather than to his father. "George was the oldest child," says Momma Mae, "and when Gerald, the second boy, was born two years after George, George refused to go home. Dr. Wallace tried to take him back, and then an hour or so later returned, driving up the street with George still sitting there beside him. It sort of stayed like that ever after. George stayed with us more than Jack or any of the others. He liked to crawl into bed with his granddaddy in the mornings, and he'd ride around with him on his calls to Baker Hill and everywhere."

In 1948, at the age of eighty, Dr. Wallace died. Up to the last, he had continued riding a horse around the square every morning, causing some anxiety among the townfolk. "We just knew that one of these days he was gonna fall off, or a car was gonna hit him. But nobody could bring themselves to say anything to him. He rode well. He was a handsome figure, even as old as he was." Lurleen remembered that "when we were living in Clayton, we could hear his horse early in the morning coming down the paved street back from town. The children and I would go to the door and watch for him. I told them, 'That is your great-grandfather on that horse.'" George was with him the night he died.

If young George felt closer to his grandfather than to his own father, it was probably because George Wallace, Sr., was almost totally absorbed in a ceaseless, savage, losing cat-fight with life. He was a frail man outrageously harried by sickness and failure, and it was as if, engaged with his own demons during his precarious existence, he simply couldn't afford to pause long enough to comprehend that he had produced three sons and a daughter, much less the time to pay them attention.

He was known in the community as "Sag." One native of Clio remembers, "He was just a little ole runty dried-up feller who was always freezin', even in the summertime. He never did get hot—never did sweat. He just seemed to have that cold blood. You'd see him all the time downtown smokin' a cigarette and drinkin' a Coca-Cola. There'd be that Coca-Cola in one hand and that cigarette in the other. I guess he drank the most Cokes of anybody I ever saw in my whole life." He spent his entire adult life near death, dodging its persistent swoops at him.

Wallace recalls vividly of his father, "He didn't have but one lung. His other lung had just died on him, and one side of his chest was caved way in. He also had this terrible sinus trouble. They finally had to carry him to Montgomery and cut out a piece of his skull right above his eyes—when they pulled the flap back, you could see his brains. It left a real bad-lookin' place there, a kind of holler. The kind of operation he had could kill you just with shock. He suffered so much from it, it affected his heart. When I was old enough to drive, I'd take him up to Montgomery every time his head swelled up again."

The only thing that seemed to sustain him, with his single dogged lung, was a sheer cold impotent rage. "He was not what you'd call an ardent church-worker," recalls an old acquaintance, "because he was too busy just concentratin' on stayin' alive a little longer. He tended to like his toddy. And he didn't like to leave folks and go home. He just went there to eat and sleep. I guess he was a damn rascal like the rest of us. Jackson's General Store was our hangout, back there around a wood stove, and he spent more time there than any of us. He was a bad one for gettin' in fights. He was a scrapper, just like little George. He'd fight 'em all. There was a fella, Paul Burnham, who was freshman football coach at Alabama for a while, who'd come to town to coach a bunch of country corn-fed boys down here. One day he dropped by the store, and George was layin' up on a counter with one of his headaches, his head on a bolt of cloth and a cigarette hangin' out of his mouth, just sufferin'. Burnham took a look at him and said, 'Why in hell don't you go on home and die?' George was up offa that bolt of cloth like a flash. Burnham just managed to get back out the door."

According to another Barbour County native, "George and a chairman of the Board of Revenue we had once, they didn't get along too well. They had a kind of difficulty once, and George chased him through the courthouse in Clayton with a pocketknife." A man who had been one of his closest friends in Clio recalls, "When we were about sixteen or seventeen, there was one girl that he was especially fond of. I did her a little favor once—something I don't even remember—but I was just being considerate, I didn't have any interest in the girl atall. But it like to tore up George. He wanted to fight me. I was a lot bigger and stronger than he was, but he didn't leave me any choice. So we went back behind the street into this public privy, and first thing I know he's pulled out a knife. It didn't scare me much, because I knew I was the best man. But he made a pass at me and nicked me here by the left eye and then come down and cut the vein in the crutch of my arm here. I bled like a stuck pig." Grinning, the old friend points to a scar which, after fifty-two years, is still long and vivid and savage. "That's the way he was. His daddy had to patch me up."

He did some amateur acting in playlets and pageants in county schools and churches; it seems his style was somewhat grand and swaggering. But most other diversions bored him. "Hell, no, he didn't fish," says his old friend in Clio. "That was hard work. He wasn't brought up to work. He was a doctor's son. He was the apple of Dr. Wallace's eye, no doubt about it. Dr. Wallace indulged him in anything he wanted." But whenever he turned his hand to any enterprise, it was like the withering touch of frost. "Dr. Wallace finally sent him up to Methodist Southern College in Greensboro. But he didn't stay long in school; he must not have been up there much more'n a year before he got it into his head to raise him some cows and make some money. He was gonna be a gentleman farmer. So he went to Tennessee and bought a bunch of fine short-horn cattle and brought 'em down here and put 'em all in a broomsage field. He didn't know no more about farmin' than that. Naturally, they were all dead inside of two years. He kept on tryin' to farm a little bit—peanuts, cotton, corn, a few hogs and mules—but he just wasn't practical. He was always losin' money at it. He messed around some as a jackleg veterinarian. But he didn't really make any money until he got that little bit from being on the Board of Revenue, and even that wadn't no more'n about twenty-five dollars a month."

They say in Clio, "If there was one thing George, Sr., took to natural, it was politics." In his only personal venture, he was elected chairman of the county Board of Revenue, but it is also claimed that he was responsible for his father's term on the bench. "Being a good Christian man and a doctor don't get you the votes in politics. It was George, Sr., that did the real dirty-work politicking. Dr. Wallace just sat back while his son put him in." A veteran Barbour County politician maintains, " 'Course, all George, Sr., ever dealt in was peanuts, so to speak, while George, Jr., now is in that high-class bracket. But the father had a natural mind for it which was just as good as George, Jr.'s, and maybe even a little better. He was just too puny and sick to move around like George, Jr., does. But was sho nuff shrewd at it. Right before he died, he was planning to run for probate judge, but he had to give it up 'cause he couldn't get together enough money."

Wallace stayed up all night with his father once or twice during local elections. "I wasn't but about ten years old, but I was fascinated. Watchin' him count those votes was like watchin' somebody water-ski for the first time." But his first recollection of his father is still his clearest one: "I don't know how old I was. I couldn't have been more'n four or five. I had gone out in a field with my daddy to watch him plow behind a mule. I was sittin' on the ground in a hot sun, barefooted, and watchin' him walk away from me, followin' that mule, goin' away so far, so far, and I didn't think he was ever comin' back."

It was not his heart, his embattled lung, or his sinuses that ultimately betrayed him, but a flank attack, Brill's fever—a mild form of typhus which, according to one member of the family, "was transmitted by fleas offa rats." Wallace was a freshman in college, and when he got back home, his grandfather was leaning over his father's scrawny unconscious form;

he looked up at Wallace and said simply, "I think he's gone this time." He died the next afternoon. It was November, and the funeral was held on a soft gentle day. "All the nigguhs on our place came by the house," says Wallace. "Daddy was in the living room in his casket, you know, and they filed by and said, 'Lawd, lawd, what we gonna do now?' "

He left behind him only his mean, unprofitable, and hopelessly mortgaged farm and the modest house which he had built in Clio, its lumber scavenged from the old unpainted frame house with its blank open corridor straight from front to back door, where Wallace was born. After he was buried in the Pea River churchyard, several members of the community quietly approached Wallace's mother and told her that if she could manage to hold the farm together, they would see that she never lacked for food. She briskly rejected that arrangement. Instead, she quickly disposed of the land—the blasted futile remains of her husband's dream of becoming a gentleman farmer, uselessly scraped and worried and raked now by a few Negro tenants—and took a job with Roosevelt's New Deal as supervisor of the local NYA sewing room. Even now she is careful to explain, "I did it just to keep myself busy. They told me, 'We aren't offering this to you because we think you need it.' I could have done without it—oh, yes. But I felt I might have a chance to help these girls from out in the country."

She had come to Clio from a female boarding academy in Mobile. She met her future husband in the waiting room of the Montgomery railroad terminal when he was on his way to college in Greensboro and she was on one of her trips between school in Mobile and her home in Birmingham. How he approached her, what they said to each other, and how long they talked remains obscure. But shortly afterward, she appeared in Clio—a small, tidy, prim girl who began teaching music—Beethoven, Chopin and MacDowell—in the high school and doughtily commandeering her lumpish pupils through seasonal formal piano concerts, but whose purpose there, everyone knew, was eventually to become the wife of the doctor's son. Two years after they had found each other, had struck their quick and probably tacit arrangement in the Montgomery station, they were married.

"My mother was thrown into a totally different environment when she came to marry my father," says Gerald, the second son. "There was some dissension between the two of them over drinking. My mother couldn't stand drinking, and my father was known to get his share." An old friend of the family recalls, "She was smooth. She was real tiny and nice. But George, Sr., he—well, we went over there one day for dinner right after he had his sharecroppers kill some hogs, he was a great pork-eater, and he asked me to return the thanks, and when I finished—he must have been checking the table while I was doing it—he said, 'Bitsy, whur's the meat?' She had laid out the table beautiful with turkey and chicken and everything. 'I'm talkin' about hog meat,' he said. 'What the hell do you think I killed them hogs for?' She was real quiet through the rest of the dinner. She never would show any sign he could get her down, leastwise not while there were other folks around."

She persevered, grim and brisk, not resigned but just adapting herself after she realized it was not to be exactly what she thought it was going to be, giving music lessons to her sons now and attending Clio's simple white-frame Methodist church with all her children in tow. "There wasn't any insisting about it," says Jack Wallace. "We just went. Mother played the piano—she had to be there, and we had to be there." Her music-teacher's dignity, beleaguered in this ruffian little country village, remained serene and unfaltering and indestructible. A long-time resident of Clio recalls with a chortle, "One Easter morning, a bunch of boys found a puddle of creosote and tar and rosin where they had just finished building a filling station on the corner in the middle of town. Everybody was still in church, and we mixed it all up and went in the privy behind the filling station and painted the seat there, and then we lay down behind a bank to see what would happen. Well, Wallace's father was the first man out of church, and he lit out straight for that privy, all dressed up in his Easter clothes. He went in and shut the door, and just a second later he came bustin' back out, with that whole seat stuck to him. Yessir. For three whole weeks, Bitsy was scrubbing Sag's behind with kerosene and turpentine. The whole town couldn't stop grinning about the thought of her havin' to work on Sag like that."

After the death of her husband, she managed to cling to the house for four years, reduced now from genteel instructions in Mozart and Bach to presiding over a hot, rank-smelling little room full of large, mute, horny-handed farm girls earnestly and monotonously blundering with recipes and needle and thread. "After his father's funeral, George said he wanted to stay home," she crisply recalls, "but I told him to go on back to school, I could get along without him. I was probably right cruel about it, but I told him I could make out." Nevertheless, in 1942, when relieved of all three sons by World War II, she promptly left Clio—the house, the community, the years there which she thought of as neither a mistake nor a blessing, because that was pointless now—and took a business course in Montgomery. She has seldom been back. She works now in a vast whitewashed state office building as secretary to the director of the Bureau of Preventable Diseases. A vigorous and somewhat brittle little lady in dresses of bright tropical colors like the plumage of a parrot, with a surprisingly loud hoarse harsh voice, she is not given to sentimentality. "No," she says, "my boys and I don't spend much time together. I hardly even talk to them on the telephone. I'm not going to be selfish and make them feel like they have to come and see me ever so often. I moved up here because I knew the boys were grown and there was no reason for them not to have to go into the war, and I wanted to be self-supporting so they wouldn't have to come back and take care of me. When you're independent, which I've tried to be, you have to be really independent. I've always had a—well, I don't want to be a burden on anybody. When I was looking at a house up here just awhile ago which I was thinking about buying, I asked them, I said, 'I'd just like for you all to come see what I think I've chosen for my home,' and they said, 'Well, Mother, you know you gonna go ahead and buy it no matter what we say.' And they were right. It was foolish of me to bother them." Seizing another cigarette from the pack on her metal desk and igniting it with a quick snap of her lighter, she mused, "Of course, somebody's gonna get George sooner or later. I've accepted that. He's gonna get it. My only consolation is, when it happens, he'll be doing the only thing he's ever cared about doing anyway."

2

George was born in the early lamplit hours of an August morning in 1919, in a small crackerbox house just outside Clio. His naps, it is reported, were "short and infrequent." Almost as soon as he emerged from infancy, as soon as he discovered there was something going on besides eating and sleeping, learned what talking was, and then found out there were other folks around besides his parents and grandparents, and then recognized that all of them seemed occupied with large invisible consequential matters beyond the simple chores and idle trivial games of children, he began interesting himself in those matters. According to those who remember him from those days, "playin' didn't take up much of his time atall—nossuh. George always seemed like he was pretty much satisfied with George." It was as if he already knew what he was going to do, and was simply waiting—calm, absorbed, self-contained, and alert—until the time arrived for him to begin.

One summer evening, his youngest brother, Jack, returned to the house after milking the cows to find him standing in the kitchen waiting for supper. Jack angrily blurted, "How come you don't ever do any of the work around here, how come I'm always the one supposed to look after the cows for you?" George replied in a quiet, toneless voice, "Because there ain't no future in that stuff. . . ."

But while he waited, he existed within the calm matrix of a village boyhood: a Huck Finn boyhood, like those classic gentle sweet scenes on jigsaw puzzles or calendars distributed by feed-grain stores. The boys plundered watermelon patches on midsummer nights and regularly raided a neighbor's sugarcane stand, often in the company of the owner's daughter, who once at a public holiday gathering bit down on some of her father's birdshot in one of the canes. "I guess we looked like something out of the Our Gang comedies," says the middle brother, Gerald. "We wore coveralls and Mother made us shirts out of fertilizer sacks, and on Sundays we put on these knicker suits." They would pass a whole afternoon, sitting beside a creek, with luxurious and tingling speculation about what they would do if John Dillinger suddenly were to stroll up to them out of the tangled brush and honeysuckle, out of the fierce rushing glory of the newspapers and radio.

Jack Wallace now lives in a comfortable brick ranch-style home on the edge of Clayton—a quiet, mild, slightly shy, but pleasant man, a bit toothy and foxy of features, with heavy black eyebrows over his dark shell-rim glasses. "There was an old man in town," he recalls, "who, every time he saw us, used to call George governor and me senator." In his mid-forties now, Jack spends a lot of his time in his workshop behind the house—a snug retreat which he carpentered himself, where, with a wood stove to warm him in the wintertime, he labors in solitude through long mornings and afternoons, hammering, sawing, drilling, planing lumber into such humble but cunning contraptions as butterbean-shellers and wire-basket fish-scalers. His work is neat, careful, stout, spare of embellishments.

Between court sessions he passes the peaceful vacant afternoon in his office at the Clayton courthouse, sometimes studying pamphlets and brochures advertising new sailboats, model blueprints spread over the legal books on his desk. "Fella always starts wanting to go to Tahiti at my age, you know," he confesses. When he reminisces about his boyhood, he talks on and on with a soft eager urgency, a steady inexhaustibility (getting up from behind his desk to snap on a light after the afternoon fades away in the windows), as someone who has been stranded for years on an island might talk to the first stranger who found them. "We'd hunt for catfish by running our hands up under creek banks, and kill possums and barbecue them and then give 'em to the colored folks. We got this old guidewire cable once and unraveled the strands and strung them from a tree at the top of a hill to another tree at the bottom, and then we hung an apple box on it with a pully and called it 'The Jolly Ride.' Boy, it would jar your teeth to ride that thing! We would break yearling calves, you know, and then hitch them up to what we called a Hoover cart, something we made out of Model-T rims with a kind of oxen yoke that we made out of poplar trees and pipes. It looked like—wait a minute—" He found a piece of onionskin paper under his sailboat blueprint, pulled his ball-point pen out of his shirt pocket, and then slowly, deliberately, almost grudgingly, line by careful line, traced out a diagram. "It looks like this, see—" He is reluctant to break off his recollections, gently protesting, "No, no—I mean, I'm enjoying it. I don't have anything else to do here." It's as if he never expects to know such innocent happiness again, such private bliss and peace, as if everything since his boyhood—his circuit-judgeship, his older brother's transfiguration into legend—has all been somehow anticlimactic. Things can never again be as full and good and real as they were when he was a boy. "We did a lot of kite-flying in the spring and fall—we got this real long string once and went out in a field and turned loose of the kite; it went up, up, up, until it was clean out of sight, we were standing in that field just holding on to the end of a string." After a moment's silence he says quietly, "It's still the most fun I ever had. . . ."

In that calendar-picture boyhood, they lived among Negroes as closely and easily and unconsciously as they lived with the weather, the landscape, the sparrows, and the rabbits in the fields. An ancient illiterate handyman named Carlton McKinnis, seemingly without age or prospect of ever dying, a kind of family heirloom, was as familiar about the house—dozing in the backyard, waiting outside the kitchen door to be handed his meals—as an old, dear, dutiful dog. He would often take the boys for walks through the fields, Wallace's mother having admonished him to switch them if they misbehaved. "One time he decided he wanted to go up to Detroit," recalls Wallace's mother. "They all get that in their heads sooner or later, you know. That's all he could talk about for days, about how he sho would like to see what it was like up there in Detroit. So we let him go ahead and even gave him a little money. He wasn't gone long. I walked out on my back porch one evening, and he was just standing there at the back screen. 'It sho was cold up there,' he said, 'and the way those folks live is sumpum terrible.' We were as glad to see him as we would a member of the family." Wallace himself remembers, "Yeah, ole Carlton—we loved him. When he got too old to get around, we built him a little house down toward Blue Springs, not too far from the Methodist Church, and on Thanksgiving and Christmas we'd take stuff down to him. I can see ole Carlton now, smilin' and tremblin' and laughin' when we toted in those hams to him. All his sisters and chillun down there been told I'm anti-nigguh now. Yeah. But I can still see ole Carlton when we'd bring him stuff to eat. We gave him money and looked after him until he died. It made us all mighty sad when he was gone."

They also played football and shot marbles with Negro boys their own age, and systematically baited a seventeen-year-old Negro helper at the local market into scuffling with them. "There were several that went around with us all the time," says Wallace's brother Gerald. "Jake and Sheenanny, and ole Roscoe French—he was a dancer and entertainer in New York last I heard of him. Hell, we had integrated swimmin' forty years ago down there; we built this dam and made a swimmin' hole, and we told Jake and Sheenanny and Roscoe they could use it if they'd keep it up. And they did. We went swimmin' with them all the time. They were regular members of our gang and went around with us everywhere. There was this other gang in town, the Brock boys—they all turned out to be servicemen—but Jake and Sheenanny and Roscoe were with us when we raided the Brock boys' tepees and threw them all in the branch. And we'd have these rock wars with the Brock boys, maybe seven or eight to a side, with elaborate trenches and bunkers just like real war, tunnels from one trench to another so you could get a resupply of rocks and change your direction of attack. You could get the hell knocked out of you. Jake and Sheenanny were right in there with us. We didn't think anything about it."

More than the children of this insulated age, they grew familiar with the implacable finalities of life. They had a friend next door about Wallace's age named Terrell Rush, and he and Wallace went to an all-day swimming picnic one Fourth of July; when they returned, Wallace was scorched, but Terrell was stricken with a fever. "I don't know why it didn't get me like it got him," says Wallace. "I was ill a few days, but Terrell got worse and worse. We could look from our bedroom window into his bedroom next door. We could see 'em ministerin' to him, tryin' to help him breathe. He was delirious. They'd try to hold him down, but he'd fight 'em, and they'd try to put some ice on his head, but he'd just flip it away. We just couldn't believe Terrell was gonna die. It took him five or six days, but he did—he finally died. It sho was sad, watchin' him dyin' like that. He used to play with my dog a lot. He was just a quiet, nice little boy, and everybody liked him."

The weekdays would pass as only a flat, fretful, noisy hiatus between the Sabbaths and the music of their stillness. They went to the simple white-frame Methodist church in Clio, which consisted merely of one large room and a smaller room in the back for the children's Sunday school; there, in the summer, with the windows open to the hot piny afternoon outside, they would pass the Sunday-school hour swatting at wasps with paper fans advertising the local funeral parlor; but in the winter, with the windows shut tight and the two-by-fours which propped them up through the hot months now lying cobwebbed and fly-specked on the ledges, there was only the smell of dust, the empty fluting of mud-dauber nests crusted to the corners of the ceiling, and the voice of their teacher mumbling like the familiar hum of a fly in the small room. After that, they would file into the sanctuary for the preaching service, with people bumping and coughing into the pews, and then the first abrupt imperious chords of the piano and the voices gathering after it a moment later, following it like the slow, steady swinging of a scythe. After church they were sometimes allowed to go out in broomsage fields and hunt for rabbits with sticks—guns were forbidden on Sunday.

There was a general happy combativeness among the young males of the community. "There were the Watson brothers," says Gerald, "Billy, Buck, H.D., John, and Clyde—they were all nineteen and twenty years old when we weren't but nine and ten. They'd be standing in front of this store in Clayton whenever we came over from Clio, and they'd holler, 'You Walruses get out of town'—they'd tell us they were gonna cut our peters off. They scared the hell out of us. Got to where, when we'd come to Clayton, we wouldn't go anywhere near that store." The fights, when they came, were quick, furious, and curiously impersonal. "There was this fella named Clyde Norton," says Gerald, "and we'd fight every time we saw each other. There wasn't any way for us to avoid fightin'. I mean, if I just saw him comin' across the street, I'd meet him halfway and we'd go to it."

Discipline, as they were growing up, was also quick, direct, and refreshingly physical, involving belt strops and switches. "The worst whuppin' we ever got," says Gerald Wallace, "was when we were about six or seven: Mother had got herself twenty Rhode Island pullets, and they'd just begun layin', and one day we found some fishin' poles and stuck some little kernels of cooked corn on the hooks and then went up on that high back porch and threw out our lines. We caught two of 'em, flappin' and pullin', before she found us. It was funny to us, but she whupped the livin' shit out of us. She never used her hand. She'd use peach-tree switches. She planted about twenty peach trees, and she never got a peach off one of 'em. That's the damn truth."

When they were little, she gave them books for Christmas—*Robinson Crusoe* and *Tom Swift*. She was distressed when their father brought them boxing gloves from Columbus, Georgia, and began giving them lessons. "I never did care much for boxing," she says. At first, they would thump away at each other for the entertainment of spectators during the halftime of basketball games in the school's wooden gymnasium, and then they built a ring of their own in their grassless, dusty, chicken-tracked backyard—a plank platform under the pecan trees with ropes attached to two-by-fours, and a big stump and boards placed on upended log chunks for spectators to sit on—and charge a penny admission for bouts with boys enlisted from the neighborhood. On some afternoons as many as fifty people would be clustered in the backyard. A young college student who was working part-time in the telephone exchange on the top floor of a building across the street would serve as timekeeper, watching the fights from his window and ringing up the Wallaces' telephone to signal the beginning and end of each round. At times, Wallace solicited Negro boys off the street as sparring partners. "He didn't really recruit any of 'em," remembers one native of Clio, "he just drafted 'em. He'd talk 'em into goin' over 'to play a little bit,' and 'fore they knew it, he'd have them gloves on them—they didn't know what was comin' off. He wasn't brutal about the thing. He just wanted somebody to practice on. He'd resort to any means to find somebody to fight. But a fella that'd get into the ring with him was in a helluva fix. None of them nigguh boys ever came back for more—he'd whale the hell out of them. One of them said one time, 'They might draft me, but I ain't volunteerin'. He just couldn't find anybody around who was as good as he was."

Wallace was equally bluff with his brothers, particularly Gerald. "We fought all the time," remembers Gerald, "but he'd always whup me. We had this system at the house where, the one who woke up first in the morning would raise up in bed and holler. 'I choose the paper,' and that was supposed to do it, you'd go back to sleep. I was always an early riser, so I was usually the one who hollered first, but a lot of times when I'd wake up the second time, George'd already have the paper. So I'd fight him, though I knew it wasn't any use—he'd always beat me, and then finish the paper and throw it on the floor. He was just mean as hell. I got a six-inch scar today on my leg, right here on my thigh, where he spiked me once slidin' into second base. He did it on purpose, too. We had a fight right there, I threw down my glove and we went to it, but he got the best of me. He was a helluva fighter. George was always a good athlete anyway, and I wasn't. I was always on the scrub team."

Gerald Wallace now operates as a lawyer out of a plain little fifty-dollar-a-month office at the top of a narrow, dingy stairway in a downtown Montgomery office building. "I could have me an office in a big ole fancy building and drive some long expensive car," he explains, "but George doesn't think it would look right. And I don't want to do anything that might embarrass him. George, he ain't gonna put up with no crap." According to a number of sources, Gerald was summoned to the state capitol not long after Wallace took office and given a savage tongue-lashing behind closed doors after Wallace learned he had appropriated a state plane for an epic spree with friends out of the state—some say it was in Las Vegas, others say Chicago, others Mexico. In any event, he has apparently committed no such swashbuckling indiscretions with state property since then. Nevertheless, within his brother's restrictions he has managed to improve his estate in life dramatically: the Ford he drives, while of a more modest size than he would like, is one of the plusher models, outfitted with all the available luxuries, and he has acquired an expensive farm a few miles out of Montgomery. "I ain't gonna say it's hurt my practice any, him being governor," he said, "but I don't do anything to take advantage of it. Folks seem to come to you on their own."

A slight, reedy, parched-looking man with thinning hair and slightly bugging eyes, as frail and light and dry as a grasshopper, there is a quality about him not quite furtive but at least elusive and uneasy and quietly desperate. Up until his brother's inauguration, he had led a star-crossed life: he spent the years from 1949 to 1955 in a succession of tuberculosis hospitals in Alabama, Tennessee, and North Carolina and was asked to pack his bags in at least one of them, he admits, because "of drinkin' and some other rascally behavior." Wallace's manner toward him throughout, it seems, has been a mixture of exasperation and despair, though one old crony of Wallace's claims that while Gerald was in law school at the University of Alabama, Wallace, who was in the legislature at that time, arranged for the state to contract for an order of cars with a Tuscaloosa dealer where Gerald was a spare-time salesman. (Wallace also introduced legislation when he was in the House to raise the daily allocation for state tuberculosis patients from forty cents to a dollar and five cents, and to construct four new tuberculosis hospitals.)

"I'm not gonna say I'm especially close to him," Gerald says. "Hell, nobody is. I just help him out whenever I can. The only person I guess he was ever really close to was Billy Watson down in Clayton. He doesn't have any time for friends, and he doesn't speak of anything except politics. He wraps up his whole existence in politics, and if you're not interested in talkin' about politics, there's just no need to be around. So I just go my own way and try to stay out of his and not cause him any trouble."

When the churches staged their regular mass county-wide revivals, George would ride the shuttle school bus out to the site every evening, according to his brother Jack, "just to be there with the girls. He didn't care anything about the preaching." Those glowing nights during revival-meeting time, with young boys and girls drawn out of the countryside as thickly as moths, were busy with a continuous delicate flirtation that proceeded through the hymns and preaching in a manner as formal and ceremonious as the flirtations conducted by Restoration dandies and belles at the opera—the same hot shy glances and burning cheeks, the random brush of shoulders and quick mingling of humid fingers—with the service itself, especially the singing, acting as the same kind of sweet and exalted accompaniment. The choir, flush with young people, a little tinny but crackerjack, cantered through each verse of a hymn and then swung into the chorus like a galloping cavalry charge, whipped along by swift licks from the piano, looping the simple melodies with lavish and intricate blood-rhythms, a unanimous blush faintly spreading over the faces of the young girls in the choir at lines like "There's no pleasure in this world . . ." Their tireless, soaring voices elicited cracked and thirsty "Amens" and "Bless 'em, Lords" from the old people in the pews beneath them, who, their shoulders stooped under faded denim shirts and flower-print dresses, their weary weathered faces rapt and uplifted, seemed to have come there to feed off the glad and oblivious vitality of their young. And all the while, the young girls in the congregation would be employing their dogeared paper fans as coyly and tremulously as powdered and ruffled court ladies once employed their small lace fans—this exquisite flirtation proceeding on through the service and the invitation and then out into the musky night under the trees with soft twitters and laughter in the dark, until the girls were finally called away by their elders.

George weighed only ninety-eight pounds then, but he

thrummed like a hummingbird. He made all the revival meetings and dances. He learned to play the guitar, tutored by an old Negro named Cazz Welch, the two of them sitting through long afternoons under a tree in nearby Ozark. They began playing together at square dances over the county. "Yeah, ole Cazz, I can see him right now," says Wallace. "He'd be going with his fiddle with that cigar in his mouth, and I'd be tagging along after him on that three-dollar guitar." An old friend of Wallace's recollects, "Dances, anywhere there'd be women and music, that's where you'd find George. He was always around the women. I mean, once he found out what they were, and what they were for, you couldn't beat him off with a stick."

About twenty miles from Clio was an isolated nightspot perched on a hill close to the highway in vast lonely countryside. It is still there, Jimmie Ballard's Tavern. Ballard himself abruptly expired not long ago—"He got killed" is the only explanation—but his wife maintains the place, and it has changed little in the past thirty years: a long, low, dim room like a cave, with bar, jukebox, booths, and a scattering of formica-top tables and kitchenette chairs with nickel-plated legs; out back, only a short scamper across a bare rutted patch of yard shaded by a chinaberry tree, there still sits a row of dumpy little wooden cabins not much larger than outhouses, nestling discreetly behind dwarf spruce trees. "We used to slip off down there in the summertime," remembers an old companion. "These country gals from all around would come there and stay in those cabins for two or three days to have them a good time and then go back home. Whenever a bunch of 'em blew in, we'd get the word and go down there jukin'. Sometimes when we heard about a new crop that'd just come in, George'd have to borrow a quarter off somebody in town before we could take off. He managed not to miss many of those windfalls. Anyway, he didn't drink whiskey, he didn't waste his time and money on that. He was all business. We'd go down there and dance with 'em, and you really danced together back then—they didn't do no frug or watusi. And them was the kind of gals that you could get close to, them knowin' that in only a few short days they would have to go back to their farmhouses and belt-wavin' daddies or waitress jobs or maybe even belt-wavin' husbands or wherever it was they came from."

When George was sixteen his father took him to Montgomery to run for page in the state Senate. "Daddy just dumped him out in front of the capitol and told him to go to it," says Jack. "He hit the ground running and on his own, you might say. He had to go shake hands with all the senators and tell them, 'Hello, my name's George Wallace, I'm from Barbour County, and I sure would appreciate your vote for page.' " While conducting this first campaign of his career, he stayed in a room in the Exchange Hotel, a slightly dowdy hive for the state politicians in town. After one particularly gratifying day of shaking hands at the capitol, he retired to a grubby tavern near the hotel, planted his foot on the bar rail, and piped, "Gimme a drink. . . ." He was shooed out. But he won his pageship by a vote of twenty-one to five, and he began taking typing lessons at night after finishing his day's duties in the Senate. It was on a hot September night while he was in his typing class—bent intently over the slow and labored and dogged tacking of his machine—that some miles away, in Baton Rouge, Louisiana, a bespectacled doctor stepped from the shadows of a corridor in that state's capitol as a group of men approached him, pistol shots suddenly clangored, and Huey Long toppled heavily to the floor.

3

In the autumn of 1937 he arrived on the campus of the University of Alabama—a small, quick, wiry youth, as thin as a ferret, with a cardboard suitcase and a quality of impatient, exuberant, ferocious hunger. All he had brought from Clio was a single pair of baggy pants, a baggy sports coat, and two thin rusty white shirts. But he had already acquired a bulky cigar, and he chewed and flourished it with what seemed an easy and long-accustomed casualness.

He worked at varied fleeting jobs: driving a taxi, waiting on tables at student boardinghouses. "He ain't too tall, you know," says an associate from those days. "The aprons they had in those boardinghouses were for average-size people, and George was so short, he was always steppin' on the end of his apron—he'd be runnin' around, and all of a sudden he'd of trompled that apron right down to his knees."

He kept his expenses down with an instinctive nimble resourcefulness. "George stayed wherever the hell he could," a classmate remembers. "I don't think he was ever a paying guest anywhere, and wherever he was eating at the time, they had to ration the ketchup. Back then, if you brought ten students to a boardinghouse to eat, they'd let you eat free. George always had a big crew with him anyway, so he'd never have to pay, and if they didn't treat him right about the food, he'd threaten to pick up his crew and leave."

He also availed himself of whatever other provisions were at hand. "If he ever owned a book in law school, I never saw it," says another old companion. "He'd borrow my books or he'd study with someone who had the books or, most of the time, he wouldn't study at all and go into classes unprepared. Back in those days, you know, we had those old-fashioned double desks where two people had to sit together, and those desks were just one more natural blessing for him. He always picked out somebody to sit with who had the books, and while class was going on, he'd read ahead and catch up on his lessons. But the thing was, he could remember stuff we had in September when midterm exams came—he could recite cases, give you the minority opinion, the judge's name, and might-near be able to tell you what page in the book the case was on. Before an exam, he'd come by and say, 'Hell, I could never learn all that stuff in one night, I guess I'll just fail,' and take off somewhere on a date. But he'd manage. He never would buy them little blue exam books, he'd just borrow paper from the dean's secretary, and set himself down at her typewriter, and come out of it with a B, while I'd get a C after staying up all night."

Before long he had struck alliances with other cheerful and enterprising country boys like himself—all of whom, it seemed, happened to be in charge of rooming houses around Tuscaloosa. Most of the boys who arrived on campus from farms and small towns, though they looked as if they had just spit out alfalfa straws from between their teeth, instantly seemed to start quietly prospering. Two of his closest friends were Glenn Curlee, a short burly youth with a placid disposition who is now a lawyer in Montgomery, and Ralph Adams, also a mild and genial soul, since appointed by Wallace president of a state college, who at the time had borrowed some money from relatives as a down payment on one of the larger boardinghouses in town.

Sitting in his office one dim winter afternoon recently, as compact and hefty as an owl, with crisply curling ash-gray hair, Curlee reminisced as he chewed steadily on a modest plug of tobacco. "Adams had to go into the service, and he told George he could run his boardinghouse if he wanted to and keep everything above expenses. Well, George managed to fill up the place all right, but he never got around to askin' anybody for the rent. He just never got around to them kind of details. Finally the power folks came out there and cut off the lights. George and the other boys simply got up some money and bought some candles. The first of the month came around again, and some other folks came out and shut the water off. So I told George he could stay at my house until they got the lights and water back in Adams' house. He showed up at my front door with all his things in a paper sack. I had a screened sleepin' porch at my place, and I offered him a bed out there, but he said he'd settle for just a pallet on the porch floor, that'd suit him fine. This was the last of September. Well, came November, it got damn cold, and he'd wake up on those frosty mornings lookin' like a droopy chicken. Finally one morning he came in and said, 'If yawl don't git me a bed and bedclothes, I'm leavin'.' Just announced that if we couldn't do better by him, we weren't gonna have the pleasure of his company anymore."

Whether consciously or unconsciously, George seems to have elicited a special affection and solicitude from those around him. They delighted in him. "Hell, I don't know," says one old friend, "everybody just liked him, he was so full of life, and nothing could get him down—couldn't catch up with him long enough to get him down. We'd do anything we could to help him." When, in the course of his hasty, preoccupied scurrying over the campus, his sports coat became worn beyond all hope of restoration, they found another for him. They lent him money—fifty dollars once to buy a suit for an upcoming football game. "Those two old shirts of his wore out after a while," says Curlee, "so he started borrowing shirts from Adams. When one got dirty, he'd take it back to Adams and come back with a clean one. We even lent him ties, but he was so short they came down to his knees."

A member of their pack was a tall, raw, bony youth named Frank Johnson, from a mountain county in northern Alabama, who now, as a federal district court judge in Montgomery, is one of Wallace's most persistent and implacable antagonists. "A bunch of us decided we'd have some fun on George and give him an exploding cigar," says Curlee, "and Frank was one of those in on it. We all gathered around to watch him light it, but it kept goin' out. I had to leave for a ballgame in Birmingham, and I told Frank to call me at a number over there when the cigar went off. Well, I finally got a call from Frank, and he tells me, 'Glenn, that cigar knocked out one eye, and the ambulance is comin' for him.' I was in a state of shock. I don't even remember drivin' back. But when I walked in the house, there was a batch of women there and everybody was havin' a good time, and he was right there in the middle of it. I wanted to hug his neck, I was so relieved."

Wallace while he was in college drank sparingly, parsimoniously, sipping only what was necessary to share the company of other people. (He does not drink at all now, more than anything else out of a lingering country boy's wariness that it will cause him to lose control of himself, cause him to lose that necessary edge of alertness and caution in the company of strangers, and something bad will happen. He once confessed to a friend, "I used to try it a little, but whenever I got a few drinks in me, I'd just go like this"—he ducked his head and threw wild blind punches in the air—"I'd rare around and holler, 'By God, when I get to be guvnuh, I'm gonna, I'm gonna—' Besides that, the taste makes me gag.") He was once invited by some other students to bring a bottle of whiskey to a party, and he amiably presented himself with a half-pint of something called "Green River." One teaspoonful promptly made him sick. On dewy Saturday nights he would sometimes accompany a carload of boys on expeditions to a honky-tonk in another county, a tiny wooden shack set back in trees, which they reached by plunging off the highway and down a gullied dirt road running through a wide moonlit pasture. Wallace, turned sideways in the front seat, would be steadily chattering without ever quite noticing where they were, and he would keep chattering, ebullient and tireless and animated, as they dusted over the country roads under a brimming autumn moon, the others drinking without dilution or ceremony or measurement from the labelless bottles of sloe gin and whiskey, the car becoming uproarious, but Wallace himself, as one veteran of those ragged Saturday-night rides remembers, "just takin' a little taste every now and then, just for the sake of form. He was already high anyway."

He calculated most of his other indulgences with the same deliberate care. According to his brother Gerald, "He got to playin' a little poker while he was up there in Tuscaloosa—never for serious money, just penny poker. But even at that, he suddenly thought one night about the political implications, and he just up and stopped, and he hasn't played since."

But whatever appetite he lacked for drinking and gambling, he made up for it in his amorous gusto. He soon established himself as something of a rooster among the young ladies of Tuscaloosa. Curlee declares, with some wonder, "He'd get meat when we couldn't even get conversation. He'd tell us he had a date and he wanted the apartment by himself for a while—after a while, it got to where we had to ask him when we could come to our own house." Curlee, his feet propped on the desk in his Montgomery office, running his fingers down his tie, sent another spurt of tobacco juice into his wastebasket. "Later, about wartime it was, they opened up this school in Tuscaloosa for a bunch of country gals from North Carolina who they'd shipped down to teach 'em how to be aircraft mechanics. They were all away from home for the first time, you know, so George goes out there and gets him a job as a tool checker. That's right. Checkin' the tools the women used out there, makin' sure they didn't steal any. It was like a weasel in a chickenhouse. But there were too many even for him, so he started up a kind of datin' bureau—you'd put in an order for what you wanted, and he'd get it for you. I told him once, just jokin', I wanted me a fine virtuous amiable Christian girl and could he get me one of them kind. He goes out there and tells this gal he has a friend who's a preacher that he wants her to date. He brought me over to meet her and introduced me as 'Brother Curlee.' Yeah. 'I'd like for you to meet Brother Curlee here.' But that was all right. It didn't take her long to find out different. I remember her raisin' up and sayin', 'Why, I didn't think preachers acted like this!' "

During his first summer vacation he toured the Depression-blasted back stretches of Kentucky, Virginia, and North and South Carolina with a gang of other youths, selling magazine subscriptions. They slept in cars and seldom had enough money to buy a full meal, and Wallace—who had won the Alabama bantamweight boxing championship in 1936 and 1937 and was a member of the university boxing team—fought occasional bouts in smoky, dimly lit basements and back rooms in Kentucky and North Carolina, merely stripping off his shirt and fighting in his trousers with a wild, furious haste, yells clamoring around him, and then, bloodied and wobbly, collecting his money and quickly vanishing before anyone could waylay him with a blackjack or baseball bat to get the money back. He once pawned a companion's razor to buy supper. It wasn't that he didn't manage to hustle his share of subscriptions. "George was the best salesman they had," says one of the old crew, "and you either sold or you didn't eat. But he never made more than enough to live on. He was the biggest bullshooter ever born with those magazines. He'd go up and tell those pore nigguhs in these little shacks, 'The federal government has passed a new law says you gotta have readin' material, and we're here to see what you'd like to pick out.' They'd tell him they had the Bible, and he'd say, 'That ain't any good, this new law says you gotta have periodicals.' They'd tell him they didn't have any money for periodicals, and he'd say, 'Well, now, let's see, maybe we can work out something else—' and kind of crane his neck around like he was tryin' to look into their back yards, and then mention, 'I speck you got some chickens or something.' So they'd give him a chicken or two, and he'd give them their subscription to *The Saturday Evening Post* or that woman's magazine, *Delineator,* with them But'rick patterns, and take off. He was travelin' with another fella in a Model A, and they finally put them a chicken coop on the top. One lady said she'd swap him a subscription for a rooster she had if he could catch it, so he chased that durn rooster all around her house for about half an hour, and when he finally managed to grab it by the neck, the lady said she'd changed her mind—so he turned the rooster loose again. Him and his buddy traveled all over Kentucky and North Carolina in that Model A with that chicken coop on the top, and when they got them a penful of chickens, they'd drive up and sell 'em in Chicago and then spend a little time up there lookin' around."

Later, when the state passed an antirabies law, Wallace got

a summer job in Barbour County inoculating dogs. He traveled the back roads with his brother in his Model A, a dog pen in the rumble seat. The pen stayed empty most of the time. "He wasn't about to take anybody's dog away from them," says Jack. "We'd treat a lot of dogs on credit, knowing we'd never get the money, or we'd take chickens or vegetables or whatever the folks had. George didn't take that job for the money anyway. He took it to get to know folks." Wallace says, "When I got the dog job, of course, I met a lot of folks, and bein' interested in politics, I remembered 'em all."

Then, each fall, he would return to the university. It is the odd recollection of many who were there with him that they never heard him talk about home. "It was like he didn't have one. It struck us as kind of peculiar, you know—at bull sessions, parties, riding to football games, we never heard him mention his father or brothers or any other member of his family. He could have been an orphan. It was probably just that inordinate ambition of his." It soon became obvious, as one of his former boxing coaches puts it, that "he would like to keep getting up in the world."

A politician who was a student with Wallace declares, "We all knew of his ambition to be governor. Everybody knew he was planning to be governor, even back then." Ralph Adams remembers, "I used to walk down the street in Tuscaloosa with him. It'd take him an hour to go a block. He wanted to stop and talk to everybody. Everywhere he went, he had a crowd following him. At football games they used George at the gate to take up student tickets because he'd know every face that passed in front of him. What they didn't know was that he was usin' that damn gate just like he used everything else to advantage that came his way—he'd let anybody in the game who wanted in, ticket or not." Another state politician who was on the campus with Wallace recalls, "Actually, nobody took him too seriously at first. He was always kind of like a pet or mascot type. He was always very friendly—in fact, he was so humble, it got to the point where it was embarrassing. He always gave the impression of injecting himself into every possible crowd, like he was never there for the main purpose, but for purposes of his own. He seemed to be a misfit who was always scrambling, scratching, trying to find a place. He wanted to run for everything."

The campus of the University of Alabama is like a farm club for the future politicians of the state, or a meadow where yearlings are put out to frisk and test their mettle. Personal coalitions are formed there which last for decades afterward. If the Battle of Waterloo was won on the playing fields of Eton, many an Alabama governor and senator has been born in the dorms and dining halls and sidewalks of Tuscaloosa.

Inside the university's artificial and microcosmic political structure—a feverish competition between the fraternity bloc and the nonfraternity students—Wallace's style began emerging. He refused to join a fraternity, says a classmate, "because he said it wouldn't look good on his record, and besides, anything he was in he had to run, or he wasn't interested in belonging to it."

As a freshman he defeated the fraternity candidate for class president. "He came on the campus running," declares a former student who was a fraternity member, "and in less than a month he had amassed a large enough following to beat the fraternity machine right off, before they could reorganize and realize what they had on their hands. He wouldn't wear a tie, and his manner, his affiliates, everything about him indicated the part of a poor country boy working his way through college. He was viewed as a real liberal by everybody, especially by the fraternity and sorority people; they were suspicious of him. There was a debate one time. I was on the fraternity team, and George was on the independent team, and before we got very far along, it became apparent that George had brought his own rooting squad with him. He had practically filled up that auditorium with his men. Thank goodness, the decision wasn't up to the audience. When the judges announced that we had won, they let out a boo that nearly lifted the roof off the place. He did things like that, you know. . . ."

But somehow, it seems, he had already discovered the peculiar alchemistic values of losing, the efficacy of defeat. Despite his initial success against the fraternity bloc, they managed to frustrate him twice when he ran for president of the Cotillion Club, an office which actually carried more prestige than president of the student body. After his second setback, he was able to read in the student newspaper, "The only good politician we ever met in four years was George Wallace, and maybe we say that because he usually lost." And another staff member wrote in a 1937 edition of the paper, "My personal nomination for best sport on campus . . . George Wallace, who was still able to smile, chew on his cigar and shake hands all around after the votes were counted election night." Defeat did not seem to leave him dispirited, but exhilarated.

He graduated in 1942 and was handed a blank sheet of paper instead of a diploma on commencement night because he was still unable to pay some old student fees. One year had passed since Pearl Harbor, and Wallace, now twenty-three years old, enlisted in the Army Air Corps. "He knew he had to go in," says one old acquaintance, "but he didn't want to be no officer. He had it figgered out that when he got back to the county, there would be a heap more enlisted men voting than officers." He lingered in Tuscaloosa while he waited for induction, collecting coat hangers and selling them for food. Finally he paid someone fifty cents to teach him how to drive a dump truck and got a job with the state highway department.

Lurleen Burns at the time was working as a clerk behind the cosmetics counter in Kresge's dime store. She was sixteen, a slight and vaguely pretty girl with smoky, drowsing eyes, the daughter of a shipyard worker and the only child in the family still living at home. She had just graduated from high school and a short business course. Her upbringing, in the quiet dreaming little town of Northport, near Tuscaloosa, had been correct, churchly, and comfortable, leaving her with modest and specific domestic expectations. She was the kind of girl most generously described, perhaps, as "a good student"—earnest, moderately industrious, sufficiently bright. She was also an eminently private person, without a glimmer of interest in polítics. "Politics," she said, "was something Daddy discussed at our house with other people, not with me."

On a warm August afternoon, Wallace, his dump truck parked at the curb outside, strolled up to Lurleen's counter—the still air filled with a sleepy whir of fans, the scent of popcorn heavy and delicious—and asked for a bottle of hair oil. He had about him then a kind of thin, dark, vivid glamour. "I remember liking him from the start," says Lurleen. "He had the prettiest dark eyes, and the way he'd cut up!" Their courtship was quiet and perfunctory—bus rides in the drab light of buses into town to the Bama Theatre for a picture show, chill autumn nights on her front porch with the slow and intimate and regular creak of the swing chains, Sunday afternoon dinners with her family. He was living in a Tuscaloosa boardinghouse—a skinny youth in old droopy pants and a borrowed coat, ravenously ambitious, impatient—and Lurleen remembered, "He ate quite a lot when he came over to our house." She also remembered, "Even then, he was talking about politics all the time. That's what seemed to be really occupying his mind. He was already talking about running for governor. While we were dating, people wanted to know why he wasn't already in the service, and this bothered him. He was nervous about that. It worried him a lot."

His orders finally arrived. Shortly before he was to report for induction, on a cold night on Lurleen's front porch, he asked her to marry him. A few days later he left Tuscaloosa to begin cadet training. Then, while he was in pilot school in Arkadelphia, Arkansas, he contracted spinal meningitis.

"I liked to died from the stuff," he reverently reports. It was a treacherous ambush by fate, and he scrabbled furiously. "They had me in isolation, and I didn't respond to sulfa, and I can remember fightin' to get up, with them fellas leanin' over me with their masks on—I was thinkin' that if I didn't get up, I was gonna die. It took six orderlies to hold me down. I fought so hard, there were bruises and scabs all over me. After I got a little better, I saw them wheelin' folks past my door with sheets over 'em, and I'd ask what the fella died from, and they'd tell me, spinal meningitis. That touches anybody, man." He survived and returned to Tuscaloosa—thinner than ever, pale, quiet—on a fifteen-day furlough.

He and Lurleen were married by a justice of the peace in a musty office in a downtown Tuscaloosa office building, the windows open to the bright May noon outside. Afterward, with Lurleen's mother, they went downstairs to the H. & W. Drug Store on the street level, had Cokes and chicken-salad sandwiches, and then walked over to the train depot and bought two tickets to Montgomery. When they got there, they visited with Wallace's mother for a few hours. They spent their wedding night in a Montgomery boardinghouse—a bleak room with a linoleum floor, a large iron frame bed, and a naked light bulb dangling from a cord in the center of the ceiling. The next day they caught a bus down to Clio, Wallace still in his uniform and carrying his flight bag, the two of them riding through the spring afternoon. They stayed, during their short honeymoon, with a friend of Wallace's, who had rented the Wallace house after George's mother sold it and moved to Montgomery. "It wasn't much of a honeymoon, I guess," recalls the friend. "George'd go into town every morning, and when he'd come back to the house for lunch, she'd be at the door waitin'. Then, after lunch, he'd go right back uptown. He spent most of his honeymoon just hangin' around town talkin' to people. I wouldn't say he was cold, exactly; he just wasn't overly affectionate. He had already moved his mind to other things. He wasn't really happy unless he was talkin' to the boys and shakin' somebody's hand, that's all."

Before Wallace went overseas, they passed through a succession of brief and shabby tenancies in large, alien cities.

Lurleen gave birth to their first child, a girl they named Bobbie Jo, in Mobile, where her parents had resettled, and then she journeyed by train with the baby back to Alamogordo, New Mexico, to join Wallace again, riding in a muggy coach through the day and a long sleepless night. Their first night together with the baby, they had to sleep on a stranger's front porch in numbing cold, keeping the baby warm between them. Not long after that, they found a chickenhouse with plank walls and a concrete floor and a small heater and hot plate. "We were in hog heaven," says Wallace. "There were folks all around us sleepin' in tents and cars. We really felt lucky."

But there still remained the matter of surviving the war. Wallace was shipped overseas as a flight engineer on a B-29 called The Sentimental Journey and immediately began flying missions from the Mariana Islands through wasp swarms of Zeros to bomb the coast of Japan. "Man, I want to tell you," he says, "You'd see all them other planes gettin' shot down all around you, you'd get nicked, and gas'd spew out on them hot engines, flak all over the place, shakin' you around in the air"—one suddenly has visions of him crouching in the belly of his bomber, nearly smothered in his flight gear, a lonely, scrawny, lost little country boy from Barbour County, Alabama, wanting nothing in the world at that moment so much as just to be back home in the bed under the familiar, heavy, musty quilts in his grandparents' bedroom—"and them tracer bullets at night lookin' like they was comin' right at you and Jap planes zoomin' all around tryin' to get aholt of you in the dark up there. . . . Man, it liked to scared me to death. My hands'd be all sweaty, my heart just athumpin' and all."

On his first mission he was assigned to empty out dribbles of shredded tinfoil to confuse Japanese radar. "It didn't take but a little bit," he says, "but I unloaded every box on the plane—at least enough for twenty missions. My earphone was out when the pilot told me to quit, so I just kept throwin' it out, really gettin' it out there, man, to get that Jap radar sho nuff messed up. I wasn't takin' any chances." When they returned to the base, someone asked him how the mission had gone, and he reported, "Well, we didn't get shot at."

Wallace now reflects, "I'm glad I didn't have to see what those bombs did. It's awful that folks have to drop bombs on other folks. You know, Japan's a great little country, they a great little people. But to see all those planes, thousands of bombers, rendezvousing in the morning sun over the coast of a hostile country, glintin' in the sun as far as you could look in any direction—it was the most colossal, tremendous sight I ever seen in my life, and I been on top of the Empire State Building." After returning from one mission, as he was walking toward the debriefing shed and unzipping his flight jacket, he noticed small huddles of men all over the airfield talking with a peculiar tense animation; a few moments later he heard that the first atomic bomb had been dropped. "Hell, I didn't know anything about it, except it was just a big bomb, and they'd just put the first one on Hiroshima." He left for home shortly afterward, and while he was in the air between Hawaii and California, the second one was dropped—the second quick, astonishing glare of light which mankind had never seen before: two rapid illuminations, after which nothing would ever be the same again.

He was discharged with a ten-percent nervous disability, a fact rather unsportingly invoked once by Senator Wayne Morse, to which Wallace replied, "Well, I have a government report that says I'm ninety percent all right. I wonder what grade Morse would make. Any problems I have come from my war service. I wonder to what Morse attributes his. I understand he was kicked in the head by a horse sometime ago." He arrived back in Mobile on the thirteenth of August, one day before V-J day. He abstained from the celebrations in the streets, sitting it out in the home of his parents-in-law. "Hell, I was too glad to be back," he says. "I wadn't about to get run over by a car downtown celebratin' the victory. I'd already come through too much for that to happen to me now." As soon as the festivities had safely subsided, he hitchhiked to Montgomery to see the governor, himself a native of Barbour County, and got a 175-dollar-a-month job as one of the state's assistant attorneys general.

That attended to, he caught a bus on down to Clio, arriving there just before dusk, stepping down once again into the familiar clutter of small stores and plain houses, the solitary water tower, the cut lumber stacked, weathered, and seemingly forgotten in the weeds along the railroad tracks. The bus wheezed away, having deposited him there—a slight dark youth, not much larger than a thirteen-year-old, wearing what looked like hastily acquired cast-off clothing several sizes too large for him, his flight bag clutched in his hand. Only a few minutes later he was standing on a street corner telling a local political elder that he figured he might run for the legislature now, or he might run for probate judge, he hadn't quite decided which one yet. "Maybe you ought to make it the legislature," he was advised; "probate judge would be just a little high for right off . . ." and he replied cheerfully, "Yeah, that's the one I was thinkin' I might go for first."

He returned to Montgomery and passed the fall and winter temporarily occupying an office in the attorney general's building, waiting for spring and the political season to come, eating for his Christmas dinner a can of tomatoes and a box of crackers.

A farmer in Barbour County remembers, "all through the war, people around here had been gettin' these Christmas cards from all kinda places—Denver one year, then the next year it'd be Guam or someplace like that—and openin' them up, they'd read, 'Merry Christmas, George C. Wallace.' I got 'em too, and I couldn't quite figger them out. I thought it was real nice of this young fella, so far away and all and yet bein' so thoughtful, but I wasn't quite sure I knew who this George C. Wallace was, and why he was writin' me. It seemed kinda strange. Anyway, when the war was over with and the local political races had done got started over the county, I was out in my field one fine spring afternoon plowin', and I happen to look up and see this young fella comin' across the plowed field from the road, like he had just popped out of nowhere, steppin' real smart and lively across those furrows, already grinnin' and his hand already stretched out, and all of a sudden I knew why I'd been gettin' them nice cards every Christmas. . . ."

Part Three

1

During that spring in 1946 he was seen everywhere in the county, trudging along the side of a road in a pair of chartreuse trousers and a vivid sports shirt and sometimes a tan gabardine jacket with a huge lurid tie haphazardly knotted around his neck. He had no car, so he would hitch rides with other local candidates. Or he would flag down school buses, cheerfully clambering aboard and walking up and down the lurching aisle hectically grabbing children's hands, and whenever the bus stopped to discharge passengers, yelling from the window, "Now, yawl tell yo mommas and poppas I said hello, heunh?" Brisk and ubiquitous, he would materialize at barbecues, church suppers, and dinners-on-the-ground on Sunday afternoons. At country sings he would inevitably wind up leading the songs himself, his hands pumping ecstatically, a wide and cozily nose-wrinkling grin on his face. " 'Course," says one old Barbour County politician, "he couldn't sing a note. Never could. All he does when he tries to sing is just make noise."

A politician who sometimes gave him rides to crossroads over the countryside recalls, "He went seven days a week, all day long. Seems like everywhere I went, folks would tell me,

'George C. was here a little while ago.' I passed him one afternoon in my car walking along the side of an old dirt road down here in this little community called Texasville, all covered with dust. He had on that pair of floppy outlandish green trousers, with a streaked or a brown checked shirt, I forget which, and a pair of ole beat-up brown loafers. There wasn't hardly a house in sight, he was all by himself out there, but he was walking like he had to get someplace fast, and he just flipped up his hand and grinned as I went by. And if you told him to meet you back at a place at six or seven in the evening, he just wouldn't be there when you drove up. There wasn't any point in hunting for him, you'd of never found him, so you'd just have to sit there in the car another hour or two, waiting. It'd be ten or eleven at night before we'd get back into Clayton, and riding in, we'd talk about the folks we'd seen, and whenever I'd mention somebody, George'd always say real quick, almost before I could get the name out, 'Yeah, now, those folks, they told me they really for you, and —uh—what'd they—I mean, they say anything to you about me?"

He managed to poll more votes than anyone else in the county. He had 618 more votes than the combined total for his two opponents, and 579 more votes than were drawn in the county by the man elected governor that year—Big Jim Folsom.

One of Wallace's current political cronies remembers that when he met Wallace for the first time, in the lobby of a Montgomery hotel not long after the 1946 races, "He was just a little gimlet-assed fella in a pair of britches with a buckle in the back. I said to myself, 'Good God, is that little boy actually a member of the legislature?' " He showed up for most House sessions coatless and wearing a loud sports shirt.

He and Lurleen were living now in the same boarding-house room where they had spent their wedding night; the other rooms around them were filled with railroad workers and drummers, with a single common bathroom down the hall, where Lurleen had to do the washing. Wallace himself was seldom there. Across the street from the boardinghouse was the Jeff Davis Hotel, where most of the other legislators roosted while in Montgomery, and, recalls an old friend, "You'd see him in that lobby all the time with that cigar of his. He didn't want folks to know he was having to live in that boardinghouse across the street, so he arranged for all his mail to be delivered at the Jeff Davis, and he'd hang around there in the lobby until everybody else had gone to bed, and then he'd slip out back across the street to Lurleen. I don't even know whether he went back to Clayton for the weekends—everybody else'd go home for the weekends, but I think he just stayed in that boardinghouse across the street waiting for them to get back. They'd pile back in on Tuesday nights, and he'd be running up and down those corridors from room to room, checking on everybody, toting that half a glass of warm Coca-Cola so he wouldn't have to drink any whiskey to talk to them." (Lurleen, meanwhile, had become pregnant again, and returned to Barbour County, where she gave birth to another girl—again alone: Wallace made a last-minute careening ride to get there, but was late.) Despite his antipathy to alcohol, Wallace would sometimes pursue fellow legislators into the hotel bar off the lobby. He was once approached there by a stranger as he stood talking to a table of politicians and asked if he could change a dollar bill. Wallace happily gathered together the change, but the stranger then refused to give him the dollar. After persisting for several minutes with a pleasant little smile—"C'mon, now. C'mon, now, heunh?"—Wallace followed the fellow out to the sidewalk, where he just lightly touched the man's elbow, his other hand still expectantly extended. "I'm gonna ask you one more time," he said, "I want my change back, or you give me that dollar bill." The man snorted, "You ain't gittin' either one, you little—" and suddenly was lying flat and unconscious on the sidewalk, not even having had time to blink at the short neat crack on his chin. Wallace stooped quickly over him to rummage the dollar bill out of his wallet, and then strolled on down the sidewalk and stopped the first person he met to chirp excitedly, "Hey, somebody just fell out on the street up there, right up yonder, see him? . . ."

Wallace may have seemed an unlikely state representative, but he had already caught the serious fancy of Billy Watson—a political version of those gristled, quiet, unobtrusive, seemingly ageless and sourceless men whose lives, since their ancient and forgotten boyhoods, have been spent leaning along the track railings of breeding farms for racehorses.

Born into a family of nine children, he was invested with no other name but Billy until he entered the Army in World War I, where he learned there weren't enough words in his name, so he decided to call himself William Winfred. After the Army he worked as a drummer over Alabama, peddling auto tires, incinerators, gas pumps (he sold the first plug of Bull o' the Woods chewing tobacco in the state). From that he naturally evolved into a drummer of political candidates. His formal business was a dry-goods store on the square in Clayton, but he dabbled in a number of other informal eclectic enterprises. He remained a bachelor until late in life, and when he eventually picked out for a wife the Barbour County Home Demonstration agent, he continued to be essentially a bachelor, childless, self-contained, as peripatetic as Faulkner's sewing-machine salesman, Ratliff—a droll and incorrigible hedonist, as humbly and casually mortal as stale cigars and bourbon in hotel glasses and money and election returns. He breathed as a Democrat. Once, at a Young Democrat convention in St. Paul, Minnesota, he began flourishing a fistful of bills, as he was wont to do in the presence of Northerners, and when someone finally twitted him, "With all that money, how come you're not a Republican?" Watson replied dryly, "Well, back there during the Depression, I was wearing shorts made out of guano fertilizer sacks. I have been a Democrat for thirty years, and now I'm fartin' through silk. I ain't about to change." He had a calling card which he would present to strangers: one side read "W. W. (Billy) Watson (Retired)—No phone—No address—No business—No money," and the other side read "The man who printed these cards for me said, 'Billy, since you have no address, no phone, no business, and no money, there will be no charge."

His calm level eye had paused on Wallace early. Watson, a well-seasoned campaign technician, was helping Barbour County's Chauncy Sparks in his race for governor, driving around with him over the state. "George was just workin' at little odd jobs there in the headquarters in Montgomery. But somehow he managed to push himself into the car with us—I turned around one day, and all of a sudden there he was in the back seat. Little later, we were in this hotel room in Montgomery, and George started tellin' Judge Sparks he wasn't gettin' out to the people enough. Judge Sparks just looked at him a minute, and then he said, 'Why, you not even dry behind the ears yet, and you come tellin' a man like me how to run a campaign. If you think you know more'n me, just what do you think I oughtta do?' George answered him real quick, 'Why don't you try jumpin' outta an airplane without a parachute?' I nearly jumped outta my shoes. Nobody ever talked to Judge Sparks like that. But George got away with it."

Soon Wallace and Watson formed a casual but enduring alliance, both political and personal. "Think it was that second time he was runnin' for the legislature, he came to me and said, 'Watson, there's these two fellas I've promised two hundred and fifty dollars apiece to, they say they know some votes they can get with it.' I asked him who they were, and he told me, and I said, 'George, you know all they gonna do is get a crop with that money.' He said, 'I know that, but we got to give it to them. I already promised.' So the whole day before the election, I just sorta messed around over there at the courthouse, and them two fellas was sittin' right over yonder across the street in front of a filling station, leanin' back in their chairs and yawnin' like they wadn't thinkin' about nothin' in the world but how they couldn't wait to get home and get in bed. But they were watchin' every move I made, all day long. They were still stuck right there in those chairs when the sun went down. I just thought I'd make 'em wait for it as long as I could, at least make 'em work for it a little by havin' to wait a fairly long time. But I finally walked over there—them watchin' me now as bright as a dollar, but still not movin'—and I handed them the money. They tipped their hats and vanished. Best I can remember, they got themselves a right good crop."

From the beginning, what intrigued Watson was that George always seemed to take on jobs bigger than he was. "He was so small, maybe he figgered it made him bigger. . . ."

In no respect could it be said that Wallace is fashioned on the tragic scale, but looking at his early years in the legislature, one is left with a sense of exuberant promise subtly and inexorably corrupted. Many still remember him from those days as a dizzily gifted young man with an air of inevitability about him, winning and eager and dauntless, with instincts that were refreshingly simple and generous. But he also was possessed by a desperate and almost embarrassing political yearning—a yearning so extravagant that as soon as he arrived in Montgomery, he asked Folsom to appoint him Speaker of the House. "But he wanted to hep out everybody," recalls a former state senator. "It was like he couldn't hardly wait to make everybody see he was for 'em. He identified with the common folks to a degree that you might have said he was almost in love with them. 'Course, it was the first time they'd ever elected him to anything."

He had not been in Montgomery long before he was described by one state newsman as "The Number-One Do-Gooder in the legislature," and another pundit cautioned, "House members would do well to look more closely at these do-good bills that are siphoning off tax funds." He presented a flurry of legislation—scholarships to colleges and trade schools for the families of disabled or deceased servicemen, additional social-security benefits for city and county employees, an antilottery bill, expanded old-age pensions, and provisions for mental hospitals and cancer-detection units. He even offered a "free hog-cholera-treatment bill." He finally managed to pass what was probably his most significant piece of legislation, a provision for vocational and trade schools. "When we were in law school," recalls his old classmate Glenn Curlee, "he'd see boys whose daddies were lawyers, but they just weren't cut out for it, though they were tryin' as hard as they could. They'd all flunk out sooner or later and be miserable. He said back then that when he got to the legislature, he was gonna build trade schools for those folks, and all the others who hadn't even been able to get into college." When a capitol reporter finally asked Wallace exactly how many bills he planned to introduce, he replied that he had about fifty in mind. "He kept his desk so stuffed with that benevolent legislation," says a capitol veteran, "that it lacked two feet of closing." He exhibited a particular antipathy to small-loan companies. "I can tell you why that was," said Billy Watson. "He'd been hunted by them boys himself. He got into a lot of tight spots with loan sharks, and there was one company that finally sent this big giant of a fella out to see him." He also continued to serve, at one time or another, on the legal committee of the state tuberculosis association, the legislative committee for crippled children, and a regional council on mental health. But it was out of his other urgency, which was a part of the same passion, that he liked to operate as a loner. "When a legislator introduces a bill," says one former House member, "he normally tries to get as many signatures on it as he can. But Wallace would introduce a bill with only his own name on it, and no others. He just wouldn't sign as a cosponsor for other folks' bills, and he wouldn't let any of them sign his."

When Wallace began his second term in the House under a new governor—Gordon Persons, a member of the state's business and political establishment whose politics were somewhat less lusty than Folsom's—a card on secret file in the governor's office bore this staccato rundown: "George Wallace. Supported most of Folsom's legislation '47 & '49. Energetic, ambitious, liberal, smart, probably will be hostile. Liquor habits: moderate. Women: Yes. Interested in legislation re Veterans, TB Hospitals, Welfare, Education. For appropriations, against taxes. Declined invitation to lunch at mansion." Another anonymous legislative grading list at the time, reportedly circulated by the state Chamber of Commerce, gave him a mark of C, one of the lowest, and added the comment: "Radical." One member of Persons' administration recalls, "He was the leading liberal in the legislature, no doubt about that. He was regarded as a dangerous left-winger. A lot of people even looked on him as downright pink."

The fact is, when Wallace first arrived in Montgomery as a freshman legislator, he was simply a part of the Folsom phenomenon in Alabama—a rowdy, yelping transition in the stale establishment politics of the state, roughly equivalent to the advent of Andy Jackson and his backwoodsmen in Hamiltonian Washington in 1829. More precisely, the Folsom years in which Wallace had his political inception were a revival of the old Populist tradition, a quaint blend of the rural Protestant ethic and a fire-brand economic discontent, which fevered the decades between Reconstruction and the beginning of the new century in the South and Midwest. It was a hectic revolutionary coalition of the impoverished rural yeomen and a few sympathetic landowners pitted against the large landowners and merchants and bankers and petty capitalists of the Gilded Age, the industrial Bourbons of the New South, the railroad barons and textile magnates and transplanted Northern manufacturers, along with their glad, glib, homegrown apologists like Atlanta's Henry Grady, who regarded the whole thing as a socialist insurgency. More ominously, Populism at first included in its sympathies the lot of the Negro. But it was racism, shrewdly cultivated by the plantation owners, which was its final undoing in the South. It was also probably doomed from the beginning since it was essentially a nostalgia for the old agrarian ideal of a democracy of small farmers; in a sense, it was a case of the country against the city. It inevitably guttered out as a serious organized movement, but the memory still lingers in the South's dusty outback, and Folsom—and along with him, Wallace—directly derives from its spirit.

In any event, the Folsom revolution in Alabama was profound—and has lasted. "You look at those people up there at the capitol today," says one former state official, "and every one of 'em of any importance first broke into politics with Folsom, were involved in his administration one way or another." In a sense, Wallace himself is merely the thickening of a plot, a story that began with Folsom. The huge and rumpled figure of that country-boy colossus has really loomed behind all that has happened since him. He was Wallace's patron saint, and if there is a tragic figure in Wallace's past, it would be Folsom. He was, in every respect, larger than life-size: titanic of stature, with titanic energies, titanic talents, titanic appetites, titanic weaknesses. And it was out of his fall, out of the massive decay of his hopes and his vision—out of his corpse, as it were—that Wallace arose.

For decades before Folsom, Alabama had been presided over by a succession of governors representing the state's power structure of Black Belt plantation owners, large industrialists, courthouse hacks, and local country-club gentility—a company described by Folsom as "the big mules." Campaigns for governor were insular and sedate affairs, largely conducted in the back offices of county courthouses and corporations' executive buildings and city newspapers, with a unanimous lighting of cigars and hats placed politely on knees and then handshakes and rounds of bourbon-and-Coke. Candidates rarely emerged for any skin-to-skin popular campaigning.

Folsom grew up in virulently political southeastern Alabama, not far from Wallace's home county—a great lumbering, galumphing youth, measuring six-feet-eight, with a size-sixteen shoe. He left college in the pit of the Depression and wound up in Washington with the WPA. Shortly thereafter, he wandered back down to Alabama and casually ran for Congress, twice—both times unsuccessfully. In 1942 he decided to enter the governor's race, and though here he found his true political dimension, he finished a distant second.

In 1946 he tried again. This time the veterans were back from the war, returned quiet and thin and grave to the cities and small crossroads, still wearing their faded field jackets and fatigue caps like emblems of their enduring isolation, tokens of their refusal to be reassimilated with a mute and passive acceptance into the old society they had left. As Folsom stumped the state—accompanied by a string hillbilly band called the Strawberry Pickers and flourishing a cornhusk mop with which, he boomed, he would "scrub out that capitol up there in Montgomery"—the crowds he gathered were thick with those gaunt and silent youths in remnants of their uniforms. And he told them, "I ain't got no campaign managers. Yawl the only campaign managers I got. I don't want no others."

When he emerged as the front-runner in the first primary, there was a general state of high alarm among the establishment. They suddenly realized that Folsom not only had in mind reapportioning the state legislature to weaken the power of the Black Belt, rewriting the state constitution, putting at least one paved road in every county, and distributing free textbooks, but also intended to repeal the poll tax. What's more, he had been endorsed by organized labor.

"We Alabamians are not going to let radical interlopers come into our state," bugled his run-off opponent, "and stir up disunity, and substitute strife and chaos for the fine and wholesome harmony and goodwill now prevailing. The people had their small fun in the first primary, but the time has now passed for clowning and hippodroming and putting on a medicine show."

Folsom, from the small junctions and village squares, answered, "They all satisfied with things as they are. They satisfied for Alabama to be way down at the bottom among the forty-eight states. They satisfied for Alabama people to make less. But they can't stop us by stirrin' up hatred and suspicion, and tryin' to divide race against race, class against class. We just finished fightin' a war against hatred and violence. So now we're startin' a good-neighbor policy right here in Alabama. The youth of the Alabama cities and towns who went forth to fight for their country in foreign lands are not going to be crammed back into the little niche they came from. They've had a taste of power from drivin' a tank and pilotin' a plane hurtlin' through space at three hundred miles an hour and whuppin' the world's best professional armies, and they gonna be the boss from now on, they the ones gonna write that new constitution up there in Montgomery. . . ."

He won by a margin of almost two to one. "Before that race," Folsom liked to reflect afterward, "there were two cliques that would meet in Montgomery every four years. They'd pick themselves out two candidates for governor, and you could vote for one, or you could vote for the uther'n. That was your God-given choice. But ole Big Jim changed all that. Big Jim talked to folks in practically every city, town, village, hamlet, hill, and gully in Alabama, and he forced every other candidate from that time on to do the same, and that's when the governor's race in Alabama became democratic. We got it away from the moonlight and magnolias, and back to the one-gallus vote."

As it turned out, his administration was essentially a disappointment. In most of his larger hopes, including reapportionment and the repeal of the poll tax, he was frustrated by a legislature still dominated by the Black Belt—a cluster of counties across the southern part of the state whose rich black loam had made them the major slaveholding counties before the Civil War; they had clamored most stridently for secession, had resisted most bitterly the Populist movement, and have served as the source of most neosecessionist sentiments and policies since. Folsom did have the gratification of seeing his efforts to reapportion the legislature eventually vindicated by the Supreme Court—"and they handed down a unanimous decision," he happily bays, "it wadn't just a half-assed decision." But he was memorable as a governor, as one former legislator puts it, "because of his great heart and his great vision. If Folsom's vision and spirit could have been sustained in Alabama, this state—and maybe even the South—would have been spared the racial ordeal that came later."

In his Christmas message to Alabama in 1949, he declared, "As long as the Negroes are held down by deprivation and lack of opportunity, all the other people will be held down alongside them. Let's start talking fellowship and brotherly love, and doing unto others. And let's do more than talk about it; let's start living it." He was given to consulting with his Negro chauffeur, on long rides over Alabama, on matters of state. He notified his people, "Now, I've sailed the seven seas of this world, and seen the seven races of man, and I want to tell yawl something: there ain't a bit of difference in any of 'em, red, yellow, black, or white. All men just alike."

In 1948 he undertook to run for President, booming that he planned to cover the entire United States with TVAs, and "I'm gonna send the professional soldiers in the government back to the departments where they know their jobs. Three good men in the State Department—one from the Cotton Belt, one from the Wheat Belt, and one from the mountains—with peace on their minds could straighten the world out in three months." But not long after this announcement, a paternity suit was filed against him by an orange-haired divorcée from his home county, who claimed Folsom was the father of her two-year-old son. The suit was somewhat complicated by the fact that Folsom, whose first wife had died in 1944, had just married a vivid black-haired clerk in the Highway Department named Jamelle Moore—an effusive and cheerful girl just graduated from high school when Folsom first spied her in a crowd during a 1946 stump rally. "There she was, and I just thought, 'Ahhhh,' and when I finished my speech, I went down in the crowd and found her and took her to a place across the road and bought her a cold drink." Folsom's marriage to Jamelle probably rescued him legally from the divorcée, but the scandal was politically awkward. "Folks," Folsom tried to explain to his constituents, "you know my enemies been fishin' for Big Jim a long time, and they've used all kinda bait. Awhile ago, a friend told me, said, 'Big Jim, they gonna hook you this time, they fixin' to get an attractive blonde, and they gonna dress her up fine and put perfume on her, and they gonna throw her out and troll her past you.' Now, folks, you know what I told my friend? I said, if that was the way my enemies aimed to catch me, if that was the bait they were gonna use, they were gonna catch Big Jim every time!" Despite this sporting admission, Folsom failed even to win a post on the state delegation to the national Democratic convention, and his presidential notions, which were perhaps a bit whimsical to begin with, evaporated.

He then turned his energies to grappling with the Dixiecrat rebellion in Alabama. "These Dixiecrats," he snorted, "all they want to do is sleep with 'em, you know, but when it comes time for breakfast, they ain't gonna sit down with 'em. . . ." He carried his challenge all the way to the Supreme Court, but in the end, Alabama's electors voted for Strom Thurmond anyway.

Confounded at every turn, his spirit still never flagged, and he continued a gradually hopeless skirmish against the massive shabby folly into which he saw the South entering. Even during his second term, after the 1954 Supreme Court desegregation decision, when the hysteria had already set in, he batted down the swarm of segregation bills issuing from the legislature and dismissed an interposition resolution, in which the legislature supposed it had nullified the Supreme Court degree, as "hogwash—it reminds me of an old hound dog hollerin' at the moon."

Actually Folsom was a casualty of his own magnificent

gusto and guilelessness. It would seem he was born to become a folk legend, the spectacular swoop of his style transcending his final political futility. Like Wallace after him, he flourished a Jacksonian indifference to aristocratic pomp and circumstance and seemed to take a country boy's relish in disconcerting, even disheveling, ceremony and citified starchiness. On one occasion the British ambassador, Lord Halifax, paid a visit to Alabama and was invited to the mansion for dinner. He was greeted at the door by Billy Watson, who always had a way of being somewhere around at such times, and as Halifax came through the door he noticed that Watson was barefooted. "Yessuh," Watson murmured, "it's customary for one to take off one's shoes when one is in the presence of the guvnuh of Alabama." A few minutes later, a welcoming delegation of state dignitaries arrived and found Halifax reclining on a couch in the mansion's living room, chatting comfortably with Watson, his shoes and socks removed and his trousers legs rolled halfway up his shinbone. "I'm very indebted to Mr. Watson," Halifax amiably explained, "for informing me that it is a custom to—" About then, the group heard a roar from the central stairway, "Whur is that goddamn limey? Let's get him fed and outta here," and turned to see Folsom sitting midway up the flight of stairs, a drink resting beside him, fumbling on his own socks and shoes. Halifax paled but maintained a thin smile, his hands folded delicately in his lap and his legs elegantly crossed. "Only," recalled Watson, "he got this look on his face right then like his feet had just went cold." Halifax proceeded, barefooted, but still game, on in to dinner. At the table, recalled Watson, he talked very rapidly and profusely, with frequent light skittering little laughs, until Folsom, bellowing a weary, "Aww, shit!" leaned far back in his chair and toppled backward, upending the table. With that, Folsom took his leave, instructing the Negro servant busily swabbing food from Halifax's lap, "See he gets everything he wants to eat and anything else we can get for him." After Folsom had gone upstairs, Halifax remarked,

"The governor, I'll have to say, is probably the most interesting man I have ever met in my life," and finished his dinner in relative silence, the thin little smile still on his face, and then went back to the living room, pulled on his socks and shoes as the others stood over him, and departed.

During Folsom's second administration, the national Young Democrats met in Oklahoma City, and one of the stronger candidates for president of the group happened to be from Alabama. "Big Jim was shippin' out planeloads of state officials and legislators for three days," says an Alabamian who was there. "They were comin' in day and night. I mean, he was gonna see to it that our boy was treated right. The only trouble was, he didn't leave anybody around to run the state. We even had the finance director flown out." While Folsom was in Oklahoma City, Averell Harriman, then governor of New York and aspirant for the Democratic presidential nomination, decided to drop by Folsom's hotel room to pay his respects, impelled no doubt by the fact that Folsom had just won reelection by a heavy margin. Folsom received him in his undershirt. After a short exchange of pleasantries, it suddenly occurred to Folsom that Harriman was cultivating him. With his huge arm wrapped around Harriman's dapper shoulders, Folsom advised him, with a benign little tilt of his head, "Now, don't piss on ole Jim's leg. You can't piss on ole Jim's leg. " A little later he appeared on a local television program with a tumbler of bourbon in his hand, a rather swashbuckling flourish, since Oklahoma happened to be bone-dry; as a political favor, he had Carl Elliott, then an Alabama congressman, sit on his left, and for obscure reasons he positioned a member of the Alabama delegation named Pete Matthews on his right. When the camera swung on him, he hoisted his glass and began, "Now, I know all you good Oklahoma folks think this is whiskey I'm drinkin', but I want you to know it ain't nothin' but good ole Oklahoma branch water. Ain't that right, Pete?" and he whacked Matthews on the back. Before the program had proceeded very far, as Folsom continued smacking Matthews on the back, Elliott discreetly slipped down in his chair, below camera range, and crawled out of the studio on his hands and knees.

Folsom's nature was expansive in more ways than one. During his first term, his compulsive pardoning and paroling of convicts finally brought a legislative investigation. He acquired a state yacht and named it after Jamelle. Expenses at the governor's mansion sometimes ran to 388 dollars a day. When his opponents accused him of indiscretions that disgraced the office he held, he would boom, "I plead guilty. I always plead guilty. Now, why don't we get on with the issues here."

For all those indiscretions, Wallace long regarded Folsom with an awe and admiration that were almost childlike. "Wadn't anybody in the legislature any stronger for Folsom than Wallace was," says one former state senator. "He really believed in all that stuff that Folsom wanted to do for the common folks. With Folsom, he felt his kind of people were getting a hook into things finally." Wallace regularly accompanied Folsom on jaunts over the state, and gleefully recounted to other legislators how Folsom, arriving one afternoon in Clayton to dedicate a new courthouse, tumbled out of his car before the assembled officials and strode directly over to the Negro janitor and shook his hand before greeting any of the dignitaries. Wallace himself asked Folsom to appoint him to the board of trustees at Tuskegee Institute, a campus which traditionally orchestrated the Negro vote in the state. "It was considered a very liberal move at the time," says one Alabama political veteran. "Naturally, nobody was thinking about race back then like they got to thinking about it later, but it was still considered very liberal of him to establish this contact with the Negro community. And he was real proud of this connection with Tuskegee; he'd tell everybody about it and all. Anybody'd said back then he would be where he is today on the racial question, we'd of thought they were crazy."

When Folsom ran for reelection in 1954, Wallace was his southern Alabama campaign manager, writing about ninety percent of Folsom's speeches, according to one estimate, including the kickoff address. "It was almost a master-disciple relationship," claims one old Folsom aide. "Everything that boy learned, he learned at the feet of Folsom. He even got to where he'd mispronounce things like Folsom, like saying 'I-dee-ho' and things like that."

But, as one Alabama politician observes, "Folsom was innocent, when you get right down to it. All along, he was innocent in a way that Wallace never has been." A veteran Alabama political analyst declares, "Folsom was a flawed masterpiece. He was almost great. But he could never be great, and the reason was, he was basically a kind and decent person. He was absolutely incapable of the kind of ruthlessness it takes to get things done in politics."

Actually, by his second term, whatever happier possibilities Folsom may have once offered Alabama and the South had already vanished. The times had turned irrevocably against him, matters were beyond him now, and the mood was inflamed and implacable. If he had not been doomed from the beginning, he had now run out of grace.

But his final fatal vulnerability was the simple and immemorial one of his kind. As was his manner in all other things, he drank heroically. "That second term, he literally bombed himself to pieces with the bottle," says a politician from those years. "A lot of times, in the middle of a reception or party out at the mansion, Jim would just quietly disappear. We'd start to missing him, and then we'd go out and find him stretched out on the front lawn of the mansion under the trees in his evening clothes, his gigantic shape spread-eagled on the grass, a bottle lying beside him. If we tried to pull him up, we might get him to a sitting position, but then he'd grunt, 'Naw, boys, I'm all right,' and swat us aside."

A northern Alabama lawyer who was House floor leader after Folsom's spectacular reelection victory recalls, "You'd have to catch him before breakfast if you wanted to talk to him about anything. He was used to risin' early, you know, before sunup. He'd come lumberin' down those steps and sit down at the breakfast table and put a fifth of liquor right beside his plate, and by the time he'd finished breakfast, that bottle was empty and he was openin' another one. Many's the time I've driven like hell toward the mansion with the light just gettin' gray, tryin' to beat the dawn there, knowin' that the lighter it got the further away Big Jim was driftin'—because if you didn't get to the mansion before the sun did, he was gone. And once he was drunk, all he'd want to talk about was Andy Jackson—'Goddamn that legislature, they against everything I'm tryin' to do, Andy Jackson wouldn't of stood for none of this.' That's all you'd hear from him—Andy Jackson. I don't know, maybe he just had too many disappointments during that first administration, because during his second administration, he was lost most every day. He would come in and inhabit the governor's office for a while, but that was 'bout all. The few days he'd show up all right—and they were rare—you'd see people runnin' all over the capitol hollerin' to each other, 'He's sober, he's sober, he's sober today!' "

But the times were growing grimmer in Alabama, and before long the people ceased even being amused by Folsom. His association with Folsom began to afford Wallace acute discomfort. Then Folsom created a major furor in the state when he hosted Adam Clayton Powell, at the time a fledgling Harlem congressman on a dramatic excursion into Deep Dixie, to a drink of Scotch at the mansion. "Big Jim had a great way of not saying anything when there was a fuss, and hoping it'd go away," says one of his old allies. "Well, that worked pretty good, until he had that drink of Scotch with Powell. That was one that didn't go away."

"When Wallace heard about the Powell thing," says an Alabama newsman, "that was the day he knew he had to break with Folsom." He availed himself of a small political frustration to do it: Wallace had asked Folsom to appoint Billy

Watson to a vacancy on the Board of Revenue in Barbour County, but Folsom, trading for votes on a pending reapportionment bill, named instead a member of the family that had been sporadic antagonists of the Wallaces in the county—in fact, it had been a member of that family whom Wallace's father had pursued through the courthouse with a pocket knife. When Wallace heard of Folsom's decision, according to one eyewitness, "he walked up and down that hall outside Folsom's office for about thirty minutes, grabbin' people by the arm and cussin' Folsom out so you could hear him at the other end of the building." That evening, he was in the lobby of the Jeff Davis hotel, still pacing, still chewing savagely on his cigar, seizing legislators by their lapels as they wandered past, and barking, "This is it. I'm through with him." Finally a canny old Alabama political broker, "Foots" Clement, motioned Wallace over to a couch and told him, "C'mon, George, sit down a minute and try to calm down." But Wallace declined to sit, merely pausing over Clement for a moment as he snatched his shredded cigar out of his mouth and spat a speck of tobacco to one side and then wiped his mouth with the back of his hand while casting his eyes about the lobby for other legislators to waylay. "I'm through with him, Foots. Why, he appointed a man who's *fought* me down there!" Clement said, "Well, if you gonna split with him, you better do it over an issue. It's gonna look a little petty splittin' over just a little home-county political appointment." Wallace answered quickly, almost while Clement was still talking, "Well, Big Jim's always been weak on the nigguh issue." Clement stared at him a moment. "You say that like you already been thinkin' about it a little." Wallace looked at him, his eyes bright. "Well, ain't he? Ain't you heard folks talkin'?"

When Folsom learned of Wallace's mood, says one of his former cabinet officials, "It hurt Big Jim bad. It hurt him deep." Two men close to both Folsom and Wallace arranged a meeting with Wallace at a small café in Union Springs, a village between Clayton and Montgomery. "He said all right," one of them recalls; "he even seemed eager to talk to us, so we thought maybe he was anxious to patch things up. We drove down that very afternoon. He was waitin' on us when we got there. We sat there in that little café by a window, drinkin' coffee and talkin', for must of been about two hours—tellin' him how upset Big Jim was, askin' him to come on back with us 'cause a little biddy political appointment wadn't much of a reason to break with a man like that. But it seemed like his mind had already been made up when he was standin' there waitin' for us. 'Naw, boys,' he said, 'folks are fed up with this entertainin' nigguhs in the mansion. Something else they fed up with too is the drinkin'. Naw, boys, I'm goin' all the way with it.' " And before long, he had begun to approach his old associates in the House, men still working with Folsom, urging them to renounce Folsom too. One of them remembers, "He kept tellin' me, 'Folsom's gonna gut you. Hit him. You better hit him now before it's too late.' "

Folsom has not won an important political race in Alabama since his second term ended, in 1959. He tried for governor again in 1962, the year Wallace was elected, and his annihilation, with that campaign, was complete. Ironically, the ultimate mortal stroke was prompted not so much by his racial attitudes as by a single absurd and freakish moment, a treacherous last-second fiasco that has become a classic in the lore of political disaster in Alabama. Right up to election eve there were clear signs that Folsom had managed to muster from the old halcyon days enough vitality to ensure himself a place in the runoff. But the night before the vote, when he was to make a statewide address on television, he arrived at the studio catastrophically drunk. The telecast was live, and it was too late to stop it. Folsom tried to introduce his children but forgot their names—"Now, lessee, which one are you?"—affectionately ruffled his wife's hair with his huge hand, and finally lapsed into making cooing noises to the cameras. "Sitting there watching it, you couldn't believe it was happening," remembers one Alabama newsman. "You couldn't really laugh. You felt more like crying."

Folsom now offers several explanations for that evening: one of them is that "somebody dropped a pill in my steak." But he seems to sense that he just messed up in godawful fashion. Talking to a visitor once, he paused, looked down in his lap, and said, his voice cracking, "I don't know *what* happened. It don't make any difference now. I'm way the hell out of the picture anyway." But to his old political allies, "that TV program" has become the great outrageous event—the isolated, capricious, demonic, devastating prank—that ended it all, and it still seems, in a way, to dominate their lives, to hang over them, though they have since scattered to the far corners of the state. But an indication of Folsom's political magnitude in Alabama once is that, even after that ghastly evening, he came within twelve hundred votes of making the runoff anyway.

Once more, in 1966, he roused himself to run for governor, but this time it was merely the antic and weightless blundering of a ghost. It was as if, having come so close to the runoff four years before, it was simply too much to accept that anything like that one monstrous accident could have deprived him of it, that so much that seemed inevitable could have been lost so quickly and whimsically, and time had simply stopped and would remain arrested for him until the chance came to do it all over again without making that mistake. So he went through all the motions. By now, it seemed the newly registered Negro vote would be a dramatic factor in the election, and Folsom, who during his two terms had probably struck the bravest and most realistic racial theme of any governor in Alabama's history, presented himself at a conference of Negro leaders in a downtown Montgomery hotel to entreat their support. But when he addressed the men, he neglected to update his pronunciation of "Negro" and talked on genially, oblivious of the hush that had fallen over the gathering. Later, in the lobby, a newsman told him, "Big Jim, I don't think they're gonna go with you. You made 'em all pretty mad in there when you kept sayin' 'nigger.' " Folsom charged back to the conference room, knocked on the door, and when it opened, implored the sergeant-at-arms who peeped through at him, "Look, you tell 'em Big Jim wants to come back in and apologize for not sayin' 'Negro' right. I just ain't used to it, but I won't make that mistake again. Can I come back in and just tell 'em that?" But the Negro vote went to Richmond Flowers Sr., and Folsom was lost somewhere in the motley, dusty pack of other trailing candidates. "I helped the Negroes, sure," he says now, "but when you help somebody, you make fifty enemies and one ingrate. Hell, when I'm speakin', my tongue just slips and I say 'nigger,' I don't mean nothing by it."

When the Wallaces were campaigning together, he appeared one morning at a rally in northern Alabama, looming over the heads of the assembled townfolk like a tired leviathan just awakened from a long nap. He drifted through the crowd aimlessly and restlessly and with a certain air of preoccupation and detachment, his eyes fastened on the ground as if he were looking for something he had dropped in the grass. In fact, he did stoop to pick up a Wallace button and inserted it in his lapel. When Wallace had finished speaking, he edged up beside him and leaned over and rumbled, "Awright for me to be here?" Wallace, flipping his hand to pat Folsom's arm backward, replied, "Sure, guvnuh, always glad to have you with us." Folsom then leaned closer to Wallace and confided, "Yeah know, I'm ridin' with Pitt Phillips today. . . ." Wallace paused a moment and then said, "That's fine, guvnuh. We glad to have you with us," and turned back to the crowd. For the rest of the day Folsom followed Wallace's party, standing off at the edge of the crowd at each stop, his hands plunged deep in his pockets, enormously alone. At one rally he sat on the tailgate of a pickup truck with his head hung drowsily, quiet and dull in the sun like a huge ancient dog, and at another rally later in the afternoon, while Wallace spoke he sat in the cab of the truck that was hauling Wallace's victory bell, unnoticed now by the crowd, his cheek lying on his palm, asleep.

In the bright, adventurous days of Folsom's political prime, his most familiar campaign call was "Yawl Come!"—a glad and jubilant beckon that he explained in one speech during his 1954 campaign for governor: "When I was a boy in knee-britches, my momma and poppa used to take me visitin' with the neighbors . . . and when it was time to go home, Momma would call me, and I'd stand by her side all tired out while she said to the neighbors, 'Yawl come,' and the neighbors would say, 'We will, and yawl come.' You know, there's something friendly and warm and sincere about that farewell; there's something about it that's deeper and bigger than even fear. And you know, nations ought to be friendly and warm toward each other, and the peoples of different nations should part with a 'Yawl come,' and maybe we wouldn't have to worry about who was gonna drop the H or the A bomb first. . . ." It's no surprise that the memory of Folsom now invokes among the minority of thoughtful liberals in Alabama the melancholy sense of a paradise lost. At the least, he leaves one with the feeling of something lost that was better than what came after him.

He lives now in the northern Alabama town of Cullman, where he has taken over a small plant which manufactures lock-nut bolts for cars—"I was the head boss of a nut house," he says, "so I figgered I'd buy me one"—and he sometimes travels down to Montgomery to hustle his product before legislative safety committees; on one such trip to the capitol, he dropped by the executive offices to see Wallace, could not get past the elaborate, evasive, polite parrying of Wallace's aides and secretaries, and had started back toward the door when Wallace walked in, saw him, and invited him in; they chatted for only a few minutes, and Folsom left his former protégé with a few samples of his product. But most of his days he spends in Cullman, arising every morning before sunup, according to his wife, and wandering for miles all through the town and its outskirts before returning to the house for breakfast.

It is a comfortably expansive wooden dwelling, neat and white, with a generous and neatly trimmed lawn shaded by chinaberry trees. On a recent Sunday afternoon in May he sat in his den, heaped in a large black leather chair, a vast hulk in soiled khakis and a white shirt with faint blue pinstripes, his left foot in a cast and propped up on a footstool. His khakis sagged from thin and exhausted-looking thighs and shanks. With his two wives Folsom sired eight children, four of them girls who are uniformly handsome, glowing, sleek, and brimmingly cheerful. The house around him seemed as full of spontaneous and careless life as an aviary, with a TV burbling in another room and the phone beside him constantly shrilling. He would sometimes snatch it up himself, listen a moment, and then clap his hand over the mouthpiece and deliver an ear-splitting yodel, "Bama! . . . Ohhhh, Bama! . . . Yeaaow, Bama! . . ." Finally he spoke into the phone to report, "She don't seem to answer. I'd hunt her up myself, but I got a broke foot." A shattered glass was lying on the tile floor beside his chair—broken how, broken when, he seemed to have already forgotten, glancing down at it with only a brief curiosity when his wife came into the room—"Oh, Jim, how did that happen?"—and swept it up.

His eyes were soft, dark, shy, dewy, faintly sad. His iron-gray hair was clipped and brushed upward in wild stray tufts, and his hands, long and tapering, looked waxy and translucent, like an invalid's or a penitent's; according to his friends, he has maintained a cautious sobriety since undergoing brain surgery two years after his 1962 television appearance, and there is about him the quiescent, chaste quality of someone who has passed through a holocaust and emerged uncertainly restored but still alive. There was a faint continuous shudder in the house from a giant cooling fan somewhere, a low and even thrumming that muffled all other noises, and Folsom, as he talked, kept yawning as if he were trying to shake off a stubborn lingering drowsiness, frequently pausing with his mouth slightly parted and his lower lip cupped out as if arresting still another yawn. When he finally reached his point after long vague floundering, his head would suddenly whip around, and in that quick movement he would seem to lose his idea for a moment, his eyes would stare blankly, and he would shake one long pointed finger once, twice, then again, like a fisherman fly-casting, until finally one cast would snag the idea, the next sentence.

"My daddy . . . My daddy was a straight old-fashioned Democrat, a courthouse politician. He fought the Populists. But me, I patterned after Huey Long. The difference between me and the other Populists, I refused to use the race issue. I can read the Constitution. There ain't no use in goin' out and lyin' to people. I coulda hung a nigger on every stump, but I just didn't go for that kinda politics. It don't get you nothin' in the long run. Folks give me hell about bein' a nigger-lover. Hell, I don't know nothin' about that. They was just against me 'cause I wouldn't hang niggers. You gotta get up there and hang them niggers. If you won't hang niggers, there ain't no use in runnin', that's all. It's an old Southern custom. Maybe if I'd taken a more positive stand—send 'em back to Africa and all that—the folks would of liked it better. I guess I just wasn't aggressive enough to suit 'em."

All through the afternoon, he was swept by abrupt dark gales of alarm and rage; he would lapse into silence, staring mutely across the room as one finger abstractedly tapped the knuckles of his other hand, clenched in his lap, and suddenly he would unload a long thunder roll of cursing. "Them Democrats up there in Washington—I raised funds for the damn sonsabitches two times a year for eight years, but I'm broke today and there ain't none of them tryin' to help me. There ain't nothin' about them low-down sonsabitches I like. Hell, this fancy-pants from Massachusetts—what's his name? They tried to put my whole family in the penitentiary. That's right. Them goddamn Democrats—them *goddamn* Democrats. Any governor they couldn't control, they'd put the income-tax people on him. That was the system, they either got you or your friends. Earl Long, they tried to get him—he was my friend. Them sonsabitches in Congress turned me in just like they did him. Them low-down sonsabitches. Hell, I'm for Johnson just 'cause them sonsabitches are cussin' him. Those bastards now, they wouldn't give me potato chips if they was rotten and I was starvin'. Hell, if *they* was hurtin', I'd help *them* out. . . ."

Though Folsom is hardly destitute, he has very little left from his days in the governor's office: only a few tokens, an old dented brass spittoon that now sits beside the desk in his den, and scalloped draperies that look like remnants from his tenancy of the mansion, faded and sleazy now, hanging improbably in a bare, bleak, pink bathroom. And it seems that Wallace now has him in a kind of gentle but absolute captivity—that he is a confined and disarmed giant. " 'Course, George, now," he rumbled, "George wadn't no race bigot either back yonder. Me'n'George was always close. My uncle and his granddaddy were Populists together. George ain't nothin' but an old Populist himself. We just disagreed on one thing: I never did want to take any credit for hangin' niggers. And he wadn't always like he is now. He just wanted to get elected to things, that's all. . . ." He leaned forward, a movement like the shifting of a mountain, to slurp from a cup of coffee, a fly crawling tinily down his massive back. "But I'm through with politics now, I'm done out of it, so I try to get along with him and not give him any trouble. . . ."

Finally he arose, with a slow and terrific surge, up on his crutches to see a visitor out. "But you say folks still mention me around the state?" he mumbled. "You know, I don't have no idea anymore, tucked away up here. I can't tell whether they still remember Big Jim or not. It's good to hear folks sometimes say they do. . . ." He waited in the doorway a moment longer, sagging tremendously from his crutches, a huge wholesome eye-crinkling grin on his face in the fine Sunday-afternoon sunshine. "Well, yawl come," he said, and turned and heaved himself back into the dim cool of the house.

Even before Wallace's repudiation of Folsom, he had decided to strike out on his own. When Wallace began his second term in the House under Persons, he was, as one of Persons' aides puts it, "banished to the two most unimportant committees we could find for him—local government and local legislation." He could not be ignored altogether, since he had been named floor leader for the League of Municipalities. But he was denied access to Persons' inner office; each time he presented himself, Persons' secretary would inform him that the governor was busy, and Wallace would turn and leave with a flat, hard little grin on his face.

So he left Montgomery to run for circuit judge in Barbour County. "Circuit judge was a little better than representative anyway," remarks an old Barbour County official. Merely by announcing his candidacy, he dislodged one opponent; the incumbent judge, who had been serving for almost forty years, quietly bowed out of the campaign before it had even begun. His other opponent was a state senator from Barbour County named Preston Clayton, a genteel politician and ardent horseman with a field full of Arabian horses just outside town. A parchment-skinned man with a long patrician face, fine, gauzy white hair, and long, languid, willowy hands, his family, a vestige of the county's pre-Civil War aristocracy, had been presiding over the community for years and had given the town of Clayton its name. The local UDC chapter had been named for his grandfather, a major general in the Confederacy, and his uncle had served in Congress; Clayton himself had served for sixteen years in the state Senate. He also had the misfortune of having been a lieutenant colonel in the army during World War II.

Clayton was blasted into political and social oblivion. Ever since that campaign for the circuit judgeship, he has been living in a kind of semiexile from the community which his family had named, which to a degree had continued to belong to them until one of them, Preston, had run against George Wallace. "Yes," remembers Clayton, "he went all over saying, 'Now, all you officers vote for Clayton, and all you privates vote for me.' He'd tell those country men that I was living out here in a mansion while he was living in a little house and paying twenty dollars a month rent, that I didn't *need* to be circuit judge. He even talked about my horses. He had all those rednecks."

Now, every morning, Clayton drives to the law office he maintains in Eufala, sitting there until noon, when he drives a few blocks across town to eat lunch with his mother; he locks the office shortly before dusk and drives back through the gathering night to the family home just outside Clayton—a small white frame dwelling, built in 1850, looking almost like a cottage, with a white picket fence enclosing a tiny front yard dense with camphor trees and oleander bushes, and a tiny front parlor cluttered with dusky portraits of his forebears, harshly and almost viciously painted, a primitive Etruscan-like flatness to their almond eyes. There he builds a fire in the bedroom, puts down the stock behind the house, eats his supper in a cold kitchen, and is in bed by eight o'clock. The townsfolk seldom see his wife. If they happen to call his home in the evenings while he is out bedding down the stock, no one will answer—his wife merely sitting motionless in their bedroom with the fire he has just kindled beginning to dull the day-long cold, listening to the phone ring until it is finally silent. Behind the house is a small fenced field, now scribbled over with brush and scrawny trees, where Clayton's grandfather once maintained the finest fruit orchard in Alabama—

peaches, pears, apples, cherry trees—but, says Clayton, "during the hard times, poor country folk from roundabout would slip in at night and scavenge for firewood, and before long the whole orchard disappeared."

It wasn't long after Wallace's election as circuit judge that Watson met him one morning in front of Clayton's city hall and casually remarked, "George, you just keep up with what you're doing, you can be governor." Wallace snapped, "I know it."

He began battering about the state in an old faltering Chevrolet to make speeches, driving all alone, sometimes leaving Clayton before dawn and not returning until early the next morning. "That damn car of his was dangerous," says an old friend. "The tires were slick, the battery was run down, it was always out of gas and water. He just didn't take care of it—he never had the time to get it serviced, he was too busy driving it somewhere to make another speech." He was still wearing the same pair of garish chartreuse trousers, now patched, which Watson had sold him years before with the assurance, "That's what they're all wearing these days, George." He now had a wine corduroy shirt to go with it. To many, he seemed, both as a judge and in his simultaneous hasty, urgent scrambling to acquire the governorship, a whimsical and unlikely figure. A former state legislator recalls, "Here he was going all over the state presenting himself as a candidate for governor, and he was still wearing his hair in a ducktail like he had in the legislature—you know, slick-combed and overlapped in the back with his ridge sticking out. I told him once that if he was really running for governor, maybe it was time to get rid of that ducktail, and he said, 'Naw. Women like 'at long hair.'" One of his townsmen also recalls, "He had this bad habit of combing that ducktail all the time. Anywhere he was, in a restaurant or church, he'd whip out that comb from his front pocket and start smoothing that hair back. I'll tell you, he might not have had any drawers on, but he'd have that comb. . . ." He made only one or two token concessions to the normal sobrieties of his office: he served as superintendent of his church's Sunday school for a while and was a member of its board of stewards. But when a friend asked him once how he liked his new position, he replied, "Fine, if it wasn't for all these damn legal problems I have to solve."

They were generally simple and humble problems, involving little more than the day-to-day housekeeping of the two counties in his circuit—and, more particularly, the small homespun quarrels of the Negroes in those counties. One case concerned a number of local Negroes who had been sold cans of Red Devil Lye by a flim-flam artist, who instructed them to plant the cans in a circle and then stand in the center of the circle, whereupon they would be cured of constipation. "All the nigguhs said they'd been hexed by the thing," says Wallace. "They were all sittin' down on the front row of the courtroom, and I asked them how many had been hexed. Every one of them shot up his hand. They all said, 'It's been 'ginst us, Judge. It's been 'ginst us.' " His disposition of such cases was usually genial and casual. When a jury exonerated a white man charged with rustling peanuts at night from the warehouse of the local sheriff, Wallace promptly released his three Negro accomplices, none of whom had been able to acquire a lawyer. "He instituted probation in this county," says one Barbour County official. "The former judge had been automatically taking the jury's verdict for almost forty years, but Wallace would probate 'em whenever he could. He wanted to give everybody a second chance." It was his habit in the courtroom to give money to the bailiff and dispatch him to purchase hamburgers for prisoners.

But when the cases were less folksy, he encountered certain difficulties. In 1947, in one of his first cases as a lawyer, he represented a complainant who was suing to sell land he held in partnership with other owners. Wallace won the case, but in distributing the money from the sale of the land, forgot to figure in his client's share. The clerk of the court called him in and said, "George, everything's fine here, you did real good, except you left your client out of the sale." Wallace swallowed. "My God. How in the world did I—what we gonna do about it now?" The clerk managed to stop payment on all the checks but one—otherwise, Wallace would have met with a financial disaster—and Wallace made up the disparity on that check out of his own fee. Accordingly, when he became a judge, cases involving complicated and bitter equity disputes caused him considerable pain. But that was not so much because of the legal subtleties they confronted him with, as because his primary instinct, even as a judge, remained, as Billy Watson observed, "Against takin' sides. I remember whenever an argument would come up on a sidewalk somewhere, he'd express his view, and then if he found out yours was different, pretty soon he'd of quietly worked around to where all of a sudden he was agreein' with you. You never could get him to be explicit about nothin'. He'd side with everybody somehow. He'd of found some excuse to side with a Russian if he'd ever come up on one." His inevitable reaction when presented with such disputes—especially disputes involving the more populous and politically significant families in his two counties—was to coax the parties into agreeing to a jury trial, and then, quickly and without comment, to accept the jury's recommendation.

A circuit judgeship would not seem a likely stage on which to engage in swashbuckling political poses and rhetoric. But in that relatively innocuous post, Wallace somehow managed to produce an inordinate amount of dramatic noise. In 1953 he availed himself of his office to become the first judge in the South to issue an injunction against the removal of segregation signs in railroad terminals. Incredibly, he began showing up in Washington testifying against pending civil-rights bills before congressional committees, flourishing at one appearance a copy of a dowdy and raucous little racist sheet from Augusta, Georgia. In 1956, when federal officials demanded to see the grand-jury-selection records of Georgia's Cobb

County, Wallace, in rather gratuitous outrage, threatened from way down in Alabama's Barbour County "to invoke the full power and authority I possess and shall issue an order for the arrest of every member of the FBI or other federal police" who might turn their attention his way. It struck many as almost an invitation.

Through such ambitious clamoring, he managed to establish some notoriety in Alabama. Actually, at that time in the state—right after the 1954 Supreme Court school-desegregation directive—it did not seem so unusual that a circuit judge should be so excited, since almost every other officeholder, from city clerk to secretary of agriculture, was delivering himself of pronouncements sounding like Leonidas' charge at Thermopylae.

Now, as the gubernatorial race approached, he began spending his evenings at Watson's house typing speeches. Watson and his wife would leave him alone in the front parlor while they finished supper, and then, after watching television for an hour or so, they would bid him good night and tell him to lock up when he left. And after going to bed, the last sound they would hear before sinking into sleep would be his slow, patient, solitary pecking on the typewriter in their living room.

2

"There were so many candidates in that 1958 campaign for governor," says one Alabama politician, "that whenever they bumped into each other and started talking about the race, the first thing they'd say was 'Now, who all's running?' " At that time the Democratic primary was still tantamount to election, and that one-party situation tended to lend itself to spectacular free-for-alls. But in 1958 the herd was exceptionally numerous, and the placard competition for telephone poles became acute. One candidate recalls, "I had a friend who had stopped to put up a poster on a telephone pole over in the next county, and he was just starting to climb up the bank when this other car pulls up and a bunch of Klansmen pile out with posters for John Patterson. They roughed up my friend pretty good. Seems they wound up in a stapling-gun fight, and my friend came back with staples all over his forehead."

Wallace made a spirited, if slightly tacky, beginning, purchasing one hundred and fifty surplus airplane wing-tanks, lettering them, "Win with Wallace," and mounting them atop the cars of supporters. "And everything," says one aide, "—and I mean everything—was painted with Confederate flags." Wallace also hit upon the idea of printing a comic book which illustrated, in primitively drawn panels of primary colors, spare of dialogue, his progression from an impoverished and mythical childhood behind the plow to the threshold of the most exalted office in the state.

One of those who attached himself to Wallace at this point was Oscar Harper, a businessman of obscure and varied interests with a predisposition for being in the general vicinity of politicians. He transported Wallace around the state in his Cadillac. "Whenever we'd pull up in a place for gas," he remembers, "George'd be the first one to hop out, and he'd hurry right over to the station attendant to let him know that Cadillac wasn't his. He'd explain he didn't have nothing but an old six-cylinder 1952 Ford. He'd look at my Cadillac like he'd never seen one before, saying, 'Nice car you got there, Harper,' standing real close to the attendant, you know, asking him, 'You ever seen anything like that? You know, I ain't got nothing but a little biddy beat-up Ford. . . .' Pretty soon, you'd of thought him and that Cadillac just happened to coincide from separate directions at that filling station accidentally at the same time. Then when it came time to pay up, he'd act astonished at the cost, carrying on about how he'd never heard of octane gas before, how all he used was regular gas and it didn't cost him more'n four dollars to fill up. He went into that production every place we stopped at."

Whether it was studied or not, Wallace seemed as indifferent to dress while he was campaigning for governor as he had been while a judge. Another old crony remembers, "He didn't know one color from another. We were goin' over to Demopolis one day, and he was wearin' this ole blue-checkered shirt, and finally Oscar turned around in the front seat and asked him to give it to some nigguh to burn, said we'd buy him a clean white one. It took us awhile to talk him into it, but we finally did, and we bought him another shirt before we got into Demopolis."

He was, in style at least, still a creature of Folsom, but there were certain odd boggles in that style during his 1958 campaign. One of his advisers recalls, "He was just usin' too big-a-words for some reason. Like, 'I am e-*la*-ted to be in this campaign.' I guess it was just one of those times he tried tinkerin' around with dignity and respectability and all that. He'd use 'mechanization' and 'modernization' a lot. Hell, it just didn't sound right, them big words comin' outa little Georgie Wallace. I don't know who it was put them big words in his head to tote around and use, but it sho was a mistake."

There emerged ominous portents of something amiss, something awry, as Wallace toured the state. Among the moil of candidates was a young novice named John Patterson, whose father four years earlier had been gunned to death in an alley beside his Phenix City law office shortly after winning the Democratic primary election for attorney general on a promise to clean up that gaudily corrupt town. The murder had generally enraged the state, and in a hot flush of sympathy and vindication, the state Democratic executive committee dramatically appointed Patterson to take his father's place as attorney general. Not only did Patterson set out to avenge his father, but he speedily proceeded to have the NAACP banished from the state. But it was the emotional propulsion of his father's murder that carried him into the governor's race. Before he declared his candidacy, Wallace in his foraging over the state would be met by people who, as soon as they had shaken his hand, would mumble, "Uh—wonder if you have any idea whether or not Mr. Patterson is going to run." When Patterson finally began campaigning, Wallace would sometimes arrive in a town just after a Patterson rally, and as one of Wallace's aides recalls, "There'd be people standing around with tears in their eyes. He finally turned to us once and said, 'I'm runnin' against a man whose father was assassinated. How'm I suppose to follow an act like that?' "

Wallace's staff still expected that he would emerge from the first primary as the front-runner and carry that psychological advantage into the runoff. But the night before the first primary, after a dinner for his campaign workers in a room above the Elite Café in Montgomery, Wallace confided, "Every one of you has been sayin' I'll be at the head of the pack, and every one of you is wrong. Patterson's gonna run first." So it turned out: Patterson led Wallace by some thirty-four thousand votes.

Though the Negro has always been the central preoccupation of politics in Alabama, that preoccupation had been for the most part a tacit and sometimes modestly charitable one. Ironically, it was not Wallace but Patterson who changed the nature of that enduring preoccupation to a volatile, unabashed, brutal irascibility. It's possible that, four years now having passed since the Supreme Court's decision, Patterson was merely reacting to the temper of the times (the immemorial chicken-and-egg riddle not only of politics but also of history is to what extent a time creates its leaders and to what extent the leaders create their time). Whatever, in the runoff that followed the first 1958 primary, Patterson—fresh, trim, dapper, with bristling gray eyebrows and small pale, squinting eyes and a tight, meager little mouth—quickly established himself as the stridently irreconcilable segregationist, while Wallace, more by default than anything else, became the muted and circumspect segregationist. "We'd never had any Bilbos or Gene Talmadges here until Patterson came along," says one Alabama political observer. "We'd always prided ourselves on being at least a little more polite and civil on those matters than our neighbors, and even enlightened sometimes. Patterson was a new departure for us. And I still think Wallace and the state both would have been entirely different if he had won that first time."

Actually, the distinction between Patterson and Wallace was one of degree, but degrees count mightily in highly charged contexts, and that difference between the candidates became sharply defined when Patterson accepted the support of the Ku Klux Klan. Wallace, after a conference with his advisers, promptly issued a denunciation of the Klan—though he was careful, at the end, to add he didn't mean to imply that *all* Klansmen were bad folks. Nevertheless, it's the opinion of one of his oldest associates that "his heart was really in it. He had a genuine aversion to the Klan. He just, in some vague way, didn't trust them. Anything that's basically uncontrollable makes him feel a little uneasy; he'd just rather stay away from it, whether it's for him or against him." After he made that move, Wallace found himself endorsed not only by the substantial Jewish minority in Alabama but also by the NAACP.

But at this juncture, all his efforts were just so much floundering in the face of the inevitable. Perhaps the most eloquent indication of the growing sense of calamity around Wallace now was that Billy Watson, the canniest and most grizzled political practitioner in either camp, who had already invested heavily of his own money in the Wallace campaign, contracted a case of the hives. But it still seemed Wallace couldn't bring himself to accept the fact that after so many years of concentration and anticipation and adaptations, after all the nimble and ingenious maneuver, after the unflagging expenditure of so much energy—after the sheer long integrity of his effort—he was now to be denied, betrayed by the happenstance of someone's father having been shot in an alley in Phenix City four years ago. Bill Jones, now chief liaison man in Wallace's national adventure, remembers, "As the campaign was drawing to an end, he was out of money, everybody knew he was beat, but he just couldn't stop tryin'—I mean, seriously tryin'. He was speakin' at this rally one afternoon in a little north Alabama mining town called Carbon Hill, out behind this little store. It was in May, a real sunshiny day, but there was only a handful of folks there, and this little band was tootin' and squeakin'. I was sitting off at the edge of the crowd in a car with Lurleen, and all of a sudden—watchin' him goin' through all the motions of a speech energetic and excited like it all wadn't already lost—the two of us just started cryin'. Our eyes just blurred over."

When the balloting was finished, he had missed by 64,902 votes. For a few days, according to one source, "he looked like a hermit who had just come out of the woods. His eyes were dilated, and he had this wild stare. He was talking wild—he was just pitiful." He dropped out of sight for a brief while. Then, one evening a month or so after the campaign, he appeared at the Jeff Davis again, wan, a little thinner, with a quiet and almost peaceful air about him, and found his way upstairs to a smoky and clamorous room full of other politicians. Not long after sitting down among them, he suddenly announced in a flat and heatless voice, "John Patterson out-nigguhed me. And boys, I'm not goin' to be out-nigguhed again."

Facing him now was a void of four years. "He just hadn't figgered on losing," said Billy Watson, "so now he was caught in this kind of gap until the next governor's race; he was caught out in the cold."

But before he went out into the cold, with only a few weeks left before the expiration of his judgeship, the U. S. Civil Rights Commission demanded to see the voting records of the counties in his circuit, and Wallace's instant reaction—like a last shrill cry, a last hectic gesture before he dissolved into invisibility for four years, to leave his image lingering in the public mind—was to appropriate the records himself and announce, "If any agent of the Civil Rights Commission comes to get them, he will be locked up." Frank Johnson, Wallace's old college companion, was now a federal district judge in Montgomery, and it fell his lot to order Wallace to release the records. Wallace loudly refused and promptly found himself facing a contempt-of-court citation. That prospect gave him some pause, and he quickly summoned the grand juries of his circuit—by now, he had only a week left as circuit judge—and unloaded the records on them, after which he placed a casual evening call to the chairman on the commission's panel of inspectors and suggested that if the commission would just contact the grand juries now, he believed somehow they might get to see the records. But criminal contempt charges were filed against him anyway.

His parting theatrics had become more complicated than he had reckoned on, and he began to engage in certain private explorations himself. Not long before his trial was to begin, so the most reliable reports have it, he got into his car in Clayton one evening after sundown and drove up to Montgomery, arriving in the still, hushed empty hours of early morning. Parking his car in a closed filling station a block or two from Judge Johnson's home, he called Johnson from a telephone booth, saying he'd like to drop by for just a minute if he could. A few minutes later—a number of Wallace's friends claim, with a chuckle, that Wallace actually drove to Johnson's with a paper bag over his head—he materialized, with a soft polite tapping, at Johnson's back screen door, with Johnson supposedly receiving him in his nightrobe.

But whatever informal accommodation Wallace sought to strike with Johnson failed. Soon afterward, in court, Wallace pleaded guilty of contempt, but Johnson ordered him acquitted, with the icy remark, "George C. Wallace, after receiving actual notice of this court's order, for some reason judicially unknown to this court, attempted to give the impression that he was defying this court's order by turning said records over to hastily summoned grand juries in Barbour and Bulloch counties, Alabama. . . . Even though it was accomplished by means of subterfuge, George C. Wallace did comply with the order of this court concerning the production of the records in question. As to why the devious means were used, this court will not now judicially determine. . . . If these devious means were for political purposes, then this court refuses to allow its authority and dignity to be bent and swayed by such politically generated whirlwinds."

Immediately after his acquittal, Wallace desperately insisted that he *was* guilty of contempt. "These characters from the Civil Rights Commission and the Justice Department were backed to the wall. . . . This 1959 attempt to have a second Sherman's March to the Sea has been stopped in the Cradle of the Confederacy." And four years later, when he began his second campaign for the governorship, he was still energetically calling Johnson "a low-down, carpetbaggin', scalawaggin', race-mixin' liar."

During that interval between 1958 and 1962, he seemed in a kind of violent suspension, filled with a ceaseless and directionless fury. Politically there was nowhere he could turn: he had no appetite for Congress, and anything else would have been regression, diminishment. Though his name had been lettered on the door of his brother's law office in Montgomery, and though he did divert himself with a few cases now and then, Wallace was actually supported during this period by discreet donations from his townsfolk. Watson alone contributed fifty dollars a month. "He didn't have anything," said Watson. "No law practice, no savings to speak of, nothing. Besides that, he couldn't take the time to bother about providing for himself, because he was too busy getting ready for the next time, so it just sorta fell on the rest of us to take care of him while he was doing it." That four-year purgatory was like a long ghastly premonition of what would become of him beyond his political existence—a premonition which he sought to dispel with noise, energy, optimism, and sheer dauntlessness—and even now, when asked about those four years, he manages to avoid talking about them. "Aw, I practiced a little law, just messed around. . . ."

At first he sat at home in Clayton and busied himself writing letters, in longhand, to the people who had helped him in the campaign. When that was done, it was still too early to start campaigning, so he spent his days at the square, talking to people. A Barbour County official remembers, "When it came time for lunch, rather than have to quit talking and go home to eat, he'd just grub him up a can of sardines and some cheese and crackers at the store and keep right on. Got to where he'd drop by my office every afternoon—he'd sit down in a chair and start up, and I couldn't get away. He just wouldn't stop talking. Finally, I got to where I'd say, when this lawyer in town, Crews Johnson, would stop by later on, 'Well, Crews, I got to go milk, I guess,' and get up and leave in a hurry, before Crews had a chance to say anything. Anybody else but George would have realized that, at three or four in the afternoon, nobody was gonna be goin' off to milk any cows. But George didn't even seem to notice there'd been a shuffle in his audience, he'd just switch over to Crews and keep on talking."

People also remember seeing him during this time on the sidewalks of downtown Montgomery, standing in front of cafés and newsstands, looking a little haggard and dingy and sour, grabbing people by the coatsleeve and talking to them with the fierce, blank-eyed, inexhaustible urgency of a street-corner evangelist. Whenever there was a convention in town, he would have a friend page him at the Jeff Davis—though he would sometimes be down in Clayton when they did. One former state official recalls, "You'd see him go into the Elite Café at least a dozen times every day. He was wearin' those little Buster Brown suits then, and he was shakin' hands every wakin' hour. He probably didn't even sleep. He probably just lay there in bed real stiff and still with his eyes open waitin' for it to be morning again when the folks would start comin' back out." A prominent Alabama politician who had been one of the candidates in the 1958 governor's race recollects, "One Fourth of July—it must have been around 1961—I took my family up to this cabin I have on Guntersville Lake to spend the holidays up there. It turned out that I had to drive back down into town for something on the afternoon of the Fourth. I had finished what little shopping I had to do, and was going back to my car, when who do I see coming down the sidewalk with a coat and tie on—shaking hands with everybody he can snatch, and no telling where his wife and family are, no telling whether they even know he's way the hell up here in the northeast corner of the state—but George Wallace. I just stood there for a minute watching him. And then I said, 'Good Lord. Good Lord . . . !' "

When the 1962 race finally began, he momentarily crumbled. Suddenly, just after his second campaign had gotten under way, he couldn't remember the names of his closest advisers. He began to be haunted by the notion that his campaign had run out of money. On a Sunday afternoon in a Montgomery hotel room, a few friends finally persuaded him to enter the hospital. "We slipped him down a back stairway after dark," said Harper. "The collar of his coat was turned up, and the brim of his hat was pulled down so nobody would recognize him. He looked like a Dead End kid." He was confined for only a few days. Some of his associates quickly rummaged up twenty thousand dollars, and one of them took the money to Wallace's hospital room, walked in without knocking, and without a word, in a motion like a planter flinging out seed, threw the money across the bed. Wallace, the reports are, simply stared for a moment at all the bills scattered over his sheet, and then bounded nimbly to the floor and started dressing. The following evening, after delivering a state-wide television address, he was on the phone until three the next morning checking reaction all over the state.

Wallace now, in 1962, was thrown into a confrontation

with his old political mentor, Big Jim Folsom, who—seemingly indestructible and eternal—had massively bestirred himself to try for a third term. It was Folsom that Wallace and his advisers assumed to be the formidable figure in the campaign, the candidate they would have to beat in the first primary and then in the runoff. In what was a final ritual of fratricide, Wallace proceeded systematically to complete Folsom's political annihilation—not head-on, not with a frontal assault, but by striking Folsom in those spots where he was already bleeding. Without mentioning Folsom's name, he launched what amounted to a temperance campaign, holding one of his first rallies in Folsom's home county on the same day Folsom was speaking in a nearby town, vowing that there would be no liquor in the mansion so long as he was governor, denouncing the state's liquor-agent system, a patronage policy. After his rally in Folsom's home county he was approached by a man in coveralls who said, "I'm hearin' you don't drink yo'self," and Wallace answered quickly, "No suh, I don't drink and no member of my immediate family drinks." At graduate speeches he would advise students, "Now, you don't have to drink to be a man or a lady." He even had it advertised about that, when he had written to the Grand Ole Opry requesting an entertainer for his campaign, he had stipulated they send him a teetotaler. Wallace, in addition, promised he would sell the state's two yachts, a reference to Folsom's expensive style of living while in the governorship.

Then, on the eve of the first primary, Folsom made his legendary television address, indignantly scuffling with aides who tried to restrain him from going on camera, and when the voting was finished the next day, he was gone. Instead of Folsom, Wallace now faced in the runoff a personable and vigorous young state senator named Ryan DeGraffenried, scion of an old aristocratic family of Tuscaloosa, an articulate moderate on segregation and a reluctantly committed Democrat. DeGraffenried's emergence as the runoff opponent caused a ripple of concern among Wallace's aides. Presenting as he did the alternative of measured, responsible, sober resistance to the federal government as against Wallace's reckless and flaring defiance, he could be expected to gain support from power structures that would have been neutralized in a campaign between Wallace and Folsom.

But such were the times in Alabama that to be moderate was to be demolished. "By 1962," says one Wallace aide, "folks understood the Supreme Court decision of 1954 would put colored kids in their schools. They didn't really understand that in 1958. Patterson just educated them for us." Alabama was still innocent of the consequences of point-blank defiance, and Wallace was an enthralling, giddy, irresistible temptation. He vowed he would place his body in the door of any schoolhouse ordered to integrate, and before long DeGraffenried was left protesting the honesty and aggressiveness of his own segregationist beliefs.

Wallace's style had improved as well. "This time," says one veteran Wallace aide, "he wadn't using them big words like 'e-*la*-ted' and 'mechanization.' He was speaking their language this time. Like, I remember the time he first called Frank Johnson a low-down, carpetbaggin', scalawaggin', race-mixin' liar. The crowd liked to went wild. People started advising him he ought not to be talking about a federal judge thataway, it wadn't *dignified,* but we told him to stay with it. Got to where, later in the campaign, ever time he started coming up on that line, the folks'd start punching and poking each other and grinning and all, waiting for him to get to it. Once he put in 'pool-mixin' just to see how that would sound. He liked to work around with things like that, and we'd watch the crowd reaction. There'd be a bunch of farmers standing around at some little crossroads, and you knew he'd scored with something when you saw them just kinda quietly nod their heads. Or even better, when you'd see those hands coming out of those coverall pockets to clap, out from behind those coverall bibs, you knew he'd reached them. Those folks don't take their hands out from behind them bibs for much they hear. It's got to be something special. So when we'd get back in the car with George and start out for the next place, we'd tell him where the hands had come out of the pockets and say, 'You wanna stick with that one, now. . . .' "

At times he would use a plane, landing in cow pastures and even cornfields. And gradually, as the inevitability of his victory became clearer, the campaigning became something else, something larger: a commemoration, a processional both of memory and anticipation; a long and luxurious celebration of final arrival, imminent consummation; but conducted still without pageant or finery, exactly faithful—as if deviation, now with it so close, would spoil or maybe even revoke it—to the simple, plain, inauspicious, persistent manner that had brought it about. He had to keep everything the same, had to keep doing everything the same way—maybe just holding his breath a little now, but that's all—until the last minute, until it came about.

"You couldn't even see some of those places we were stopping at," says one of his old aides. "Anyplace they had three buildings, he'd go into a store and get a can of sardines and some crackers, or maybe some Vienna sausages, and then sit down on a drink crate with a bottle of Big Orange and talk to the folks that gathered. We got lost one time out in the country trying to find this school he was supposed to speak at, and while we were riding around lost, he spotted some men putting up lights on these utility poles. He said, 'Stop a minute, let me get these fellas,' and jumped outta the car. He had to go across this big deep ditch to get to them, but he didn't hesitate, he went right on down into it, disappearing clean outta sight for a second, and then he was coming back up the other side—he flowed in and outta that ditch like a hound chasing a rabbit. Then he stood at the bottom of that utility pole—he had those fellas treed, all right—until they climbed down and shook hands with him. We'd stop at another place, and he'd see this mechanic under a car, he'd go over and tap the fella on the leg until the fella came up to see what was bothering him, and then he'd shake his hand."

Toward the closing days of the campaign he began softly murmuring to his aides as they drove from rally to rally, "You know, I think we got this thing won. Yessuh. I think we got it won. . . ."

The night of the election, sometime after it had become apparent that he would receive the largest number of votes of any gubernatorial candidate in Alabama's history, he disappeared from his campaign headquarters in Montgomery. His staff finally found him in a small diner a few short blocks down the street from the capitol, perched on a stool at the far end of the counter under bleak and flickering lights, disposing of a charred hamburger steak lavishly splashed with ketchup.

The governor's mansion is a vast white-columned hulk built in 1900 by a Confederate general, filled with slightly forbidding Victorian furniture of velvet wines, maroons, yellow ochers, and moss greens, with marble fireplaces and enormous gold-leaf mirrors and friezework done by French artisans, its drawing room complete with piano, its long dining room presided over by a somber portrait of Robert E. Lee. Wallace and Lurleen moved in with nothing but their clothes. The night of the inaugural ball, he put on a tux for a while but finally looked out the front door at the guests still chattering and milling over the lawn under the lanterns, turned to Lurleen, and said, "How much longer you reckon these folks are gonna want to stay? I gotta turn in. You can tell them I said just to go ahead with everything, but to 'scuse me." He then made his way upstairs, swiftly got into his pajamas, and by nine-thirty was asleep.

Part Four

As governor, Wallace proved to be, aside from his racial aberration, essentially a Populist. In this sense, his administration was an extension of Folsom's, a projection of his own days in the legislature.

He built fourteen new junior colleges and fifteen new trade schools, initiated a one-hundred-million-dollar-school-construction program and a free-textbook policy. He pitched into the largest roadbuilding project in the state's history, devised plans for new nursing homes and medical clinics, and introduced an ambitious act to keep all the waterways of the state twinkling clean. And the proportion of Alabama citizens—338 out of every thousand—participating in public welfare programs at the end of his term was exceeded by those of only one other state, Louisiana. One of Wallace's old Folsom allies admits, "His economic programs surpassed the fondest dreams of every liberal in the state. He did what all the Populists have always dreamed of doing." Judge Roy Mayhall, a loyalist Democrat who was once chairman of the state party executive committee, maintains, "Wallace is the most economically liberal politician I know of. He's more liberal than Johnson, I tell you—more liberal than Folsom or Kennedy ever were. We owe per capita in this state *twice* what we *ever* owed. And we have to pay more interest on it, because it's not a general state obligation which entails all the state's revenue—a general state obligation has to be voted on, but Wallace hasn't submitted a one of these bond programs to a popular vote."

A Northern reporter once proposed to Wallace that, though he generally had the image of a conservative, most of his programs really seemed rather liberal. Wallace eyed him for a moment, not suspiciously, but with just a special alertness. "Whatcha mean, now? If you askin' me—well, of course, I'm not one of these ultraconservatives. They against everything. The only thing they for is the dollar, that's all they want to conserve. Well, that's not me. . . ." During the 1966 governor's campaign, he declared, "They talkin' about yo guvnuh borrowin' money to build roads and bridges over this state. Well, whatever it takes, we gonna build those roads and bridges. And they talkin' about all the other money we spent. Well, spendin' money for the blind and crippled and elderly and disabled—that's what we *spose* to do. That ain't no giveaway, that's easin' sufferin', that's *heppin'* folks. Yessirree, and I'll tell industry, 'We'll borrow five million dollars *more* and build you a bridge straight up in the air if you want.' "

Actually, he is a somewhat altered incarnation of the Populist mentality. Though he entertains the old Populist notion that "cities do something to people—really do—makes 'em mean, or something," he vigorously set about industrializing the Alabama countryside as soon as he became governor. After a paper mill was built in a little town only some twenty miles from Montgomery, it wafted, on particularly muggy mornings, a squalid scent all the way to the capitol, and Wallace, when asked once about the odor, replied, "Yeah. Sho does smell sweet, don't it?" Also, the larger share of his taxing programs—on cigarettes, beer, sports events, automobile tags and gas—have fallen on the "common folks" to the benefit of big business in the state.

While governor, his style as a day-to-day administrator was somewhat fitful and distracted. One of his aides allows, "He don't like to fool around with work. He likes contact with people." A former state senator under Wallace declares, "He was a miserable man trying to sit down there and run that office. He'd go out in the hall and shake hands with anybody he could find rather than have to sit behind that desk. Of the three governors I've known, Wallace knew the least about actually running the state." Wallace himself admits, "I'm a policy man. I can't sit down and work out problems. That's what you have people around you for."

Pleas for stays of execution afforded him a special anguish. Glenn Curlee remembers, "When he had to make a decision on these capital-punishment cases, it really upset him. He'd walk up and down his office chewin' that cigar and sayin', 'I don't know—I just don't know.' Then he'd rationalize a little by sayin', 'You know, it ain't me pullin' that switch, it's the jury.' Then he'd start repeatin', 'I don't know.' Finally, he'd call the warden and talk to him a little bit, sayin', 'Yeah, but this here's a man's life. We tellin' a fella he's got to die.' Then he'd hang up and ask somebody if the federal courts had done anything. He'd stay right by that phone till the last minute, and we'd try to make him feel better about it, but he'd keep starin' at that phone and sayin', 'Yeah, but I could stop it.' "

There were a few mutterings of corruption during his administration. The state paved a road to the farm home Gerald bought shortly after his brother took office, and a number of Alabamians cite the fact that one of Oscar Harper's brothers is selling all the gravel to the state for road construction and that a florist who was a Wallace partisan suddenly went into the asphalt-mix business when Wallace became governor. But in dramatic contrast to previous administrations, not a single significant scandal arose after Wallace assumed office.

It is generally conceded that he would have become one of the most beneficial stewards ever to preside over Alabama if it had not been for his mutation into racism.

Shortly before Wallace was inaugurated, he informed a group of state senators one evening, "I'm gonna make race the basis of politics in this state, and I'm gonna make it the basis of politics in this country." One of his old allies from the Folsom days later approached him with the suggestion, "You know, with all these Klan bombings and shootings and all, you got a great opportunity now, just going in, to condemn all that stuff as not a matter of segregation or integration, but just as a matter of law and order." Wallace's reply: "Well, I've gotten sick and tired of that kinda talk. The folks have already heard too much hollerin' about law and order."

Even before the inauguration, static began crackling between Wallace and the attorney general elected with him, hulking, rusty-haired Richmond Flowers, a former Folsomite from the southern Alabama town of Dothan, not far from Wallace's own county. On inauguration day Flowers issued a statement shortly before Wallace's inaugural address: "The officers of this state must stand up for their people. But the people of this state must discern and distinguish between a fighting chance and a chance to fight. . . . To defy the same federal arm that speaks for America to Castro, Khrushchev, and Mao Tse-tung, to preannounce that any decision concerning us that is contrary to our likes will not be heeded, is only a chance to fight and can bring nothing but disgrace to our state, military law upon our people, and political demagoguery to the leaders responsible."

Flowers now explains, "I had already realized he was gonna make the Big Hate campaign for the next four years. All those legislators who'd been seeing him between the election and the inauguration to talk about legislation came away saying all he'd tell 'em about was the Big Hate. So I made my little ole statement, and when he heard about it, he said I was a demagogue." Through the crises that followed in Alabama, says Flowers, "The Justice Department kept telling me, 'You're the bright light down there, see if you can't do something with him.' So I'd go to him and say, 'Look, George, you gonna be whupped all through the courts. And when you're whupped in the courts, the Klan's gonna come out on the streets and the killing's gonna start. You know that's what's gonna happen.' But, hell, he didn't want peace. George'd tell me, 'Damnit, send the Justice Department word, I ain't compromising with anybody. I'm gonna *make 'em* bring troops into this state.' That's exactly what he told me."

So the metamorphosis was complete. In abandoning himself to the immemorial dark obsession of Southern politics, he was as much a casualty of that obsession as Folsom. Shortly after returning from the war, Wallace had confided to a Sunday-school teacher in his church in Clayton, "You know, we just can't keep the colored folks down like we been doin' around here for years and years. We got to quit. We got to start treatin' 'em right. They just like everybody else." But only two years later, when he decided to run for alternate delegate to the 1948 national Democratic convention, his campaign cards read: "Unalterably opposed to the nomination of Harry S. Truman and so-called Civil Rights Program." He seemed to mesmerize himself with his own posturing. "He made himself believe what he had to believe out of political necessity, out of that inordinate ambition of his," says one of his old associates from the Folsom days. "He used to be anything but a racist, but with all his chattering, he managed to talk himself into it." The day he took office was bleak, gaunt, and stunningly cold, and Wallace, improbably attired in hickory-striped pants and a cutaway coat, blared in what was one of the most incredible inaugural addresses given by a Southern governor since Reconstruction: "This nation was never meant to be a unit of one, but a unit of the many . . . and so it was meant in our racial lives. Each race, within its own framework, has the freedom to teach, to instruct, to develop, to ask for and receive deserved help from others of separate racial station . . . but if we amalgamate into the one unit as advocated by the Communist philosopher, then the enrichment of our lives, the freedom for our development is gone forever. We become, therefore, a mongrel unit of one under a single all-powerful government. And we stand for everything, and for nothing. . . . Today I have stood where Jefferson Davis stood, and took an oath to my people. It is very appropriate then that from this Cradle of the Confederacy, this very heart of the great Anglo-Saxon Southland, that today we sound the drum for freedom. . . . Let us rise to the call of the freedom-loving blood that is in us. . . . In the name of the greatest people that have ever trod this earth, I draw the line in the dust and toss the gauntlet before the feet of tyranny. And I say, Segregation now! Segregation tomorrow! Segregation forever!"

The man who was the chief architect of that bizarre speech is an elderly Montgomery lawyer named John Kohn, who lives, after the manner of an eighteenth-century English squire, in a large white country home, with two smoke-colored mastiffs, among tawny fenced fields a mile or two out of Montgomery. He has continued to function as the sole consultant-intellectual, the Arthur Schlesinger, Jr., the discreet guru of Wallace's administration. He achieved a minor but permanent local fame when, on the day Kennedy was assassinated, he danced a jig down Montgomery's Dexter Avenue.

At his home one cold, windless, sunless afternoon, settled on a couch with his long legs crossed atop a small table and his hands folded formally across his vest, he said, "Some men like bird hunting, raising dogs, and all that. I like political tactics, strategy, and psychology. I suppose I wrote ninety percent of Wallace's campaign platform. I reckon you could call me the coach of the campaign. But I myself am allergic to politicians. I don't even like to shake hands with them. I simply choose not to mingle with ass-scratchin' politicians."

His voice was like an old church pump organ, measured and deliberate and staunch. A tall and rather formidable figure, rigidly erect, he has a classic Roman head, craggy and balding, with hair combed in thin and faintly rippling streaks across the pale skin of his pate, and rather fierce watery, glaring eyes.

He was wearing a black coat and an unbuttoned black vest loosely held together by a gold watch chain, with a gray silk tie that was just a bit spotted. His baggy gray flannel trousers were also a little stained, and—as if the care and odd formality of his attire began to relax and dissipate as it approached the ground—he ended with a pair of scuffed gray desert boots. The room was cold and faintly drafty, but it had a certain tropical atmosphere about it: the furniture was dark and heavy and cluttery, and there was a large Persian rug, and rattan blinds, and an archaic black ceiling fan which hung now arrested and motionless as a fire rustled quietly at the end of the room.

"Governor Wallace has his hangers-on, but I don't fault him for that. My dogs wag their tails at me, too, and I think I'm a big shot. But adulation is not a virus with him. I have the highest regard for Wallace. You always have a certain number of rats around a governor. Oscar Harper? He's a second Christ compared to some of those jerks Wallace has got with him at the capitol."

He seemed to talk always through clenched teeth—enunciating precisely, carefully, almost with pain sometimes, his lips forming a small thin smile with the effort—while his eyes would flare and squint with a faintly manic intensity. "These Rotary-type politicians are so scared of being criticized, they won't do anything. They're merely potbellied men living on coupons. We've got no senators now. That applefaced Sparkman—he's a phony. My wife and daughter thought the world of John Kennedy. I'm glad he's dead. He was the most dangerous man in the history of our country. Eisenhower was a great general but a dumb president. Nixon clawed his way to the top. He's a jerk, but he's tough. As for LBJ, he ought to be tried in the docks as a traitor. . . ."

Kohn lightly stroked his taut lower lip with thumb and forefinger. "If this country is going to be saved, it'll take a man like Wallace to save it. He's the Andrew Jackson of 1966—the closest thing to Jackson that's ever come along. He would have ridden with Forrest or Jeb Stuart. He's permeated with the spirit of the Confederacy. . . ." He paused a moment and recrossed his legs. "Now, George Wallace is not a racist. I am. My grandfather was born one hundred feet from the state capitol. He was a banker and in real estate, half Irish and half Jewish, and brought up as a Catholic. I myself was reared on the capitol grounds. Whenever I get in a deal, I call on my Jewish ancestry. And if you've got Jewish, Scotch, English, Irish, or German blood in you, it would be stupid to compare you with my nigra cook. I give them all a fair chance, but don't tell me they're as smart. They never put a sail to a boat or a wheel to a wagon. About all they've ever done was jump up and down and eat each other. I'm not for burning anyone, but I'm an absolute racist. You either have the right momma and poppa the day you're born, or you don't. It's as simple as that. . . . Wallace, however, is not a racist. But he knows this state is the last stronghold of the Anglo-Saxon civilization. He's well-grounded in Anglo-Saxon Western civilization. And he had enough practical political sense to know cussin' nigras was popular. The mass of people were looking subconsciously for someone, and now they have him. He created a devil and then slew him—Hitler used the Jews the same way, Jacob Javits did the same thing with the South. Hitler, of course, was a paranoid. The Germans are either at your ass or at your throat. But this country's full of little Hitlers—people with animosity toward everybody. The Klan, now, they're a little different: they're just poor boys that can't get in the country club, so they put on a sheet and have a little fun."

He sneezed and produced a huge soiled handkerchief, which, after swabbing it once across his mouth, he stuffed back into his coat. "Excuse me. I'm allergic to everything that grows out here." He lunged forward on the sofa and propped his elbows on his spread knees, his long arms in the narrow black stovepipe sleeves of his coat forming a stiff and almost perfect triangle. "Man, right where I'm sitting now was once the center of the Greek nation. The Judeo-Christian people ran them out and stole the whole United States. They put the Cross here"—he made a stabbing motion downward with one hand—"and they put the sword here." He repeated the gesture with his other hand. "You know that. The greatest curse that ever happened to man was Christianity. It's been Christian nations that have caused the wars. They stole this country. Now, I'm a dues-paying church member. I'm not an agnostic, because there's bound to be something superior to man. Man is the worst beast that ever trotted through the jungle. There's bound to be something superior. . . ."

Leaning back, he lapsed into dark and moody contemplation for a moment. "Well, if I die tomorrow, I haven't missed a damn thing. Life's been good to me. I was the only man who went into the Army a captain and came out a captain. If I liked what they told me to do, I'd do it. If not, I'd tell them to blow it. I've challenged two bastards to duels in my lifetime—to shoot it out. I respect a man's intelligence and a woman's virginity. The last time I got drunk, I knocked a fellow down at the country club for killing his wife's dog. I called him a dog-killing sonuvabitch. I challenged him to a duel. I'm not hurting. I'm in my seventies now, but I still get my exercise most every evening." He produced a pale quick glimmer of a smile. "I am also writing a book. I've done about four hundred pages on it so far. I'm going to call it *The Cradle*—Montgomery is the Cradle of the Confederacy, you know. It's a combination of Faulkner and *Peyton Place,* about all the creeps and phonies in this town. . . ." As Kohn described his book, it is to be a collection of miscellaneous oddities, snatches of lurid gossip from around Montgomery, anthropomorphic comparisons between Alabama's larger cities, disguised—for some reason—with fictitious names, and certain random definitions: What is a redneck? What is a slut? What is a bitch? Kohn explained the project at length with stiff and courtly gestures—his hands were long and impeccably clean, and they made single cleaving chops through the air from his shoulder to his lap when he reached a point. He would also sometimes hold one hand up beside his face with two fingers lifted straight upward in a strangely stylized and almost religious gesture, like the poses in Russian icons or medieval paintings of saints. "I'm going to tell it all," he intoned; "I don't give a damn."

Kohn is seldom seen at the capitol; he appears only for such momentous occasions as major addresses by Wallace, standing alone against the wall in the balcony of the House chamber, his coat folded over his arm, gazing down with a steady, tight grin and glaring eyes, and then, when Wallace is through, swiftly departing. But Wallace readily acknowledges, "Oh, I call John about once a week. He's a good springboard for your opinions. When I'm havin' a tough time makin' a decision, when I want to do something and everybody else is wishy-washy about it and tellin' me, 'Now, that might be a little rash, you better kinda hold off and temper it a little,' I go home and pick up the phone before I go to bed and call John, and he tells me to go ahead and give 'em hell. You talk to him, and you feel like you can do anything. He's sorta our morale builder."

In the months following his inaugural address, Wallace seemed occupied with little else than engaging in racial skirmishes. All over Alabama, it was a season of sudden furious disarray, in which there was more than a suggestion that Wallace had actually proceeded, with a gleeful hectic haste, "to make race the basis of politics in this state."

He had only to wait until the end of the winter for his first authentic grand-scale crisis. Negro demonstrations erupted in Birmingham, led by the man who was to emerge as his single great symbolic adversary in the years ahead, Martin Luther King. The two of them were like embodiments of the two popular psyches of the South's racial conflict—a conflict which had actually begun, had its inception, in the Negro church only a short stroll down Dexter Avenue from the state capitol. It was an unlikely bit of stagecraft: from that church, King had led the Montgomery bus boycott during the Patterson administration, and the two buildings—a plain brick church and a domed political citadel on the hill above it—seem to have been set down with just the right exquisite sense of dramatic spacing to challenge each other, serving as the nucleus and source for a confrontation eventually magnified over the rest of the South and then the nation. And all through that confrontation, Wallace and King continued in a kind of unwitting personal collaboration, though they have never once spoken to each other, as the mutual foils, the mutual catalysts of the Negro revolution.

Birmingham's public-safety director, Bull Conner, managed to keep the demonstrators at bay for a while with his celebrated firehoses and police dogs, but after a particularly tumultuous Saturday night Wallace dispatched his state patrol into the city. The force had been outfitted shortly after he took office with steel helmets painted with Confederate flags, and Confederate-flag license tags affixed to the front bumpers of their cars. They had been renamed State Troopers instead of State Patrol. They now swooped into Birmingham, over the protests of a number of local officials, with carbines and shotguns, and before long, the demonstrations subsided. But the summer simmered with bombings and shootings. On a Sunday morning in September, four small Negro girls were killed in a dynamite explosion at a Negro church. Wallace, while deploring the incident, hinted that it had likely been the handiwork of Negro militants—a suggestion he invoked in all the violence that attended his four years as governor.

Only a few months after sending his state troopers into Birmingham, Wallace learned that Judge Frank Johnson had ordered the desegregation of schools in Macon County in the Black Belt. The site of Tuskegee Institute, the county has a preponderant Negro population, and the racial attitudes of the white minority approximate those of the whites in Southern Rhodesia. But surprisingly, when Wallace instructed the county's Board of Education to ignore Johnson's order, they voted instead to desegregate the high school in Tuskegee, the county seat. The day the high school was to open, more than one hundred state troopers surged in before dawn with orders for the local officials to close the school. "We hit 'em early and caught 'em off guard," recollects Al Lingo. "We went up on their porches and rapped on their doors and got 'em up out of bed—they came to their doors with their pajamas on, and we handed them the governor's order and then went and ringed around the school to make sure it stayed closed." The maneuver was effective for about a week; court orders finally broke up the occupation of Tuskegee, and thirteen Negro pupils began attending the high school. With that, state troopers began transporting white students from Tuskegee to still-segregated high schools in nearby Shorter and Notasulga. Wallace released them from that special duty by confiscating two buses from a northern Alabama trade school and putting them to the shuttling service. He also had the state Board of Education authorize financial aid to the parents of white students boycotting the Tuskegee school.

There were other, rather more elemental gestures, such as Wallace's paroling of a Klansman convicted of emasculating a Negro whom he and a carload of other brutes had picked up at random beside a Birmingham highway one night. Robert Shelton, the glum, drowsy-eyed, lank-jawed chief Klansman in Alabama, was discovered to be working as a petty contractor for the state Highway Department. Though Wallace may once have entertained a distaste for the Klan, they were seen frequently prowling through the state capitol, and in no administration within recent memory in Alabama has the Klan lurked so close to the corridors of power. But they were still kept carefully at the fringes of the administration. When a delegation of Klansmen volunteered their services during one civil-rights crisis, Wallace told them, "Naw, boys, I 'preciate it, but I 'spect you better let us handle this—I do 'preciate yawl comin' by, though."

In the spring of 1963, when a federal judge ordered the enrollment of two Negroes at the University of Alabama, Wallace's finest hour was at hand. The order presented him with a spectacular opportunity to make good on his campaign pledge to stand in some schoolhouse door, and it also offered the heady possibility that he might manage to have the state occupied by federal troops. It was even more: in personally striking the pose of hopeless defiance, he sensed he was on the verge of becoming the apotheosis of the will of his people.

Wallace's political psychology essentially derives from the Southern romance of an unvanquished and intransigent spirit in the face of utter, desolate defeat. It has become a dogeared cliché about Southern leaders, but the fact is, the Civil War is still quite alive to Wallace. As he chatters about the days between 1861 and 1865, one is inevitably reminded of the Reverend Hightower in *Light in August,* whose gray head, as he sits by his window at dusk, is filled with the flash and roar of the old glorious doomed charges, the lifted sabers and bugles and grimy howling faces above gaunt, galloping horses. Wallace seemed to regard his career as governor merely as an invocation and projection of the old aboriginal glory and valor. It was all still happening to him. In fact, one got the feeling that, for him, what was happening was not quite as *real* as that great primeval conflict.

There is one moment in the history of that war which has for Wallace an almost religious meaning. "When it was about over, they captured Jefferson Davis down in Georgia and put him in jail, and one day several Union troops come around to clap him up in chains and manacles. He was sick and nearly starved to death by then, and old, but he told 'em he wadn't lettin' *nobody* put chains on him, he had been the president of a country, and that country might be beat now, and they might have him in jail, but he would not allow them to put him in chains. They grabbed him, and he started fightin'—that old man, weak as he was. It took a bunch of 'em to hold him long enough to get it done, and when they turned him loose again, he was still goin', still fightin'. . . ."

It has not mattered to most Alabamians that in his series of confrontations with the federal government Wallace has met with consistent failure. What matters is that he fought, and continues to fight. He answers the romance of defeat. That role has been one of Wallace's central political inspirations: he seems personally to lust for chains. As the University of Alabama crisis approached in 1963, he proposed to a group of legislators in his office, "By God, you watch now, they gonna send federal troops all over this state. We gonna be under military occupation. . . ."

While Wallace regarded President John Kennedy with a certain measure of awe, his attitude toward Robert Kennedy, then the Attorney General, was one of bristling suspicion. When Bob Kennedy tried to contact Wallace at the governor's mansion one evening shortly before the University of Alabama confrontation, Ralph Adams, Wallace's old campus crony, happened to answer the phone. Wallace told Adams to inform Kennedy he didn't want to talk to him. "So I told Kennedy the governor was unavailable," says Adams. "Kennedy kept saying, 'I don't see why he won't talk to me,' and Wallace—he was standing just a few feet away from me—kept whispering, 'Adams, just tell him I plain don't want to talk to him.' "

But Kennedy finally managed to set up a private meeting with Wallace at the state capitol. Before he arrived, Wallace had the local contingent of the United Daughters of the Confederacy place a wreath over the iron star embedded in the front porch of the capitol marking the spot where Jefferson Davis was sworn in as president of the Confederacy. "He didn't like the idea of Bobby maybe steppin' on it," says one Wallace intimate.

To some, Kennedy's mission to Alabama seemed a curious exercise in naïveté. But after the unseemly and embittering spectacle at Ole Miss only months before, the White House desperately wanted to avert another garish rhubarb between a state and the federal government. In a day-long group analysis in the Justice Department of what had gone wrong at Ole Miss, it was concluded there had been a disastrous lapse of communication with Governor Ross Barnett and the other Mississippi officials. So, haunted by the nightmare on the Ole

Miss campus, and impelled by the mystique of the face-to-face dialogue, Bob Kennedy flew to Montgomery.

It was a bright lush April morning when Kennedy arrived at the capitol. The governor's outer reception room was as hushed and empty of incidental people as a funeral parlor. Kennedy, quiet and thin, himself looking a bit funereal, had with him Burke Marshall and Ed Reid, the old Alabama political broker who had picked out Wallace to represent the state's League of Municipalities while Wallace was a legislator. They were conducted into Wallace's office, where they found the governor waiting for them with his finance director, Seymore Trammell. The five of them shook hands and then closed the door.

Reid observed, in reference to the army of state troopers outside the capitol, "Governor, you got quite a crowd out there this morning."

"Have we?" murmured Wallace. "Well, I don't know, I came up the back way. . . ." Wallace then notified Kennedy that he was taking the precaution of taping their confidential discussion, and would furnish the Attorney General's office with a copy. "We might wanna save this conversation for posterity. . . ."

Kennedy replied in his almost shy, flat, fast voice, like the twanging of a rubber band, "I don't know anybody who would want to listen to it."

There were light laughs all around, and a chuckle from Wallace. "I expect you're correct. I doubt it." After a pause, Wallace said, his voice a little louder, "This is a fine city. Hope yawl enjoy your visit here." His tone was easy, idle, casual, as if he were merely a Barbour County boy chatting with fellows on some street corner, though his enunciation had assumed a certain careful and studied preciseness. But he waited, passively, almost luxuriously, for Kennedy to extend himself.

"I just came by to pay my respects to you as governor of the state," said Kennedy.

"Well, we're glad to have you in Alabama," Wallace allowed. "We feel like we're the courtesy capital of the nation, and so if you want to pay a courtesy visit, this is the courtesy capital of the country—" and he suddenly asked, "That right, Eddie?"—the first of several small moments in which he gave Reid a tactical, psychological tug toward his side, though Reid had accompanied Kennedy to help him explain his position. "That's right, governor," said Reid.

After another awkward little pause, Wallace said, "This is the Alabama flag over there. This is the governor's flag, I beg your pardon. Of course, this is the Stars and Bars, and that's the state flag over there. You all know what the American flag is. We all recognize that. . . ." He cleared his throat.

"This is a beautiful office," offered Reid.

"This is not as ornate as some offices at all," Wallace hastily protested. "The mansion at Mississippi is the most magnificent thing I've ever seen. They got twenty-nine rooms in it, spent a million dollars or something renovating it last year. It's a landmark. Eighteen-thirty-nine was when it was built. . . ."

Reduced to hopeless triviality, Kennedy said, "This is a terrific-looking building." From a corner, Trammell whispered reverentially, "Yes. . . . Yes. . . ."

This tortured patter lasted approximately five minutes, ending in a final long pause. Abruptly, clearing his throat, Kennedy delicately proposed, "I don't know whether we might discuss the problem that we are perhaps facing here in the state in connection with the integration—"

"I don't hear good," said Wallace.

Kennedy raised his voice just a notch higher. "I said, I don't know whether you would care to discuss the problem we might face here in the state in connection with the integration of the university . . . and perhaps the . . ."

For Wallace, it was an almost sensuous moment of triumph, a soft small warm inward explosion of glee and gratification which he sought to prolong as long as possible. "Well, uh, of course, in other words, your telegram said you wanted to come by and see me. Of course, I assumed that you would decide what to discuss, and that's up to you. . . ."

"It was primarily a courtesy visit, governor, but I don't—I mean, it's up—I would be glad to discuss this matter. I think it might be helpful, but I think it's completely up to you, whether—I'm here as your guest, and I just—"

"Well," said Wallace, "that's—that's the reason, you're here as my guest. I thought I would leave that up to you as to what you want to discuss."

"Fine. Well, then, I think we might discuss that."

Exquisitely, Wallace inquired, "You want to discuss that?"

"That'd be fine," said Kennedy with what seemed considerable relief.

"Well, uh, what—you have anything—?"

"Well, I just thought that—perhaps I'd just explain our position that, uh—that, uh—I would hope that all of these matters could be handled at a local level . . . without any outside influences at all. I have a responsibility that goes beyond integration and segregation to enforce the law of the land, and to ensure court orders are obeyed. . . . If you were in my position, you would do no less. . . ."

Wallace, insisting that he made a commitment in his campaign to resist the integration of any school in Alabama with "a legal course of action," said that it was up to the governor of a state to ensure the welfare and safekeeping of his state, and "you just can't have any peace in Alabama with an integrated school system."

Kennedy snapped, "You think it would be so horrifying to have a Negro attend the University of Alabama, governor?"

"Well, I think it's horrifying for the federal courts and the central government to rewrite all the law and force upon the people that which they don't want, yes. . . . I will never myself submit voluntarily to any integration of any school system in Alabama. And I feel it's in the best interests of the country and Alabama, and everybody concerned, that these matters ought to be—attempts ought to be—at least, delayed. In fact, there is *no* time in my judgment when we will be ready for it—in my lifetime, at least. Certainly not at this time."

By now Kennedy seemed to have the growing suspicion, the growing realization that, in this office confronting Wallace and Trammell, with the lawn outside swarming with state troopers, he was actually in another country. But he persisted. "It transcends, as I say, the question of segregation or integration or anything like that. If the orders of the court can be disobeyed by you, governor—in all respect to you and your position—then they can be disobeyed by anybody throughout the United States who doesn't happen to think that a particular law of a federal court applies to them, or feels it's not the kind of law that would be good for them. I don't know what you would have other than complete havoc and lawlessness throughout the United States if that philosophy is accepted."

"Well, let me say this," declared Wallace, "we have more peace and law and order in Alabama in one minute than you have an entire year up in Washington, D.C. And that's the place where—you can't maintain law and order in a sort of system that exists, for instance, like you have in Washington. I believe that we should obey the law, but I also feel"—he clamorously cleared his throat, and then spat, presumably into the wastebasket beside his desk—"that the governor of a sovereign state has the right to—" At this point, a secretary stuck her head through the door to inquire cheerfully if she could get anyone anything. Wallace grunted, "Yawl want anything?"

"I might have a Coke," said Kennedy.

Orders were quickly taken all around, and then Kennedy resumed. "I think we've got a lot of problems in Washington, D.C., governor—no question of that. I think a lot of it arises out of the fact that we have difficulty between the races. I think we have problems in Chicago, my own city of Boston. . . . There's a feeling between whites and Negroes, I think—"

Wallace interrupted, his voice quiet and hurried. "We don't have that problem here, though. We have safety and peace and goodwill, and there's no place in Montgomery, Alabama, or Birmingham that you cannot walk at night—white or colored section. . . . But you can't do that in Washington. You can't do that in Chicago, or Philadelphia. We think that too much politics is involved in it. We people feel that eventually this whole effort is going to bring a breakdown between the races."

Kennedy began speaking at a faster and higher clip, with a mixture of urgency and despair. "I don't know how politics really gets into it, governor, because we don't have any control over the fact that somebody's going to come here to the University of Alabama. . . . Just let me give you an example. I never heard of Mr. Meredith, governor, until—"

"Who?" said Wallace, cupping his hand behind his ear—another immemorial little tactic of countrymen in debate.

"Mr. Meredith at the University of Mississippi," said Kennedy. "I never heard of him until three weeks or four weeks before we had the difficulty there. I couldn't tell you for the life of me the names of anybody that's gone to this University of Alabama—"

"I imagine you're sorry you ever heard of him, frankly," Wallace murmured deliciously. "I would think that, uh . . . well, I also think that in the Mississippi matter, if you want to just get right down to it, there were more civil-rights violations in Mississippi as a result of the troops shooting at students and the gassing of students and search and seizures. . . . They opened people's suitcases and belongin's, they had colored troops stoppin' white women and searchin' their belongings, and there was no martial law declared . . . Why, the courts are so disrespected here in our part of the country, that it's the popular thing to defame the courts. . . ."

Kennedy's voice had sunk to almost a whisper. "I would say to you that probably the most painful thing the President has to do or might do, and that President Kennedy did, is to use troops in any of these matters. I think the matter can be handled at a local level, and South Carolina indicated that, Georgia indicated that."

Wallace replied a bit hotly, "Well, let me say this—we don't want you to be under any misapprehensions or misconceptions of our attitudes. I am not, as the governor of this state, going to use the courts of the state to integrate any institution. And Alabama is just different from South Carolina in that respect. I'm sure they had their reasons for no more legal resistance than they made, but that will not be the case in this state. . . ."

Kennedy finally snapped, "Would you get angry if your orders were not obeyed? Did you when you were judge? Did you care?"

"Did I care?"

"Yeah."

"I don't recall any were ever disobeyed. . . ."

"Oh? What would your reaction be if they did disobey?"

"If they did what?"

"Disobeyed your orders."

"Well—of course, you are assuming that my actions as contemplated would be an outright disobedience of a court order. . . ."

"Ultimately, after that's litigated, governor, will you follow the orders of the court?"

"I will never submit to an order of the federal court ordering the integration of the school system. . . ."

"How would you feel if your orders were not obeyed?"

"It's not an analogous situation—"

"But don't you think it's fundamental?"

"—because we're dealing in great constitutional questions in this matter. . . ."

Wallace was rescued by the fortuitous appearance of the coffee and Coke. As they were being passed around, Reid said, "One thing that Mr. Kennedy was talking about coming up here, he doesn't know whether he wants to say anything to the press. He thinks it ought to be left up to you whatever is said to the press."

"Well," said Wallace, "I think that—I think that whatever Mr. Kennedy wants to do about that—I mean, I can't tell—

these Washington folks won't listen to me about anything—" He sniggered, and there was a general round of laughter.

"No, we'll listen to you," said Kennedy, and then, rapidly, as if striking at what he recognized as a psychologically propitious moment, he announced, "I think the President will be down here. He's going to come to the state in the next few weeks—I don't think that he's disclosed it yet, perhaps we could keep it among ourselves. I would hope that you would have the opportunity to see him."

But Wallace answered cautiously, "I know the President. He doesn't know me, he's met so many people just like I met 'em in the campaign for governor, but I carried him to the airport once in fifty-seven. . . . I voted for him in the national convention for Vice-President. In fact, we defeated Kefauver in the Alabama delegation. In 1960 I spoke wherever I was called upon to speak within this state for the party—"

Reid interrupted to mention that Wallace had raised money for the national Democratic ticket in that campaign, and Wallace hastily added, "Didn't raise *much,* but I gave two hundred and fifty dollars myself, I think it was, I'm not sure of the amount, maybe that may be a—anyway, that's not much." It had probably occurred to him that the tape recorder was still quietly twirling over in the corner. "But I raised one thousand dollars in my little rural county."

"Yes, I heard you were very good," Kennedy remarked dryly. "I have read indications that that's not going to be true in 1964."

"What's that?" Wallace said—of all his Barbour County devices in debate, this is his fondest.

Somewhat louder, Kennedy said, "I have read indications that that's not going to be true in 1964."

"Well, let me say this, I—uh—I do feel that both national parties are beginning to consider the attitudes of people in our section of the country. I feel that we've been kicked around by both parties, and especially by our own national Democratic party. . . ."

Finally Kennedy murmured, "Well, uh, governor, I just

say we're going to enforce the orders of the court for the reasons I've stated, because I think it gets to the integrity of the whole system. No matter what the political ramifications or the political losses, I don't think we have any choice. . . ."

Wallace now seemed to sense Kennedy's weariness. Suddenly he ventured, "I think you could use your influence, though, and in Washington or the Justice Department, because the NAACP and all these groups feel that you people" —he paused again to spit into the wastebasket—"are almost gods." He gave a brief, barely audible snigger. "I believe you could exert some *influence* on them. This business of marching, the registration, this business of registration suits—every registration suit that's filed does the Kennedy administration no good because it—all you're doing is making the white people solidify for whatever efforts they're going to make politically in the future. . . ."

"I think everybody in the United States should be permitted to register and vote, governor," said Kennedy. "We never come in—I mean, I'm—I mean—" There was almost a desperate and pleading tone in his voice: "I'm in *favor* of states' rights. I'm in favor of the people, and—and the President is, and this administration is, trying to get people to make these decisions, remedy the situations themselves."

"But you might give 'em some time," came a voice from offside. It was Seymore Trammell, the governor's finance director. A taut, quick, brisk little man with a quick, tight grin full of round little teeth, a cap of sandy wiry hair kept closely cropped, and shell-rim glasses which, when reflecting the light, stamp a certain opaque blankness over his face, he is given to wearing dark pinstripe suits with white ties and glossy shirts, and his movements have the abrupt sharp quality of a mechanical toy. His voice is clipped, harshly flat, and savage; it sounds somewhat like the gnashing of teeth. Of all Wallace's aides, he seems the readiest, the most eager, to reduce all confrontations to the terms of a street rumble. "But you might give 'em some *time,*" he said, his tone faintly agonized and squeezed.

"We do," said Kennedy.

"Maybe in a year," persisted Trammell softly, "maybe in five years, maybe ten years—"

"What, permit somebody to register to vote?" Kennedy's voice was suddenly sharp. It seemed that, after carefully restraining himself with Wallace, these hisses from the side of the road had finally caused his patience to snap.

"In view of what the overall circumstances are, looking at it objectively," Trammell continued, "the inflammatory nature of it, and how it'll upset the—"

"Now, the governor said that he thinks everybody should be able to register to vote—"

"*I* do," insisted Trammell. "*I* do. And the governor does . . . so we would educate 'em accordingly."

"Would you keep a Negro college professor from registering to vote in an election for five years?" Kennedy demanded.

"I certainly—I wouldn't want to myself, nor would the governor want to," said Trammell. He seemed to realize now that he had eased himself in too close to Kennedy. "And I think it can be worked out on the local level without intervention."

"Well, that's what we try to do, we go to the local level," asserted Kennedy.

Wallace, stepping in to extricate Trammell, said quickly, "Well, about the integration matter. Of course, I understand your position and I—I'm sure you understand mine, and it looks like we may wind up in court."

Kennedy's voice was soft again. "As long as we wind up in court, I'll be happy, governor. That's all I ask. . . . I just don't want it to get into the streets. I don't want to have another Oxford, Mississippi; that's all I ask."

"I don't want another Mississippi myself," said Wallace, "but you folks are the ones that will control the matter." And then, as an idle, fleeting lure, he added, "Because you have control of the troops."

"We have a responsibility to ensure that the orders of the

court are followed, and all the force behind the federal government must be used for that purpose."

It was like the snapping of a trap. "I know that. I know you're going to use all the force of the federal government. In fact, what you're telling me today is that if necessary, you're going to bring troops into Alabama."

"No," said Kennedy, "I didn't say that, governor."

"You didn't? Well, you said all the force of the federal government."

"To make sure that the orders of the court are obeyed." Kennedy's voice was low and anxious as he began to realize what had happened.

"But all the force includes the troops, doesn't it?"

"Well, I would hope that would stay in the courts and be litigated."

"But it does involve troops if the law is not obeyed?"

"I'm planning and hoping that the law will be obeyed."

"But I mean," insisted Wallace, "so if it's not in your interpretation of obedience, you will use troops?"

Kennedy repeated that he hoped the court order would be honored.

"But you gonna use all the power of the federal government, which involves troops—"

"I had hoped that wasn't necessary," said Kennedy. "Maybe somebody wants us to use troops, but, uh—we're not anxious to—"

"I can assure you," Wallace said quickly, "*I* do not want to use troops. I can assure you there's no effort on *my* part to make a show of resistance and be overcome. . . ."

Kennedy replied crisply, "I'm glad to hear that, governor."

"I mean to stand," continued Wallace, "as I said in the campaign for governor, because I believe we've got to wake the people of this country up to the fact that this business of the central government, every time you turn around, moving in with troops and bayonets. I believe the people don't like it. I believe all over this nation—" Incredibly, only four months after he had been sworn into office, there were already glimmerings of a larger hankering. "—we get thousands of letters from Michigan and former Southerners in California, in Michigan—automobile workers—" The litany was already forming, that early "—who say, 'We gonna stand with you people in the South.' "

"I don't blame people for not liking it, governor," said Kennedy in an almost inaudible whisper. "I don't like it myself."

Wallace quickly, gently, bizarrely proposed again, "Well, why don't you use your good influence in the Justice Department to persuade these people who want to integrate school systems, especially in the Deep South—why can't you be patient and hold off and let things evolve? And—why don't you? I've been trying to get some new industry, we've gotten one hundred and fifty million dollars' worth of it in the past five or six months since I was elected governor. . . . That's the most important thing you can do for the Negro people, is enhance their standard of living. . . . We're trying to do some *real* things for them, but all this agitation and all this business of Martin Luther King—who's a phony, and a fraud—marchin' and goin' to jail and all that, they just livin' high on the hog—"

"Purely a commercial venture," Trammell interposed.

"It's a commercial venture," echoed Wallace. "I would—why don't they organize an industrial-development committee and go sit down and say, let's bring some industry to Atlanta and Montgomery and Birmingham, we got people out of work? We just don't get a bit of help from them—do we, Mr. Reid?"

There was a long pause. Finally, in resignation, Kennedy said, "Well, I appreciate your seeing me, governor."

"Well," said Wallace, "I appreciate you comin' to see me. I wish we could—I wish that you could feel that you could use the influence of the Justice Department to stop the integration movement—" There was only a stunned silence from

Kennedy. "—of course, I'm against integration at any time, but at least for the next ten years, at least."

Trummell again injected, in a hushed and stealthy voice, "Use some *persuasive* powers and not force. Per-*suaaa*-sive powers on both sides. This thing can't be overcome overnight."

"Well, of course, let me say this," Wallace added rapidly, "let's be gettin' it straight now. 'Course, I'm not for usin' persuasive powers on us to persuade us to integrate. I'm against integration—"

"So just use the persuasive powers on the other side," said Kennedy, giving a short laugh.

"That's right," declared Wallace solemnly. "I think integration is bad. I don't think it's good, and you don't have any bona fide integration in this country, we know that. In fact, you don't have it in Washington. Everybody's fled to Virginia. Why don't the government make all them officials come back from Virginia and Maryland and go to school in Washington? Wouldn't that be a—they flee integrated schools. I sorta feel like that's sorta a mockery of the situation, and our image is not good in other parts of the world. . . . Looks to me like Congress can push anything else across they want to, it'd look like they'd push home rule—but there's another item of high-pocrisy. . . ."

"Would you be in favor of home rule in Washington?" inquired Kennedy.

"I think it would be *good* to have home rule in Washington, yes, I think it would be good to have an example set for the world and the nation what happens to a good city and a big city when you turn it over to colored control. Now, it may turn out to be a model of perfection. It may turn out to be the finest city government in the whole world and, on the other hand, it may turn out to be the right opposite. I think the American people should have a right to look at the city of Washington bein' controlled by its local inhabitants, and therefore, because I would just like to see what would happen, I think you ought to have home rule."

Kennedy spoke with a curious low, dull uncertainty, as if not quite sure that he was actually engaging with the governor of Alabama in the kind of discussion about the kind of question he seemed to be engaged in. "I've seen a lot of cities throughout the world, governor, that aren't controlled by white people that are doing pretty well."

"Not controlled by white people? But they're not controlled by Negroes—"

"Oh, yes. I've seen a lot of those."

"Oh, have you?"

"Yeah."

"What—name some of them," Wallace demanded.

"Well," said Kennedy, "any place on the Ivory Coast—"

"You think they're model cities?"

"They're very impressive cities," asserted Kennedy.

"You know, two-thirds of the world is colored, but it's not Negro," Wallace offered. "In other words, the Japanese and the Chinese people— Listen," he said suddenly, "I have nothing against people of opposite color, I believe that God made all of them, and I believe that anybody who hates anybody because of their color, I feel sorry for them. I'd hate to die hatin' people because of their color. I just don't believe in social and educational mixin'. . . . It creates disorder, and we're tryin' to keep order. . . ." And then, once again, he submitted with a kind of deathless optimism, "I wish it were possible to have those folks in Washington to say, we're gonna side with you Southern folks for once, and we're gonna ask 'em to slow up on this integration business. But there's no chance for that, is there?"

Kennedy replied, still a little numbed, "Well, I think I've made it clear, governor, that what's involved is the integrity and orders of the court. . . ." He was clearly ready to end it now and leave. "Could we just decide perhaps what we might say outside that would be satisfactory to you? That we paid a courtesy visit, and that we discussed some of the problems involving, uh, uh, some of the—uh—" There was a long, dangling silence. "Well, I don't know how we'd describe it—"

He gave a nervous and awkward laugh. "I think it's—what do you say, Ed?" He turned to his press aide, Ed Guthman, who along with Wallace's press aide, Bill Jones, had now been called into the room. There was a general flurry of recommendations.

"Well, we had a *frank* talk," said Wallace. "But, uh—"

Trammell quickly inserted, "Don't lead, we don't want to lead the people to any *fallacious* thinkin' as to what may have come out of this. . . ."

Wallace suggested a simple statement that "Governor Wallace still stands in the position that he held the time he ran for governor, and you still stand in the position that you held all the time. Seems like that's the way it is, isn't it?" he said.

"That's it," said Trammell.

Kennedy said, "I'd rather not get into what your—you can speak for yourself—"

"As far as I'm concerned," said Wallace, "you can say anything you want to, Mr. Kennedy. . . ."

"Yeah," said Kennedy, "it would be a mistake to create any controversy. Whatever I say, I want to make sure that you approve of. . . ."

Wallace then innocently mused, "Of course, it depresses me and makes me very sad to think that we—we have these strained relations between the states and the federal government, but it's that way, and we feel very strongly about this matter. . . . In fact," he added casually, "according to yawl's attitude, of course, it's we may have to send troops and jail you as governor of the state—"

"We never said that, governor," Kennedy said quietly and rapidly. If it had not been clear to Kennedy in the beginning, when he walked into the office and discovered that Wallace had set up a tape recorder, that any agreement was hopeless before the discussion even started, that Wallace had consented to it only on the chance that he might come out of it with a threat to further dramatize his stance—that was clear to Kennedy now. For Wallace, the conference existed only for that purpose. And he had almost managed to pull it off. He and Trammell had snagged Kennedy just by the cuff of one pants leg, as it were, and they were reluctant to let him go; they sought to induce him further into the trap.

"No," said Wallace, "we didn't say that you said that, but we do feel that—"

"That's what's been attempted in one state," Trammell almost whispered, "and this situation is very little different—"

"Since he's gonna have a press conference—" Wallace added.

"I'm gonna walk out," said Kennedy with an edgy laugh. "I'm not planning on a press conference, I just thought I'd— I can't get out of here without saying something."

"Well, what do you have in mind to say?" Wallace asked curtly. "Go ahead, let us hear it."

Kennedy said something about a mutual exchange of views, and Trammell interrupted almost abjectly, unctiously, "The people are very interested in this thing, they've got to know, they're entitled to know. . . ."

Kennedy protested, "I don't think that what I think is going to help any if we got into any kind of controversy—I leave here and say something, and you leave here and say something, and then we start the next two months discussing what we said to each other. . . ."

"I continue to stand as I've always stood," Wallace relented for a moment, "and let's let it go at that. . . . The people in this state talk to you folks who have so much *charm,* and *wit,* you know, out of Washington, you know, and they [the people in Alabama] feel like they [the people out of Washington] gonna get you [himself, Wallace] in a compromisin' position. Of course, I don't intend to compromise on anything."

"I understand," said Kennedy. "Why don't we just leave it, I'd speak for what I said and not get into what you said, and you could get into what you said and what your position is, without getting into what I said."

"I agree," said Wallace. "I can speak for myself and you can speak for yourself."

But Trammell gently, officiously persisted, "Well, well, I think, though, I think you're entitled to your opinion and so is Mr. Kennedy—"

"Oh, sure," said Wallace.

"—as to what the opinion of this conversation is."

"Well, I don't think it would be helpful to get into an analysis of it," repeated Kennedy.

Trammell continued, "You don't want the people to be led into thinking maybe that Mr. Kennedy agrees with the governor—"

"There's no agreement," said Wallace.

"Well," proposed Trammell, "I think that the people of Alabama and the South should know—"

Wallace picked up his cue. "Let's get it straight, now. You will *not* use—"

Kennedy wearily reiterated, "I will hope and expect that the orders of the court—there's no plan or idea of using troops. I think as you said, these are going to be resolved in the courts. . . ."

Wallace suddenly ambushed Kennedy by asking him why he had men taking pictures of the University of Alabama campus, if it were not in anticipation of the use of troops. "We'll give you a picture of the school if you ever want one. I mean, you won't ever have to—uh—" He ended with a small laugh.

"I understand that," said Kennedy. "It could have been handled better."

"Well, I'll say this," Trammell doggedly tried again, "the governor has made his position very clear, and he's asked what your position would be, whether or not troops would be used—"

Kennedy replied quickly and testily, "I don't plan to. You seem to *want* me to say that I am going to use troops—" Trammell hurriedly and gently protested. "No," said Kennedy, "but that's what you seem to think and that's what you seem to *want*—" He gave an incredulous little laugh, a faintly harried and cornered little laugh, recognizing that he was faced by a kind of implacability that was beyond both his understanding and all his rational references. "You're pushing it so much, I sort of get that opinion. In any case, so we understand each other, we haven't the use of any force prepared, we haven't the use of any troops prepared. . . . So I want to make sure that we don't get out of here—I mean, I didn't say anything to the contrary, and I don't want to have any inferences about—"

For the last time, Trammell whisperingly insisted, "Just that one statement in there that you would use whatever powers the central government had to carry out the court order—"

"Well, that's the implication," Kennedy said. "I mean, you can decide whether the federal government is going to use troops, and that's your decision."

"Well, past history—" Trammell began.

"Yeah, but don't apply it to me or any statement that I made here in this room, now." Kennedy's voice now was cold and brittle. "That should be understood with Mr. Jones, too. So that we all understand each other, I think that would be most unfair—"

"Well, then," said Wallace, "we can say that you're *not* going to use troops in the—"

"I have no plans to," replied Kennedy.

"Well, that's fine," said Wallace. "You're in charge—" He then thought it meet to confide, "Let me tell you something, I'm not trying to trick you, and, uh, of course, I wouldn't want you nor anyone else—'course, I know you wouldn't want to trick *me*."

"Well," said Kennedy, with the tape recorder still humming, "that was why I wanted to have this conversation."

"We not trying to *trick* anybody," Wallace kept on. "But of course, we do know that troops were used in Mississippi, and they were used in Arkansas, and we do know that you took photographs of the University of Alabama, and for what other purpose I can not comprehend than the use of troops' ingress and egress, and you did say, Mr. Kennedy, that you would use the full power of the federal government to enforce the order of the court and to protect the integrity of the court. And the full power of the federal government necessarily means military power also."

"You can reach that conclusion," snapped Kennedy. "Anybody's entitled to a conclusion, but I didn't say that. Based on what I said here today, you can say for a long line of reasons that you've reached the conclusion that the federal government's going to use troops. I think you're mistaken on it, but I just want to make sure as far as my statement and our conversation here today—I don't think that that's very helpful for the state or the federal government or our relationship with one another. Did you—" He turned now to Ed Reid. "—did you get the impression I said I was gonna use troops?"

"No," said Reid, "I didn't get that impression."

Wallace, who may have assumed he had effectively neutralized Reid with his earlier subtle little pleasant tugs, now turned on him. "But he did say that he was gonna use the full power of the federal government to enforce the court order, didn't he?"

"But he said he hoped and assumed that that wouldn't be necessary," replied Reid.

"He said, he hoped," barked Wallace. "But he didn't say he would not use troops. . . ." But with that, Wallace relinquished the point: he had almost managed it, but not quite. Now, again assuming that outrageously hopeful, wistful air, which must have been maddening to Kennedy, he remarked, "Well, you feel it would weaken your political position if you talked to these people who are trying to get into the school here at the University of Alabama, and asked them to withdraw their applications in view of the attitude and demeanor of the people and the state government here? Would that—uh—anything wrong with that?"

Kennedy briskly repeated that it would neither be proper nor possible for him to do that.

"If you as the Attorney General would say," Wallace wheedled, "this Martin Luther King is doing things he shouldn't do, and he's advocating lawlessness, and that you call upon him to obey the law like anyone else, and be emphatic about it—" But he finally surrendered even the pretense of that possibility, and satisfied himself with the rueful observation, "Yawl make an easy little statement, and then the President talks to Mr. King over the telephone, and all those kind of things—" He chuckled.

The conference then ended. Kennedy, as he turned toward the door, said, "I don't know how I'm going to do out here. Will you go out and stand with me?" There was an explosion of laughter.

But as Kennedy left the capitol in a cab, he muttered to a newsman riding with him, "I suppose I can understand the governor's position politically. But that Trammell is a son of a bitch. He wants somebody killed. . . ."

Wallace's staff had already journeyed up to Tuscaloosa, where, with grave and momentous deliberation, they had selected a doorway. Al Lingo, Wallace's head trooper, had made the mistake of ordering that press coverage be limited to members of the Alabama capitol press corps. As Bill Jones, Wallace's press aide, puts it, "Lingo misunderstood the governor's plan to dramatize his position to the nation." Adjustments were quickly made. The Attorney General made a last-minute call from Washington to Montgomery, but was informed Wallace was not available. Instead, Wallace's executive secretary, Cecil Jackson, put him on the phone with John Kohn, after telling Kennedy, "He is one of the governor's leading counsel. . . ." Kohn informed Kennedy, "Well, first, for the record, this call was not initiated down here—it was initiated by yourself, and I am just repeating that for the record, and I don't think any human being can tell what is going to, in all reasonable probability, going to happen."

Before the event Wallace seemed filled with a kind of twittering exhilaration. It was something like the air of a small boy about to embark on a colossal mischievous prank. Waiting for Assistant Attorney General Nicholas Katzenbach to appear on the campus, says one of Wallace's aides, "he was wisecracking all over the place." He chuckled to the general of the Alabama National Guard, when it was federalized, "Now you sonuvabitches are on the other side, ain't you?" Only an hour or so before his public confrontation with Katzenbach, as his staff was standing in the hall outside his hotel room waiting for him to emerge, he called out, "Say, boys, I don't feel so good. How about one of yawl goin' out there and handlin' this?"

What followed that glowering June morning was like a dream: Katzenbach, hulking and rumpled, emerging from a car and proceeding on up the walk between banked hushed newsmen and law officers who formed a long aisle of mute and tense expectation, which ended before a stumpy little man in a black suit (poised behind, of all things, a lectern), who solemnly threw up his hand, halting Katzenbach; the two then exchanging vaguely irritable and exasperated phrases, like a short, idle, haphazard argument on some street corner; Katzenbach with arms folded tightly and a faint expression of pained sufferance, beginning to glisten a little with sweat, then turning and going back down the aisle between the dumb, watching faces while the stubby little man turned from the lectern and disappeared inside the auditorium behind him. Four hours later he reappeared to confront the general of the Alabama National Guard, snappily returning the general's salute and then reading from notes scrawled on the back of a calendar pad, and finally stepping aside. Shortly afterward, the two Negro youths—Vivian Malone and James Hood—were registered as students at the University of Alabama. By that time, Wallace was on his way back to Montgomery.

It had been little more than a ceremony of futility—and, as a historical moment, a rather pedestrian production. But no other Southern governor had managed to strike even that dramatic a pose of defiance, and it has never been required of Southern popular heroes that they be successful. Indeed, Southerners tend to love their heroes more for their losses. After the University of Alabama, Wallace entered a new political dimension—both in his state and in the nation.

The whole affair left Wallace with a tingling sense of national involvement. He felt quite gratified by his encounter with Kennedy, and his brief exposure to the country posing in the doorway at the university brought speaking invitations from all over the United States—mostly from campuses, where the interest in him was largely as a grotesque amusement. If Wallace was not exactly aware of that, he recognized they offered him at least heady walk-on parts on the biggest stage of all, in the biggest play of them all. With his instinctive nimbleness, he accepted as many campus invitations as possible.

It was his first venture beyond the snug politics of Alabama, the first audacious extension of his vision of the possibilities for himself into the national contest.

On almost every campus where he appeared—at Harvard, where he was hustled out of an auditorium through a dank basement full of pipes, at UCLA, at the University of Oregon—he was greeted with memorable melees. The old cronies from Alabama whom he carried along with him—Watson, Harper, Adams, Curlee—regarded the free-for-alls in these alien climes as the fearsome gyrations of exotic tribes. Stranded outside the auditorium at Harvard among a crowd of pickets who suddenly began singing "We Shall Overcome," Watson turned to Harper and muttered fiercely, "Sing, you fool. Sing! I'm too old to run," and the two of them joined hands with the demonstrators and lustily chorused in. During the college tours, there was about Wallace and his entourage the air of reckless little horsemen on forays into enemy encampments, and reconnoitering later in the evenings in their hotel lobby, after having plunged precipitously through hostile, awesome uproar, they huddled together and chattered breathlessly and exuberantly, most of all just feeling lucky to have survived it, to still be intact, recounting to each other, "You see me put that elbow in that fella? Goddamn, man, two of 'em tried to crowd in against me, and I put a shoulder in one, and then I just slapped the other'n. . . ."

Wallace himself was subject to the most bizarre personal humiliations—one woman in California, when he reached to shake her hand, stuck a lighted cigarette into his palm—but he remained impervious to embarrassment. It was not so much out of calculation as just a simple lingering dauntless country innocence; he seemed to regard such affronts merely with an abstract astonishment, the gentle assumption in the South being that political notions should have nothing to do with good manners. His only conclusion, when he met with such abuse, was that "those folks just hadn't had much raisin'." Ralph Adams recalls of a two-week speaking tour in Wisconsin, "Our last stop was there at the University of Wisconsin, and it was so cold, the lake had froze up solid. Wallace had this all-night bull session with students at the resort hotel where we were staying, there were about forty or fifty of them sitting around on the floor, and the rest of us turned on in. Then, when we got up in the morning and looked out the window where that froze lake was, we saw that somebody during the night had wrote in huge letters across the ice, 'Fuck Wallace.' The way they fixed it up, I bet it lasted until the spring. It must of still been on there when he came back up to campaign in the primary." But Wallace is initially oblivious to insult—or, as when he is asked subtly vicious questions by newsmen, doesn't recognize it when it happens. It's only later, mulling things over, that he decides he's been insulted. Days later, many miles away, he discharges his resentment at accumulated slights with almost peevish tirades (when he failed to receive the customary certificate of appreciation after an appearance before the National Press Club, he blared in speeches over Alabama, "Well, they can take their certificate and they know what they can do with it") against intellectuals and professors and newspaper editors and all other members of that hostile, cold, inscrutable estate whose disdain he has not been able to disarm.

Occasionally in his campus addresses he essayed aesthetic flourishes. "Let us look at the 1954 school case, Brown vs. Topeka, the lawyers call it," he once intoned. "It did not, I assure you, as some seem to think, spring instantly into existence full-grown and ready for action equipped with injunctive processes, preferred appeals, set bayonets, and all its accouterments like Botticelli would have us believe Venus came to the shores of Greece full-grown and full-blown on the breath of Boreas." Such unlikely phrases were obviously the handiwork of unseen advisers, designed to make him somehow more palatable to his campus audiences. The effect, instead, was one of baroque implausibility. And he would inevitably deliver himself of at least two unblinkingly gross pronouncements before the evening was over. On one occasion he carefully explained to his audience how the mulatto children born of Union occupation troops and Negro women during Reconstruction took on the characteristics of their fathers, and that the mulatto was the image most Northerners had of the Negro, "whereas, when we speak of the Negro in the South, the image in our minds is that great residue of easygoing, basically happy, unambitious Africans who constitute forty percent of our population, and who the white man in the South, in addition to educating his own children, has attempted to educate, to furnish public health services and civic protection. . . . The people of the South do not hate the Negro. They have carried him on their shoulders and have endowed him with every blessing of civilization that he has been able to assimilate. . . ."

Wallace's own manner, among the howls and hoots that attended his speeches, was a kind of detached playfulness. In the midst of enemies who have a particular blatant and unappeasable hostility toward him, his instinct is to become almost cuddlesomely kittenish, to innocently spank and paw at their rage. At Harvard he told his audience, "You left-wing, pinko liberals should appreciate me puttin' money into your treasury." When the din would begin to rise around him, he would pause and lean on the lectern with both arms and tilt his hips and grin, with a little shake of his head. "Well, it's gonna be a hot time in the old town tonight!" And whenever the tumult became impossible, he would throw up his small arms and blare, "I accept the nomination!"

Besides his facility for puckish disconcertment, Wallace also discovered during his college tours that he generally had the asset of antagonists who underestimated him—who regarded him as a kind of animated caricature. That is, of course, the classic advantage of the wily country boy dealing with supercilious sophisticates. This revelation enheartened and galvanized him.

The prospect that he might be able to enlarge his tribuneship to a national scale had, actually, long been a dimly flickering idea in his head, and with his campus excursions, the possibility became more tantalizing. As the 1964 national primaries approached, a Montgomery newspaper editor, Grover Hall, directly proposed to Wallace, back in Wallace's office one afternoon, that he enter some of the primaries. "He grabbed it and ran like a hungry fish," says one Wallace intimate.

Late one afternoon, after a speech at the University of Wisconsin, someone called Wallace's suite at the hotel in Madison and declared that he had a plan for Wallace to run in the upcoming presidential primary in the state. "I thought he was a crackpot," remembers Ralph Adams. "I told him thank you, and to send his plan on down to Montgomery. But he kept on calling back, saying he just had to speak personally with the governor about running for President. Wisconsin seemed like the last state we wanted to run in—they had no Negro problem, and they had their own civil-rights law. The whole idea seemed like a joke. We'd been on this speaking tour for two weeks, and everybody was ready to get on back home. It was snowing. But this nut wouldn't quit calling, so we finally told him to meet us at this radio station downtown where Wallace had to appear on a call-in program before we flew back to Alabama. He said, okay, he'd meet us there. He was from Oshkosh, seventy miles away, but he drove all the way over in that snow, with us sitting around that radio station for an hour and a half, all ready to leave but having to wait on this nut."

That's how his 1964 primary campaigns began. Wallace's conversation with the man was hurried, but it left him feverishly excited, and he emerged from the radio station with an outline of the primary qualification requirements tucked into his briefcase. Waiting for him in a limousine outside in the snowing twilight was Wisconsin Governor John Reynolds, a large hunk of Wisconsin cheese in his arms, and he offered to drive the Wallace party to the airport. "I guess he was pretty happy to get us on out of the state," says one Wallace aide, "but if he had known what we were all sitting there thinking about on the way to the airport, he probably would have told us to get out and walk the rest of the way in the snow." As soon as Wallace had clambered aboard his plane, he snapped open his briefcase and took out the primary requirements. He studied them all the way back to Alabama.

Through the campaigns that followed—first Wisconsin, then Indiana, then Maryland—it all seemed a faintly desperate and hopeless adventure. "We started in Wisconsin with exactly eight hundred dollars," says one Wallace staff member. "We couldn't even negotiate television time. I paid my own expenses." Wallace says, "We didn't even know what town we were going to next half the time." In many places they found that the hotels would refuse to accept them as guests. "I guess," says one Wallace aide, "they were afraid we'd short-sheet 'em." In Baltimore, they had planned to set up headquarters at the Lord Baltimore Hotel but were suddenly informed there were no rooms for them, so the party transferred to a motel in nearby Towson. "We had all these desks and typewriters we had to get out of the Lord Baltimore," says John Pemberton, one of Wallace's national liaison men. "We called every mover in town and were told they couldn't get to us till the next week. I finally called up this moving company that was owned by a nigra and asked him if he could move us. 'I think you better know,' I told him, 'it's Guvnuh Wallace you'll be moving.' He said, 'I don't care if it's the KKK, as long as you got the money.' But he showed up faster than we'd figgered he would. Later that day, about eight of the biggest nigguhs you ever saw in your life walked into our suite at the Lord Baltimore dressed in these rough work-clothes with no markings on them, and one of them looked around and then said to another'n, 'Is this the place we supposed to clean out?' I thought they'd come in there ready to have at it. My mouth went dry, and I could see some of the others in our party, their eyes kinda buggin' out. . . ."

In each campaign Wallace met with total rejection from the state's establishment—political, religious, and journalistic. In Wisconsin the editor of a Catholic newspaper, Msgr. Franklyn J. Kennedy, suggested that a vote for Wallace would be a sin. There were the natural accusations of racism. Quoted in one state as describing all non-Anglo-Saxons as "lesser breeds," Wallace quickly dispatched someone back to Alabama to rummage up a congenial Syrian, Jew, Pole, and Greek, and trotted them out at subsequent appearances to declare their affection for him. But he moved through a constant weather of outrage and tension. His bodyguards carefully Scotch-taped the hood of his car at each stop so that, when they returned, they could check to see if anyone had wired it with dynamite.

For all the haphazardness of their expeditions, they accomplished a political mayhem in the primaries. In Wisconsin Wallace spirited away almost thirty-five percent of the Democratic vote. In Indiana he captured almost thirty percent. Then, in Maryland, the last campaign, he came chillingly close to actually taking the primary; leading in the early returns, he finished with about forty-five percent of the vote—and he now maintains that Maryland Governor Millard Tawes confessed to him privately that he *did* win, and that there was some feverish sleight-of-hand on the precinct level that night when it became apparent he would. There were, no doubt, domestic politics at work in each state which helped to enhance his showing, but it was also clear that Wallace had invoked, had discovered a dark, silent, brooding mass of people whom no one—the newspapers, the political leaders, the intellectuals—no one but Wallace had suspected were there. The effect was to transform his national hankerings to an obsession.

Charles Morgan, a liberal refugee from Birmingham who now heads the American Civil Liberties Union office in Atlanta, remembers that while he was following Wallace through Indiana trying to impart to citizens there some idea of the nature of the man who had ventured among them, the sudden cold realization struck him in a plane one afternoon, "My God. The galoots are loose."

Part Five

Back in Alabama, there still remained ahead of Wallace the mortal crisis of his political existence.

It finally occurred to him, sometime in the summer of 1965, that his term as governor was due to end in about a year. "Once he was inaugurated," says one Wallace intimate, "he just seemed to forget the fact he would have to leave office in 1966. It was one of the few things that ever crept up on him." The provision in the state constitution which confined governors to one term seemed to him an outrageous intrusion into his communion with the people, the arbitrary impediment of an abstract technicality to a marriage of true minds. He briefly considered running for the Senate and then dismissed it; for a politician of his nature, the Senate would have been a kind of gilded exile. Further, according to his closest associates, he had the touchingly naïve suspicion that once he arrived in Washington, he might not be seated, or might be subjected to some other formal and official humiliation.

In September, 1965, he notified the state legislature that he wanted them to design and then submit for popular vote a constitutional amendment removing the constitution's one-term restriction. "To those so-called liberals who are voicing mock concern over what they call the growing power of tyranny and the washing tides of anarchy, I would suggest further that they are not concerned about me—but about the growing power of the people." He then appealed to the people, in a state-wide radio and television address, to bestow on him their blessing—by letter, by wire, or in person. "I want to speak for you and champion what you would have me champion. I want to know that you are with me in our cause for the law and civilization. If you feel a need for me in the job I try to do, then I want you to know I feel a need for you."

This gambit was the most audacious stroke of a political career that had always, since he had asked Folsom as a freshman legislator to appoint him speaker of the House, been characterized by startling audacity. To a number of state legislators it appeared that his brave and solitary ambition had now passed into a kind of giddy hubris. He had ventured beyond the pale. In private conferences with legislators before the succession session, he even reversed the astrology of an old Alabama political aphorism, "A setting sun gives off no heat," to boast that his sun was giving off more heat than ever—that, in effect, he had arrested his sun at high noon.

Those legislators—most of whom were in the Senate—who quickly decided to resist were, no doubt, acting out of their own individual political interests to a degree: many of them had already made investments in candidates who were preparing to run in the 1966 campaign. Whatever, they were also armed with legitimate reservations. When Wallace asked one of them for support, the senator replied, "I'll do it on one condition—you make it start with the next governor." Wallace snapped, "What's the matter, you afraid to let the people vote on it?" The senator answered, "Hell, frankly, yeah."

Sensing deeper complications than he had reckoned on, Wallace set out to carry the matter by sheer windy, breathless speed and momentum—simple kinetic energy being one of his basic political resources. Before the month was over, he called a special session. "He declared an emergency," snorts one state senator, "a special emergency session so he could succeed himself. Now, isn't that something? An *emergency."*

His tactic was to open the session under public gaze by means of a televised evening address to a joint gathering of House and Senate members in the House chamber, with the necessary preliminary parliamentary procedures carefully choreographed to finish at the precise moment of his introduction, seven P.M. air time. Dissident legislators raised a flurry of parliamentary distractions, hoping to sabotage the timing. Before the opening prayer, one senator demanded that the floor be cleared of all but authorized persons, but the House speaker, a Wallace ally who was presiding over the session, barked, "All you're entitled to is what the chair gives you, and right now we're going to give you a prayer." The tumult subsided for a moment to let the minister scamper through his remarks to the Almighty, but with his "Amen," bellows for recognition erupted from succession opponents. The clamor became deafening. From the balcony, brimming with Wallace partisans, who sported "Wallace for President" buttons, rose an ominous rumble. The speaker recognized a pro-Wallace representative, and his resolution to invite Wallace to address the joint session was briskly hammered through after a voice vote. The representative was again recognized, and this time he proposed a resolution calling for a delegation to go fetch Wallace. The decibel outcome of this vote was more dubious, but it was hammered approved. With the clock ticking perilously close to air time, the same representative, amid almost berserk baying from the dissidents, introduced his third resolution to make the governor's address the first order of business, and Wallace came through the doors into the chamber just as the on-lights of the television cameras glowed red.

His address was short. He invoked his Northern primary expeditions and declared, "If you send me again . . . I will go again. The liberals say George Wallace wants to be President. What's wrong with that?" He insisted, "The issue is the right of the Alabama people to vote to amend or not to amend their own constitution. It is a precious right. I shall do all in my power to see to it that they do not lose that right." And he challenged the assembly, again and again, "Let the *people* speak! . . . I say, let the *people* speak. . . ."

Actually, before the session had even opened, the House Rules Committee had passed the bill unanimously, with no untidy discussion. There was a spatter of complaints from other representatives, though: one of them declared, "This is raw political power that you can see and feel and touch," and another cried, "This is a banana republic!" When the bill reached the Senate, the Rules Committee there, also dominated by Wallace courtiers, cleared it with even more alacrity—it took them exactly twenty seconds to receive, approve, and pass it on. When the measure reached the Senate floor, though, it immediately ran into a filibuster, and it was at this point that Wallace had his first dark hint of disaster. While he needed only twenty-one votes to have the bill approved by the Senate, he first needed twenty-four votes to invoke cloture and extinguish debate; early in the maneuverings, he concluded he had twenty-three commitments and one other vote almost certain—miscalculation, as it turned out. With their first cloture challenge, Wallace's forces could muster only eighteen votes. Appallingly, somewhere along the line, six votes had melted away.

With a sense of alarm now, Wallace exercised all his political arts. Senators report, "He'd work on you this way—first he'd call you into his office and tell you how great you are and how much he likes you, all the while pattin' you, strokin' your arm, blowin' smoke up you. Then he'd start bringin' out all these letters—he had them in cardboard boxes sittin' on his conference table during the succession fight, with each box lettered county by county, and he'd dump them out on his desk and run his hands through them. Then he'd start on about how he was spit on in Wisconsin, how he suffered up there in the cold and how those mean people treated him ugly up there. Finally, if you're still just sittin' there lookin' at him and not sayin' anything, he gets to hollering and rantin' about how he's gonna take away everything in your county. There were three or four counties he actually stopped road construction in. In that last phase of his, he's out to destroy you completely—morally, physically, financially. His folks would put the finger on you back in your home community as aiding and abetting the demonstrators. They'd call your clients, they'd offer you all kinda personal considerations. He'd even call up and talk to your wife and children—he'd know you weren't there, but he'd ask for you anyway, and then just start up chattin' with your whole family for a half-hour or so. . . ."

But it wasn't enough. He had met with other frustrations during his administration: in trying to get Communists banned from speaking on state campuses, in trying to abolish the board of trustees at the University of Alabama, in trying to change the process of selecting boards of registrars from one of popular election to gubernatorial appointment, and in a punitive maneuver to snatch from Richmond Flowers the authority to appoint attorneys for highway-condemnation proceedings. But those were only incidental irritations in which he had nothing really personal and vital at stake. The succession bill, however, was a politically mortal matter. Now only a maddening handful of minor politicians stood between him and what he knew to be the popular will, and that torment caused him to lose for a time the uncanny poise that had marked him all his political life, plunged him into his most graceless, blundering, ignominious hour. Everything he touched now seemed to topple down on him, to compound his hopelessness. It was as if, for a period, he was turned inside out.

"Our strength would have been diminished if he could have kept from making mistakes," recalls Robert Gilchrist, one of the filibuster leaders. "We had to count on his making mistakes. And he made his first one immediately." Confounded in his attempts to snuff out debate and in his efforts to lure more senators to his side, he set out to alter the Senate rules on the number of votes needed to override a filibuster. He failed. He then appealed to the state supreme court to do it for him, a garish proposition which they summarily dismissed. In the meantime, one recalcitrant senator, Julian Lowe, announced on the Senate floor that Seymore Trammell had phoned the president of a junior college in Lowe's district and told him the institution would not be receiving five hundred thousand dollars which Wallace had promised it. Lowe declared, "Trammell told him that he and the governor had found other uses for the college's capital-outlay money." The reaction to this news among the other opposition senators was gleeful. "No man has the right to use public funds to corrupt a man in such blatant fashion," roared one of them. "My God! Is the price of victory worth your morality?" Trammell, for his part, never denied the charge.

Such indications of ragged desperation served merely to fortify the resistance in the Senate. That resistance now—that perverse refusal to be intimidated by what Wallace regarded as the popular will, a defiance entered into by men with no evident longings for political suicide—was like an intimation that perhaps the popular will was not what Wallace had assumed it was, that he may have actually overreached himself. He had those letters in the cardboard boxes in his office, he seemed to feel a glow of popular empathy, but with each rebuff in Montgomery, the earth trembled under him a little anyway. For a while he pondered calling for a Selma-style march of his supporters to the capitol. But he finally decided to make a series of raids into the home counties of the opposing senators. "We are going to the people with this issue," he declared. "I don't mind the people telling me where to go, but I'm not going to let a few senators tell me."

One of those senators recalls, "He didn't announce his plans on this until one morning when he sends a telegram to my home and tells me he wants to debate in Florence at nine A.M. the next morning. He knew I was in Montgomery and not at home. My wife called me at three P.M. to tell me about it. There was no time to prepare—so I dictated some remarks to my wife on the phone, and then drove all the way up that night." Wallace was met by cheering crowds everywhere. They were, he found, apparently as anxious to remove the senators and the constitutional technicality as he was. A state senator who showed up at one Wallace appearance in his home county barely escaped being mauled by the throng. "He got 'em all worked up, and then he turned and pointed straight at me down in the crowd and said, 'There. There he is.' They really converged on me—'You sonuvabitch' and that sort of stuff. They had closed in all around me, but Wallace finally called them off." Wallace's attitude at this point, reflects one state politician, "was a matter of 'If I'm ruined, by God, I'm gonna take all these sonuvabitches with me.' " But as his tour wore on, Wallace saw signs that it was beginning to backfire into resentment at a governor so conspicuously bullying local politicians, and he suddenly abandoned it.

The situation now, of course, was unsalvageable anyway. Actually, after the tactics to which he had finally resorted—one opponent even charged Wallace had threatened a senator with cancellation of funds to a school for the blind in his district—it was probably just as well he didn't win. His uncharacteristically clumsy and hectic intimidations would have made it a victory he could ill afford. One of his admirers, Grover Hall, now editor of the Richmond *Post-Dispatch* but then a kind of journalist-laureate for the Wallace administration as editor of the *Montgomery Advertiser,* observed, "This must be a crestfallen and melancholy time for Wallace. To console himself over the loss of battle, he is entitled to reflect that it is remarkable that such a battle could even be fought. . . . Simply, as is the way of daring, resolute men, Wallace overreached himself. He asked that he be reelected governor in order that he might run again for President. This was somewhat too outback for his supporters. It was an excess that generated just enough combined opposition to tip the balance. . . ." Hall compared Wallace's succession maneuver with Franklin Roosevelt's attempt to pack the Supreme Court: "[Roosevelt] was diminished by attempting to pack the court and diminished by the defeat of the effort." But the fact is, if Wallace was diminished by his defeat, he would have been diminished even further by victory.

The coup de grace was dealt on October 22, almost a month after Wallace had convened the legislature. Some three weeks of Senate filibustering came to an end, and the Senate voted on the succession amendment: Wallace missed by three votes. This final day of deliberations was the occasion for the most spectacular speech of the entire debate. Senator Kenneth Hammond, a burly former football player from the little northern Alabama mountain village of Valley Head, caused an abrupt hush to fall over the Senate chamber when he charged that Wallace had used "Nazi tactics," and described him as "one of the greatest political manipulators this century has known." Anyone who resisted Wallace, declared Hammond, was identified as "a nigguh-lover, a pinko, or a communist." Wallace was out "to destroy democracy at its best" and had in mind "a dictatorship which would make Huey P. Long look like a piker." Not only had Wallace confirmed Alabama as "a haven for hate-mongers," but he had the same designs on the rest of the nation. "In order to pick up support, he is going to pit the white race against the minorities in this country," Hammond prophesied, "the same way Adolf Hitler pitted the master race against the Jews." By now a number of legislators, frozen in their seats, had paled noticeably, and the lieutenant governor had stalked out. Hammond suddenly produced a small package, wrapped in a paper bag, and clunked it down on the press table immediately in front of him. "When he came out with that little bag," recalls one state senator, "mouths dropped open and eyes bugged out all over the place. That was when that chamber got sho nuff quiet. They just knew there was a pistol in that bag." After a dramatic pause, Hammond pointed to the package and announced that it contained a tape recording. "It's got on it every damn promise the administration made to me. I understand the finance director wants to play rough. That suits me." Legislators let out their breath, but only a little. Hammond concluded with the suggestion that he might be assassinated for voting against the succession bill—"The hate-mongers may kill me before I leave the capitol."

Wallace, when asked about the speech sometime later that evening, after the defeat of his bill, replied with a silent glare and scurried out of the capitol into the chill October night.

After his desperate and profligate expenditure of energy and concentration in the succession fight, there followed for Wallace a period that was like a long and careful inhalation. On his way to some factory opening or graduation exercise outside Montgomery, he would ride for hours in absolute silence in the back seat of the car, pulling on his lower lip as he gazed out the window. In his office, he would pause in the middle of dictation and stare blankly off into a far corner, sitting very still behind his desk, as the minutes passed and his secretary waited with poised pencil. Facing him again—and more imminent than ever before—was absolute nothingness: the void.

Then, like a sudden small soundless concussion in his head, it came to him that he might run Lurleen.

She had remained, throughout her husband's four years in the governor's office, an obscure and rather lonely figure, pleasant enough on public occasions, but essentially a private person, unassuming and unprepossessing. A small, tidy woman with a fondness for blazers and turtleneck blouses, which made her look like the leader of a girls' college glee club, she was attractive in that hard, plain, small-faced, somewhat masculine way that Deep Southern women tend to be attractive—in fact, over the years, she had even acquired a certain resemblance to her husband.

When the last of her four children, Janie Lee, was born in 1961, it was as if she went into a kind of private, resigned semiretreat, like so many other women approaching middle age—like the women, perhaps, for whom Anne Morrow Lindbergh wrote *Gift from the Sea*. With her eldest daughter, Bobbie Jo, married and in college, and her son, George, Jr., and another daughter, Peggy Sue, absorbed in teen-age worlds of their own, she spent a lot of time by herself outdoors, hunting, swimming, water-skiing. She was happiest when floating in a tiny boat in shorts and a baggy shirt out in the middle of a wide lake on a drowsy afternoon, all by herself, fishing with a cane pole. "I'd just sit out there on the water, and if they bit, that was fine, and if they didn't bite, that was even better, that was the finest thing in the world. Because you could think then."

As soon as they were married in 1942, when Wallace took Lurleen down to Clayton for a quick and humble honeymoon, he seemed already to have moved his attention, energy, and concentration to larger things. An old associate admits, "I guess he neglected his family pretty bad. It was always like he kinda felt Lurleen would get in his way. . . ." They lived meagerly while Wallace was in the legislature. "The money just wasn't coming in for them back then," recalls an old friend. "We'd visit the two of 'em in Clayton sometimes. We went over there one night, and Lurleen called my wife out of the room for a little while, and then when we got back home my wife told me that Lurleen had bought three new dresses on credit, and she didn't want George C. to know about it. She had 'em hid way back in some closet—the poor little girl was scared to wear 'em."

In 1952, after Wallace had left the legislature and won his circuit judgeship, she wanted him to stop there, to settle for that. "I would have been content," she delicately allowed, "for him to stay circuit judge from then on." But almost immediately, he began pursuing the governorship. "He was making speeches all over the state," said Lurleen, "and it was a matter, for me, of sitting home and waiting for George to get back." She spent a lot of her time now in church work. One woman in Clayton remembers, "At Christmas, she would be Mary in the little church pageants. She would wear a shawl over her head, and she was so lovely, and she read her part so pretty. . . ."

There are reliable reports that more than once during this period Lurleen was on the point of leaving George. A couple once close to the Wallaces recalls, "She wasn't well—looked awfully anemic—and she had a baby to care for, and she was alone most of the time. She really had thought that he'd settle down after he was elected judge; his salary would have kept them comfortably. She thought this was good enough. But, of course, he looked on it as just another stepping-stone on the way to becoming governor. This was the reason she wanted to quit him. She was bent on divorce. We tried to talk her out of it—one time we were at this fellow's house down there, one of Wallace's helpers—and we all tried to talk her out of it, but she just wouldn't hear anything we had to say."

Finally, Wallace and his "helpers" managed to dissuade her—though, as one of them now admits, "It got a little hairy for a while there." Lurleen then tried to enter into his life. "I started traveling with George," she said. "I had this feeling, that if I campaigned with him, it would draw us closer together. But I was frightened every time I got near a crowd. Most of the time, I'd just sit in the car and wait for him."

It was in the deep, long, silent winter after the succession-bill disaster that he began to talk of running Lurleen. The first people to whom he posed that possibility, including Lurleen, thought he was joking. But he began to insist more frequently and seriously, "Why not, now?" He finally had a small delegation of his aides meet with Lurleen in an office at the capitol. Formally, gingerly, they proposed it to her, negotiations made all the more delicate by the fact that she was soon to undergo extensive uterine surgery. She balked, but only half-heartedly; she had no real choice, of course. With the approach of spring, he began taking heart that he might be rescued after all.

Though he finally won Lurleen's consent, he still hesitated. He sent informal emissaries over the state to check what the reaction might be to such a ploy, and the reports they brought back were inconclusive, at best. Probably the most troubling factor, though, was that Ryan DeGraffenried was planning to run again. He had been steadily and quietly building support throughout the state during Wallace's four years at the capitol and had behind him the newspapers, big business, the city politicians, and educational leaders—the establishment coalition. One Wallace intimate says frankly, "George was scared to death of Ryan." Several polls gauging DeGraffenried's potential with the general mass of voters were also disquieting. "It got right down to the lick-log," says one Wallace aide. "One day he was gonna run her, and the next day he wasn't. He was gonna have to make a move now one way or the other."

DeGraffenried was already making speeches in the state, winging from one stop to another in a small private plane. Then, at the end of one day's junket in the mountainous reaches of northern Alabama, he returned to the small local airport where his plane was waiting to fly him to his last engagement only a few miles away across a looming ridge. It was a dark and gusty evening, and the airport manager pleaded with him to make the trip by car. DeGraffenried turned to his pilot. "You think you can make it?" The pilot said he could, and the two of them scrambled into the plane and took off. They rose up into the night with a tiny diminishing winking of lights. Then, as the airport manager watched, the frail and weightless craft seemed to hover for a moment in the air just above the top of the ridge, almost over it, but suddenly, like a kite abruptly plunging in a crazy smack of wind, it dropped, was batted back, and he heard a small brief explosion. When they found the wreckage, both the pilot and DeGraffenried were dead.

"George was very remorseful," says Glenn Curlee. On the day DeGraffenried was buried, Wallace was scheduled to speak in the House chamber to a women's group. "He didn't know exactly what to do," says one of his aides. He wound up sending someone from his office to represent him.

After a short but respectable passage of time, Wallace announced Lurleen's candidacy.

A member of Wallace's family says, "If Ryan had lived, it's highly possible George would not have run Lurleen." Wallace himself admits, "The more in a race, the more considerations. I would have naturally had more considerations if Ryan hadn't got killed." He hastily adds, "He was a fine man. I never said anything but kind things about him. . . ."

Through the spring and fall campaigns of that year, then, she tagged after him as he scuttled over Alabama with the tense urgency of a squirrel. They put her, with one female companion, in a separate car behind his, and she was borne from town to town like some irreplaceable ceremonial fixture, a token to lend the enterprise a measure of legitimacy and sanction, like those provincial plaster madonnas snatched from the gloom of medieval church naves and carried by the grimy, red-eyed, sulfurously profane, leek-breathing crusaders into flames and pillage. She submitted to it with an air composed, patient, somewhat inert, and remote—a small, quiet figure, smiling pleasantly and a little uneasily, with an expression sometimes, as she squinted in the sun, faintly perplexed and querulous.

And, of course, only the uninitiates—those excellently reasonable people behind desks and typewriters regarding the whole thing incredulously from afar—supposed that it was too baroque to work. Through the first and second reconstructions, Alabamians like most other Southerners had developed a high appreciation of the art of the solemn masquerade, the straight-faced ruse. Segregation itself has probably been one of history's most elaborate and durable disguises, a colossal facade constructed around what is really an irreconcilable blood belief in the innate inferiority of the Negro, and the maintenance of this improbable edifice of law and logic has become, in a way, its own perverse tribute to the industry and ingenuity of the Southern mind. Whatever the task may have cost in character, it has left Southern society with certain talents and certain tolerances. In fact, Wallace's deft stratagem probably had an endearing effect on Alabama voters.

Lurleen went through both campaigns bravely enough, but in the second one, in the fall, she began to get a little tired. The winter before, she had undergone major surgery for cancer. There were moments now when she seemed to flag. After one particularly strenuous morning of rallies, the party stopped at a high school to eat lunch, and Wallace, not thinking yet of food but rather of all the children collected there in one place and the family supper tables they represented, bolted off down the corridor toward the classrooms, leaving his group behind. Lurleen, who had been beside him coming through the door, stopped and watched him for a moment. She slumped foward as if something inside her had caved in a little, and then she called wearily, her voice just edged with exasperation, "What are you going to do now, George? Where are you going now?" He turned, as if suddenly reminded of something he had forgotten to fetch, and came back and took her aside, and as the rest of the party watched, engaged her in a brief moment of animated whispering, the two of them standing alone together a few feet down the hall. She mostly listened, her face turned slightly away, and then she seemed to sag forward a little more as he took her arm and led her to the first classroom.

But she endured. The tight little cavalcade of cars sped from one crossroads rally to another, with the crowds always gathered and waiting in the windy fall weather. At one rally shortly before nightfall in a village in central Alabama, she mounted the flatbed trailer, acknowledged the applause with a single wave of her thin slight hand, and then, without further flourish, read her speech. It was short, toneless, metronomic, without humor or any of her husband's kind of raw passion, her syllables slow and deliberate and enunciated with an unchanging expression of vaguely scowling earnestness—she sounded, really, like a high-school valedictorian delivering a laboriously crafted commencement address. While Wallace himself spoke, she sat off to one side in a corner of the platform, looking blank and irrelevant and a bit bored, gazing fixedly over the heads of the crowd, as if she were musing on grocery lists and school clothes for her children. Wallace's voice blared electronically in the twilight: "My opponents say they don't want no *skirt* for governor of Alabama. That's right—no *skirt*. Well, I want you to know, I resent that slur on the women of this state. . . ." Her expression did not change. She sat rigidly and a little primly, as if she hadn't heard, her hands in her lap, still gazing off into nothing. The wind feathered her hair. And suddenly one had the impression that when it was all over, when Wallace's people had gotten back in their cars and the townsfolk had scattered, she would still be sitting up there on that platform, all alone, straight, composed, smiling vaguely, gazing blankly off into the distance, to be hauled away finally with the platform to the next town.

The morning of her election—and the morning of Wallace's climactic, triumphant translation into a political phoenix—dawned splendid and lyrical. In Montgomery, in the mansion's huge white-tiled kitchen, Negro cooks bustled about preparing breakfast for the bodyguards as a soft sweet breeze came through an open window. (The Negro servants at the mansion are all convicted murderers furnished by the state's penal system, and they move about the house and over the grounds, fetching the morning newspaper or carrying breakfast trays, with a composed and eternal serenity, their faces vague and blank and peaceful, having now abstracted themselves into a kind of quiescence that is beyond the cares of this world.) Wallace appeared, wearing a shiny black suit, pale blue shirt, black tie. Lurleen joined him outside by the car, and Wallace asked the patrolman who opened the door for him, "How's it look?" The patrolman answered, "Real good." Chomping on his cigar, Wallace said, "You done voted?" The patrolman replied with an uncomfortable little laugh, "Well, the polls hadn't opened quite yet, governor, but I'll vote just as soon as I get a chance." Heading now out of Montgomery on the way down to Clayton to cast his ballot, Wallace immediately began looking for bumper stickers on the passing cars and trucks. "Hope there's enough of 'em today," he said.

He turned to Lurleen. "You got to bed mighty late last night," he said. "You should of been in bed earlier than you were." She protested that she had spent the time tucking in the younger children. She was wearing, this morning, her customary dark blue blazer and white turtleneck sweater. "Yeah," Wallace continued, "and at that rally last night, you didn't introduce me right. You should of introduced me as governor. I was shocked when you said 'George.' You said, 'And now, I give you your governor and my husband, George.' I was shocked." She only leaned back in the seat and turned her face away, gazed out the window with a steady, patient little smile on her face. But he did not notice; he was perched now on the edge of his seat, still talking, with his small stubby hands lying flat and side by side on the back of the front seat, where a reporter was riding.

Lurleen listened to him raptly, and with a small and strangely proud smile. It seemed that she had finally arrived at a kind of solitary, contented affection for him, not only deferring to him but actually doting on him. ("When we were married," she said, "he had to borrow a tie for the ceremony. But he has lots of shirts and ties now. People are always giving him shirts. And he has *so* many suits. . . .") All the way down to Clayton, Wallace chatted ceaselessly and jubilantly, seeming only incidentally aware of Lurleen beside him, while she—who that day was to be elected governor of

Alabama—wordlessly and tenderly and steadily picked invisible pieces of lint from his sleeves and brushed dandruff from his shoulders.

When they emerged from the car in front of the Clayton courthouse, they were immediately greeted by three frantic, scurrying photographers, who, their faces crammed against the back of their cameras, swam madly and dizzily around them with persistent discreet little clickings. Empty bleachers from the rally the night before were still sitting in the sun on the lawn before the courthouse. It was a sensuous autumn day, with a light warm breeze. The trees were bare, spread over the rooftops of the town like dainty fans, and the grass, though faded now with November, was thick and lush underfoot.

On the courthouse steps the Negro turnout was quickly reported to Wallace: "We been here about an hour, and we ain't seen the first one yet." He went on into the lobby, with its black-marble pillars and liver-colored marble floor and tall glass windows faintly tinted against the glare. Someone asked him, "You gonna sit with us today?" and he replied, "Little while. Brooks is still down at the Railway Express, ain't he?" He went in to vote, stepping into a booth that looked a little like a Parisian *pissoir,* only the cuff of his pants visible under the black curtain. He had trouble getting the curtain yanked completely shut at first, and as he was giving it furtive little tugs, a Negro woman came into the room to vote—she stood off to one side looking a bit awkward and embarrassed and startled to find Wallace there, her hands folded in front of her, the light reflecting blankly off her glasses.

Back in the courthouse lobby, Wallace, his heels clicking busily on the marble floor, made the rounds of all of the townsfolk with Lurleen. Presently she wandered outside and began walking toward their car. Wallace came out after her and called from the courthouse steps, "C'mon back here a minute, honey, fella here wants to say hello." She returned, shook a few more hands, and then seemed to vanish suddenly, as if, at the conclusion of her final and complete service to him, she had evaporated into the air. She had left the day now to Wallace.

It has become his custom to celebrate election days in the same manner he had been preparing for them, anticipating them, since he was a youth: by simply hanging around downtown with people. He took a long and leisurely stroll through the courthouse, and then sat for a while in one office talking with a collection of local officials, the windows open to the fresh autumn day, he smoking a cigar and twirling a Coke between his blunt little fingers. The chatter was casual and idle, as a damp warm breeze blew gently in through the window. "Yeah," said Wallace, "I hear Bernice is pregnant again. She don't seem to do nothing but spend her time gettin' pregnant. Heard she got pregnant this time out there under the schoolhouse—that right? That place is a regular social club. Her daughter went up to Rochester, you know. She wrote my wife to send her twenty dollars, said she wanted to come back home. Didn't seem to find things quite suitable up there in Ro-ches-ter, New Yoke. My wife's always been givin' her money, went and cared for all her chillun when they were sick. They'd come to her whenever one of their chillun got sick, and my wife'd go out there and get 'em well. She was outside there this morning, Bernice was—wanted a dollar. I had Hellier give her a dollar out there in front, and she went on in and voted. Guess we got that one, I don't know." There was laughter. Wallace continued, "Ole Nook last night, I heard he was fussin' 'cause they didn't give him any fried chicken last night, just some weenies. I gave him a dollar, too. Thing about Nook, he won't stay bought. You got to buy him again right before he goes in to vote." There was laughter again. Billy Watson wandered in at this point, slow and fragile and watery-eyed, freckled with age, looking convalescent and barely revived from an insulin shock of the night before. The bottom leaf of his tie was about six inches lower than the top leaf, and Wallace chuckled, "Somebody get some scissors and let's even up that tie for Billy." Watson merely stared at

Wallace and wheezed. The morning wore on. Once, as everyone seemed to rise together on some signal to change their sitting positions, Watson, remaining in his chair, invited them, "Why don't yawl come on out to the house and eat a little ham with me?"

Finally Wallace went outside, pausing to arrange for the lifting of an old man out of a car and into the courthouse to vote—he was as small and shriveled as a monkey, in a crisply starched white shirt that fit him like armor plating, he seeming as slight and fragile inside it as a matchstick. He had been brought to town by his daughter, a trim young, harshly pretty girl with bleached hair, and her husband, fortyish and balding and burly with tattooes on his arm, wearing a black knit shirt. The old man sat in the car waiting for assistance, spitting tobacco juice into an empty Champagne Velvet can. "Ed," Wallace called to someone behind him, "you hep 'em get Mr. Garrett in there, heunh?" The girl followed as two men carried the old man into the courthouse in a chair, his legs dangling down as uselessly as a doll's. Two old Negro women, sitting on a low wall along the sidewalk in the sun, watched the girl go up the steps. "Now, that's the oldest one," one of them said. "She married?" said the other. "Yeah, she married," said the first. "Well, lawd, I didn't know that."

Watson came out of the courthouse and sat for a while in the bleachers, his wispy pate bare in the sunshine, his cane between his legs. A woman headed for the courthouse greeted him, "I swear, dead last night, and here you are downtown this morning!" Watson gave a dry, weak, rustling chuckle. "Yeah, George told me to come on down this morning and vote as quick as I could while I was still alive. . . ."

Wallace had made his way around the square and now was sitting on the front porch of the Republican headquarters, a flat brick building that was a little newer than its neighbors. Among those gathered around him were the three leading local Republicans, a married couple and another man. With Wallace having decided to alight for a while right on their front stoop, they sat very straight and did not look at him but laughed rather loudly and abruptly at his remarks. He merely leaned back in his metal folding chair with his hands folded behind it, his dark glasses on now, a cigarette dangling from his mouth, his coat buttoned tightly across his middle, and his legs crossed with his elevated foot constantly twitching like a cat's tail. "Yeah," he said softly, "this is the exact spot the Republicans were headquartered after the Civil War. Right here. Should have mentioned that last night and watched the crowd sort of move over in this direction." The third Republican, a tall and gangling and sunburnt young man in white shirtsleeves, laughed. "Sho am glad you didn't do that, Governor." Wallace grinned under his dark glasses, his cigarette pinning the grin together in the middle, and turned to repeat the line. "Yeah, if I had just thought to say that last night. The Freedman's Bureau was right here during Reconstruction—all them nigguhs and carpetbaggers and scalawags, right here." His grin spread wider at the edges, the cigarette still pinched in its exact center, never quite looking at the three Republicans there, and, in fact, nobody during the conversation was really looking at the object of his remarks, in that curious, oblique, ceremonial way of casual but tense Southern exchanges. He was unmistakably presiding over the situation, and enjoying it enormously. A rickety drunk doddered past them, and Wallace muttered, cigarette ash flaking down over his black suit but he not stirring to remove the cigarette from his lips, "There goes yo man right there." The woman had ceased smiling now. She finally got up and went into the building, without a word. Wallace did not seem to notice her flight, as if she simply had not come into his range of vision. He remarked, " 'Course, I didn't say that last night, but I could have. This little corner of the square here has had quite a history. But you can always be magnanimous when you're beatin' 'em." The Republican beside him leaned forward quickly and blurted, "Yes, magnanimous, yes, well, how about ostracization, judge? You using the big words, there's a big word for you, let's talk about ostracization a little bit." Wallace said, "What's that? Hunh?" The man repeated, a little louder, "Ostracization, judge. You want to use the big words here, now, how about that one?" Wallace replied quietly, "Say it again one more time. My hearing's bad, you know. I can't hear good outta this ear." Now, with rather an impaled look, the man fairly bellowed, "Ostra-ci-*za*-tion!" Wallace, his hands still tidily folded behind his chair, paused a long moment, looked at everyone gathered around him, and finally remarked in a low voice, "Ostracism. Well, now, I don't think I know what that one is. Ostracism. Nossuh, I don't believe I ever heard of that one."

Abruptly he rose, and with a parting flip of his hand, left the porch and walked back across the square. It was now early in the afternoon. The traffic in and out of the courthouse had thinned somewhat, and the square was nearly deserted. Wallace motioned to his bodyguard, and they got into a car and headed back toward Montgomery.

Lurleen Wallace was closely surrounded by her husband's men after election. "I guess," she said with a small smile, "that I'm just one of the boys now." Though it was known that she regarded some of his aides with a cold distaste, Wallace's old staff was kept intact, and Lurleen existed as little more than a legalizing accessory to the extralegal extension of the George Wallace administration. Though, as Wallace heatedly points out, all the constitutional proprieties were observed, he still acted as the governor from his office directly across the hall from the executive suite (sometimes, late in the day after Lurleen had returned to the mansion, he abandoned even that appearance, quickly crossed the hall, and serenely continued his work, his telephone calls and conferences, from behind her desk). He still personally drew up the programs and strove with the legislature to get them passed, and the lobbyists and legislators still approached him directly, convivially pulling a chair over to his table in the capitol's bleak little basement cafeteria, where he hastily consumed eighty-eight-cent lunches of mealy peas and fried steak and cornbread and then held court with a toothpick, just as in the old days, just as if nothing had changed. The only difference was that now Lurleen served as head of state while he acted as prime minister; she attended to the ceremonial functions, leaving him that much freer for his maneuverings.

She seemed to be constantly, rigidly afraid that she was going to do something wrong, make a wrong move, blurt out the wrong thing. She drank coffee obsessively and manfully, and after becoming governor she also began to smoke raggedly, incessantly, carrying her pack of Benson & Hedges in a demure cigarette case in her hand wherever she went. "We been worrying about it a little bit," said one of Wallace's aides. "She really ought to cut down on some of them cigarettes. Why, when she goes to make a speech, she's stubbing out a cigarette when she gets up to talk, and as soon as she's done, as soon as she's finished shaking hands, she's grabbed another one out of her pack, and she's lighting it up." She was brittle and tautly on guard before newsmen, and Wallace's people carefully shielded her from political interviews and dialogues. It was as if, having been a private and nonpolitical person for most of her life, she was simply accustomed to delivering the direct and flat-footed truth and had not yet mastered the calm, intricate minuet of evasion and equivocation and sanctitude at which natural politicians are more or less born adept. "She ain't all that sharp," Wallace allowed, "but she can take care of herself." She read all her speeches. Her own political notions are a dutiful one-dimensional duplication of her husband's—in sum, rather on the order of an essay on states' rights that might be entered in a local high-school contest sponsored by the UDC. In fact, she seemed puzzled that anyone would inquire into her political beliefs. Asked once what figures in history had made the greatest impact on her, she answered, after a long pause, "Well, I suppose the women of the South who fought such hardships and tried to hold things together back during the War Between the States, and that period afterward." A little later, asked what books had been most important in her life, she replied, "Well, I suppose those stories on women of the South and the hard role they played back during the War Between the States and Reconstruction. . . ." Visibly uncomfortable as she was with conversations that had to do with anything other than her family and the business of running a household, she did not want to attend the conference of governors that President Johnson called in the spring of 1967, and Wallace had to reassure her. "Now, honey, they not gonna ask you to stand up and give your ideas about Vietnam or the balance of payments; all you got to do is just sit there and listen, that's all." Left, then, with little more than a figurine to analyze, some of the press, most notably the women's magazines, indulged in wry little smiles about her dress and drawl, and Wallace affected a politically effective indignation about such stories. But for her part, she maintained a brave, if slightly baffled, cheerfulness about the articles. "It's all just a part of politics."

There hung on the wall of the breakfast room at the mansion, right behind her chair, a small framed legend which says, "She Hath Done What She Could." The speculation that she might prove more assertive than her husband or his advisers ever reckoned on, while irresistible, was really rather fanciful. She was not so naïve a girl as to forget it was her husband who put her where she was, that the people elected her as a stand-in for him, and that without him she would have been absolutely lost and helpless in the office. What's more, if she had tried to take over the show after her election, it would have struck the people of Alabama, not to mention herself, as surpassingly unladylike. Finally, such a stunt simply wasn't the nature of the woman. She submitted to everything, surrendered even herself to her husband's furious public passion, much as an evangelist's or missionary's wife might, after so many years, finally surrender herself to attend her husband's lonely and obsessive communion with God, thereby accepting forever her own diminishment.

Whatever, the fact that she was the governor, and not Wallace, left Wallace in a state of vague nervousness. He called off the customary inaugural ball because, a friend declares, "He didn't like the idea of not being right smack in the center of the spotlight, of having to act as the escort for the new governor—he told everybody it was a racial thing, that he didn't want any nigguhs showing up and dancing with Lurleen, but that wasn't it." Not long after her election, says Glenn Curlee, "I told him, 'George, you better start sleepin' with that woman.' He said, 'Yeah. Wouldn't it be a helluvva note if she run me off?' Back when he was governor, every time she'd call him up at the office, he'd say, 'What the hell you want? I'm busy now, don't be botherin' me.' But he's even talkin' sweet to her on the phone now."

Part Six

Wallace emerged from the succession crisis—his closest brush ever to oblivion—miraculously revitalized, and in the process, he completed his personal appropriation of Alabama.

Not only did he assimilate virtually the entire governmental structure of the state (the appointive terms of most state agencies are constitutionally phased to spread over several administrations), but he eliminated the last vestiges of any political opposition. The senators who had frustrated his hopes of a succession amendment met with unanimous political extinction. Some of them simply did not offer for reelection; those who did were demolished by Wallace candidates. The capitol is now absolutely clean of them.

One of those senators was a mild, balding, bespectacled farmer named Charlie Montgomery, from Greene County, in the Black Belt, who had placidly supported most of Wallace's other programs. When he unexpectedly balked on the succession matter, says one of his former fellow senators, "he was considered a traitor back in his home area." It was known to Wallace's people that Montgomery at one time had a critical drinking problem and had been maintaining a fragile abstinence for only a year or two. "Seems like they picked out

Charlie to bear down on more'n anybody else," says his former colleague. "Wallace people started contacting his family, his neighbors, and all these people started calling him all hours of the night. About the middle of the succession debate, Charlie started drinking again. Two days before the final vote, he came to me and broke down and cried, and told me what Wallace's people were doing to him back in Greene County. The last day of the fight, he was absolutely, totally blind drunk. He could hardly talk." A few months later, back in Greene County, Montgomery shot himself to death in his home.

Kenneth Hammond, the senator who delivered the last-day speech charging that Wallace was following "the same cycle as Adolf Hitler," also found, when he returned home, that "friends would give you these various looks, empty stares—you could tell when you walked into a place they had just been talking about you." He offered for reelection anyway, and was trampled. With a kind of desperate irreconcilability, as if unable to accept that Wallace had actually made him an exile in his own community, Hammond ran for mayor of his town—a village of some 460 people in the mountain vastness of northeastern Alabama—and managed to win that. But there remains about him an air of pent rage. A thick, burly thirty-five-year-old man with light thinning hair, usually wearing a black windbreaker and nursing a cigar stub with a match, he careens defiantly among his townsfolk, seeming to have abandoned all caution and discretion, talking loudly about Wallace along the sidewalks and in his family's small dry-goods store as gunfighters talked recklessly and heedlessly in frontier saloons about sheriffs they knew they were going to meet someday in the middle of the street. His parents quietly fear for him. He lives, with his parents and his wife and two small children, in a white-columned galleried house built in 1845, set on a high knoll under massive trees and surrounded by a white picket fence. On a wintry May afternoon recently—a chill and sunless and blowy spring afternoon—he sat in his kitchen, a plain and bare room with a high ceiling which seemed to lend itself to long talk and coffee in such weather, and declared, "Naw, I didn't fear for my safety during the succession thing. I wadn't about to get any trouble from anybody. During my lifetime, I've left many a whupped one over this state. When Trammell was making all these promises to me in his office, he said, 'Kenneth, if I'm not telling you the truth, you can beat my ass—I know that.' Naw, my danger's now, while everything's quiet. Wallace knows I'm just a redneck sitting up here without a law degree. But even so, they couldn't really get to me, except to kill me. Horton, now, he's the biggest cattleman in this part of the country, all they would have to do is slip in there and poison his ponds at night. But three men pick me up and follow me whenever I get in Montgomery these days. If I announced against Wallace for governor, I'd either be killed or put in Kilby prison. The next man that runs for governor in this state, two things he can't do: get in a helicopter or get in an airplane. It's all a game of chicken, California style. Me and Wallace, we're on a collision course. I'm gonna see him ground down—I mean, ground down, so he won't ever get up." He paused. "If I didn't have my family, there are times —you know, I'd just flip my wig."

It has been one effect of Wallace's complete appropriation of Alabama to create a scattering of such desperate men who, seeing no hope of defeating Wallace inside the state, are separately maneuvering, with assorted feverish schemes, for support from *outside* the state, from parties who might have an interest in neutralizing Wallace. Wallace's one-man rule has created a vacuum inside Alabama which politics, no less nature, abhors, and that vacuum has engendered a dizzying variety of opportunities for his enemies to sign themselves on, to become the agents for, important outside interests. It's something like Cuban exiles clamoring for the patronage of the American government with the promise they can accomplish the destruction of Castro. Curiously enough, most of these hopes revolve, not around President Johnson, but around Robert Kennedy, and it is Robert Kennedy who stands to gain the most from his demise.

The men engaged in these maneuvers range from Hammond, who would offer himself as a gubernatorial candidate in the form of a political human bomb, to Richmond Flowers, attorney general under Wallace, who was obliterated along with everyone else when he ran for governor against Lurleen. Flowers still gamely insists, "I thoroughly intend to run again." The outlook is glum for him, though. He conspicuously identified himself with the ambitions of the newly registered Negro voters in the state and the dreams of the white liberal minority when he ran for governor, and though it earned for him substantial support from Kennedy interests and a spot as runner-up in the primary, he probably erased himself as any serious factor in future campaigns. He now maintains an office in a Montgomery office building only a few floors above Wallace's own presidential campaign headquarters. There he receives the occasional visitors who drop by—Northern lawyers and politicians, African exchange students, sometimes reporters. He tends to dress somewhat like a Mississippi riverboat gambler: a soft dove-gray suit and a gray shirt monogrammed on the pocket with maroon thread, a satiny white tie, a white silk handkerchief stuffed in his coat pocket, a diamond tie stud and gold cuff links bearing the Alabama seal. He has pale blue eyes and sandy hair parted in the middle after the fashion of the twenties, and a dainty, impish way of ending his anecdotes—"Bull Conner's always been a tool of the Big Mules up there in Birmingham. He's a two-hundred-dollar-a-month man. All he wants, they give him crackers and a drink above the train station, he's happy"—by fingering his tie, with his little finger raised, and snapping his head to one side.

He himself happily proposes, "We all got our human frailties, you know"—a phrase that seems to be a popular admission along all those who emerged from the Folsom years, including Wallace. At the least, people in Alabama tend to look on him as a flagrant opportunist: before his political reincarnation as Alabama's most significant and gallant liberal, he achieved some state-wide fame as a teller of Negro dialect jokes. But Flowers maintains, with apparent sincerity, "My opinion began to change first as I got into the legalities of the matter. I was going strictly on the legal basis, but the more I got into it, the more I realized there was no moral basis for Alabama's resistance. It was just as wrong morally as it was legally." With a kind of doughty optimism, he has managed to extract encouragement from Lurleen's shattering victory: "The number two, three, and four candidates combined to get forty-two percent of the vote. That's an indication we haven't got far to build. There's a place for a man of reason, and I'm gonna be that man on the scene until some other individual has guts enough to stick his head up. I'm stronger today. I've hit the bottom, and I'm comin' back."

The likelihood, though, is that the possibilities for any other kind of leadership in Alabama were preempted even before Wallace. Also among the politicians snuffed out by Lurleen's election was former governor John Patterson, the man credited with initiating the state's shrill segregationist politics. He has been forgotten as swiftly as he flared and now lives quietly in Montgomery in peaceful irrelevance. In his law office one afternoon not long after the campaign, he made the surprising confession, "In fifty-eight, now, I was the champion of segregation, because there just isn't any way to run as a liberal in this state and get elected. That's all there is to it. I couldn't be what I wanted to be. You were either for the white folks or the nigras. If you didn't appeal to prejudices, you'd get beat. It was something you just had to live through. Nothing disappointed me more than having this millstone hanging around our necks. We were just born with it, and we can't get it off. During my administration, because of this millstone, Alabama was deprived of the opportunity to have any voice in national affairs. We were just too hot on the racial matter. But even when I was attorney general, I knew we were just fighting a delaying action. I had to keep my tongue in my cheek on some of those cases we argued before the Supreme Court. It wasn't anything more than a delaying action, but it looked good in the headlines. Those nigra lawyers knew their constitutional law better than anyone. A lot of times, you didn't *want* a decision, because you knew which way it'd go. I guess you gotta give the devil his due: if it hadn't been for some of these outside factions like the NAACP and Martin Luther King, the nigras just wouldn't be where they are now. Sure, my views have moderated. There's nothing that would please me more than to see the nigras have equal opportunity to develop the state. You just can't defend any system that treats one group of citizens different from another group. When you allow the nigra to participate in government, you can demand that he obey the law and stay off the streets, but deny him participation in government, and you can't make any demands on him atall. I never in my life believed in segregation because one race is different or better than another. How can anybody seriously defend the accusation that nigras are inferior?"

One former state official laments, "I just don't know of anyone left of any political significance with the will to fight George now." Even the state's two U.S. senators have shown a profound reluctance to antagonize him, and his own manner toward them is faintly contemptuous and imperious: he was heard recently on the phone barking irritably to Senator Lister Hill that he expected from him quick and hearty support on Alabama's school-guidelines defiance if he, Hill, hoped to preserve his political health in Alabama. Only a few months later, Hill announced he would not run for reelection.

He has singlehandedly isolated Alabama from the national Democratic party. In 1962, through a long January night in a Birmingham hotel, he persuaded the state party executive committee, composed mostly of national loyalists, to alter its rules to allow him to run his own slate of unpledged Democrat electors who would be free to withhold their votes from the national nominee and cast them for someone else: namely, Wallace. "After that," says a party loyalist, "it was like watchin' a freight train go by." Wallace's maverick slate defeated the loyalist slate by a margin of almost six to one, and the national Democratic party was devastated in Alabama. "They didn't spend one dime down here in 1964," declares another loyalist. "What could they do? Hell, their man wasn't even on the ballot, Democratic congressmen were swept out of office right and left, and took eighty years of seniority with them. George Wallace busted the Democratic party in Alabama. The only political organization in Alabama right now is George Wallace."

There is a Republican party in the state, but it exists only at Wallace's sufferance. The fact is, the most recent campaign between the Wallaces and the Republicans was largely conducted on the common premise of who could do the most damage to Washington, who disliked Lyndon Johnson the most thoroughly—politics in the state having been reduced to a singleminded competition of ill-tempered enmity against the federal government. Wallace's executive secretary, Cecil Jackson, ruminates with some gratification, "It's just a tough situation now to distinguish between Republicans and Democrats here. Everybody in the state thinks the same way, and people feel the same way."

Indeed, if there is to be found anywhere in the United States today a totalitarian society, it would be the state of Alabama. Whether the condition is Wallace's personal handiwork or whether he has merely served as a political accomplice, the truth is that the state was transformed, during his administration, into a psychological and ideological monolith, more insular and intransigent than even Mississippi in that the popular mentality has been given consistent and undistracted political articulation—the final deep foxhole of the South. It would seem that what Wallace has managed to do is convert the Folsom revolution—the immediate and personal involvement of the masses in the politics of the state—into a kind of popular totalitarianism: the Folsom revolution simply set the stage for this in the manner that some divines like to imagine that the Roman Empire existed to facilitate the propagation of Christianity.

In any event, the racial conflicts of the past ten years and the solitary apostolic histrionics of Wallace have left Alabama with a single provincial vision of itself in the nation and the world, and a single ruthless expectation for unanimity—not only in ideas but also in habits, in morality, even in dress: most youngsters in Alabama classrooms regard any deviation from short hair and neatly pressed clothes as a sign of perversion. The archaic specter of the unkempt beatnik still hovers over the state and conglomerately connotes everything that is sinister of the Alabama mind: communism, miscegenation, dope, illicit sex. It is a mentality cultivated not only in the pulpits of Alabama but also in the schools: it pervades everything. A Montgomery editor was shocked during the 1966 gubernatorial campaign when his five-year-old son informed him, "I'm not gonna vote for Richmond Flowers, because he's that man that'll make you change color." In public restaurants, any out-of-state visitors who may fall to chatting casually but critically of Wallace and his policies will suddenly find people at tables around them turning and glaring with venomous mutterings. There is a general psychology of martyrdom, or at least harassment, which Alabamians actually seem to savor. They cherish visions of their persecution. After a restaurant fire in Montgomery in which some twenty-six persons perished, it was announced that investigators from a fire-inspection firm in Boston would be journeying down to examine the rubble, and one lady phoned a local radio talk-show to suggest, in a high thin voice, "I just wonder had it not been Alabama, if these people from Boston would have been sent down here. . . ." As recently as 1966, the then Alabama superintendent of education, Austin R. Meadows, composed a remarkable philosophic essay which he mailed as an inspirational epistle to educational and political figures all over the state. Some of its observations: " 'Segregation' is a perfectly good word. . . . The Lord set aside or segregated fruit from the apple tree in the Garden of Eden from Adam and Eve. . . . Matrimony, the most sacred of all bonds for man and woman, is the highest type of segregation. In matrimony, husband and wife bind themselves to cleave to one another, even to the extent of forsaking all others if necessary. . . . Segregation is the basic principle of culture. The good join together to segregate themselves from the bad. . . . Animals, in many instances, join their own kind to defend themselves by numbers against other animals that would destroy them without such segregated bond. Birds of a feather truly flock together. Wild geese fly across this continent in a 'V' formation, but they never join any other flock of birds. The wild eagle mates with another eagle and not with any other bird. Redbirds mate with redbirds, the beautiful bluebirds mate with other bluebirds, and so on through bird life. . . ."

Perhaps the most melancholy aspect of Alabama's massive preoccupation under Wallace has been the toll it has taken in the vitality of the whole state community. Such a bitter obsession enervates any people, exhausts any society, and steals from the spirit of its citizens, narrows their lives. In Alabama, segregation has acted as a great succubus. Former state senator Robert Gilchrist declares, "I once led a filibuster for seventy-two hours just for a resolution saying the Alabama Senate was for upholding law and order. That's what you have to do in this state now on a simple little decent thing like that—a seventy-two-hour filibuster. It cramps everything. Even efforts to change local option on routine little county housekeeping duties, they involve race—county option is opposed because of the fear the nigras might get a majority rule in the county. The hours of conversation and debate and energy wasted on this racial thing—why, I must have spent a third of my time in the legislature debating this question, instead of concentrating on creative and useful things for our people. But everybody—I mean, businessmen, preachers, teachers—they're talking about it all the time, too."

Another former state senator notes, "Anytime in history when civilization was the lowest, two groups have had to band together—the schools and the churches. But both of these groups in Alabama are gutless now. The preachers are intimidated by their congregations, and Wallace has used money to neutralize the teachers. He's combined the political theories of Hitler, Jim Folsom, and Huey Long. He's the greatest politician this state has ever seen." Those dissenters left in Alabama—serious and sober men not given to hyperbole, many of them conservatives and segregationists—have begun to talk about the Wallace phenomenon in Alabama and the nation in terms of the Third Reich. One of them declares flatly, "*Mein Kampf* is the Bible of Alabama politics today. It's the textbook for the prejudice and propaganda. And when George starts nationwide, you just watch him. He'll pick an enemy—maybe a new one—and he'll run against that enemy." Another simply remarks, "Hitler's vote, you know, was proportionately larger than Lincoln's. Mussolini was given a vote of confidence by ninety-eight percent of the Italian electorate." Senator Hammond's speech on the last day of the succession fight no longer seems quite as intemperate as it once did. In the last year or two, a number of Alabamians have taken to carrying around books on Nazism, the most popular being Shirer's *The Rise and Fall of the Third Reich.* So acute has the sense of alarm and despair become among certain people that, at a party in a Montgomery apartment one evening not long after Lurleen's inauguration, a gentle, bespectacled, exquisitely civilized Montgomery dowager suddenly blurted, "I wish he were dead. I wish someone would kill him. He ought to die. He's awful, terrible. I would kill him myself if I just had the chance—I would." There were tears in her eyes.

Alabama belongs to him now. He is all alone with the people, and they are all alone with him. But having accomplished this—and now in his attempt to enlarge awesomely the scale of his incarnation "of the majority of the folks"—he seems to have acquired a peculiar air of final personal loneliness and isolation, as if he has withdrawn more and more into himself.

When he was not foraging about the country, "he just stayed cooped up in that hot office in the capitol all day long," his brother Gerald reported unhappily. "He's been gettin' lots of colds lately. He don't get enough sunshine and fresh air." The governor's outer reception office—a large high room with slightly dingy yellow walls, furnished with busts and chairs and bookcases whose style seems to be nicked and cigarette-scorched Ancient Egyptian—was constantly filled with a babbling collection of politicians, admirers, tourists, and aides; in one corner, a legal assistant explaining to a visitor how segregation is even justified by evolution, though he doesn't happen to believe in evolution; in another corner, a capitol employee telling a bodyguard about the phenomenon of a seventy-four-year-old man whose forty-nine-year-old wife had just borne a baby—"He's just as jealous of her as he kin be. Seventy-four-years old. Says when he ain't on her hisself, his hand is, or his shotgun is close by"; a secretary glancing out of a window, "Huh. Looks like it wants to rain. . . ."; another secretary talking over the phone in a loud bulging voice, "We gonna say, 'Congratulations and best wishes on your production of *The Tempest.*' Only, would you say the name of the play? Huh? All right, then—'which plays at Troy State tonight.' I don't know, should we say production or performance? It's a play by Shakespeare, you know, I think. If it was being given for the first time, maybe we should say production, see, but since I believe it's a play by Shakespeare, maybe we should say performance, since this isn't the first time. . . ." (One morning a gaunt and spectral Negro, elderly, dressed in a shabby coat with an open shirt collar, a Bible under one arm, strode suddenly into the office—which was filled with the usual assembly of courtiers, whispering in corners or leafing through the dentist's-office assortment of dogeared magazines—and, as everyone stared astonished and motionless, delivered himself of a five-minute tolling Zechariac denunciation of Wallace, his eyes wild and red, his long arm flailing. When he finished, he bowed formally to everyone in the room, gave a curt salute, and departed. It had been an unsettling materialization.)

The governor's office is a long somber room full of dark wood, suggesting somehow the executive office of the president of a venerable but slightly seedy railroad, with gold-scalloped drapes and a sea-green marble mantel above a cold fireplace and wine leather chairs sitting around a massive conference table under a splendid crystal chandelier, and Wallace, occupying this room, stumpy and quick and chewing ceaselessly on a tattered cigar, in his dark shimmery suit and bulky Masonic ring and tab-collar shirt with buttoned cuffs sometimes double-secured with heavy ruby cuff-links, suggested perhaps a rugged little switchman or flagman who relentlessly made his way up to become head of the whole operation. Behind his vast desk, he looked not much larger than a midget, and it seemed he tried to answer all the deep and imposing space around him with a constant violent business. Talking to visitors, he would yank out a middle drawer in the desk and prop his foot on it, scrabble out a cigar from the box on his desk and unpeel it and lick it and quickly get it fuming, fumble up a letter-opener and tap it over his telephone and papers and then at a Boy Scout medallion suspended in a tiny hinged frame until he had it spinning madly, suddenly lean forward to spit into a wastebasket, lean back again and almost in one motion drop the letter-opener and snatch up a wooden gavel and proceed to jam it into his cheek and midriff, then balance the head of the gavel on his desk and twirl it with one hand while he picked up the letter-opener again and kept the medallion spinning at a blur. When he got a call, he would wedge the receiver between his cheek and his shoulder and continue chomping on his cigar while one hand worked the gavel handle into his side and the other shuffled the memos on his desk or tugged the lobe of his ear. He kept a meager and eclectic array of books on a table by his desk: a history of Alabama and an Alabama encyclopedia, a history of the International Longshoreman's Association called *Men Along the Shore,* a study of *The Prohibition Movement in Alabama, 1702–1943,* and an odd volume called *The Formation of the Negro* by an author with the last name of Lynch. Sitting on the marble fireplace mantel was a white plaster bust of himself, done by some female admirer, which vaguely resembled Cro-Magnon man. He also had a small framed color photograph of the last two Confederate veterans holding a proud if rickety salute to a lowered Confederate flag against a lonely cold blue autumn sky.

The aides who surrounded him and insulated him were a disparate lot, each of them like some less pleasant and less engaging fragment of the man they all complemented.

Cecil Jackson, Wallace's executive secretary, is a generally humorless sort with a lean slack face and a perpetually anxious expression, who looks hauntingly like Robert Shelton; when he does laugh, he pulls his lips back with a surprising swiftness and simply hisses. Wallace's chief legal aide, Hugh Maddox, a Baptist boy with an aversion to alcohol and the theory of evolution, wears the same dour, houndlike expression with the same stitched brow; both he and Jackson cultivate the careful gloom of funeral directors. But Wallace's other aides seem to share the curious childlike naïveté that essentially characterizes Wallace—as if they were all basically overgrown children being led by someone who was himself half child and half man. Ed Ewing, who has served sporadically as Wallace's local press secretary, is an untidy heap of a man with a chubby cherub's face and small curling locks of brown hair, who lives in a constant state of harassment and aggrievement at the indignities endured by his boss at the hands of a hostile world; he spent one afternoon recently passing back and forth through Wallace's reception room with a clipping from a New England newspaper clutched in his plump hand which referred to a speed trap in Alabama named Ludowici. The town is really in Georgia. Ewing was convinced the mistake was malicious, and he was readying a letter to the newspaper threatening to sue. A reporter found Ewing one drizzling afternoon in late October during the 1966 gubernatorial campaign in a back room of Wallace's campaign headquarters in downtown Montgomery, elaborately snuffling with a bad cold as he bent over a well-thumbed copy of *Esquire* which contained a less-than-enchanted article about Wallace—the issue had come out the summer before, and seemed to be registering only now among Wallace's people, and Ewing was trying to figure out whether the writer of the article had been white or Negro. "We just been laughin' about it," he professed. "I guess they thought it would make us mad or something, but it didn't."

Wallace's current national liaison man is Bill Jones, a pleasant little cricket of a man in heavy bug-glasses who has always served off and on as Wallace's press secretary. He took a sabbatical in 1965 to run for Congress, and was defeated. More than any of the others, Jones seems to live vicariously through Wallace, likes to lend him his own suits to wear, and derives a certain personal swaggering gratification from Wallace's political vitality. When asked once about the prospect that Wallace might not get the endorsement of Lester Maddox in Georgia, Jones chirped, "It don't make any difference, we gonna run slap over 'em all." He recounts his own role in the melees that Wallace has provoked in appearances out of the state with flair and relish: in a reverent biography of Wallace, Jones wrote shortly after losing the congressional race that "most civil rights pickets are cowards and will not press their cause if they meet any resistance at all. I earned a Southern-type nickname during the [Indiana] campaign because I liked to test picket lines; many times to see how lively the sign-bearing crowd would be I walked into the line, stopped and disrupted the marchers. The nickname was 'Cotton-Pickin' Picket Plucker.' "

When Wallace ventures beyond Montgomery now, he always carries with him a platoon of his oldest cronies, the more the better, and he doesn't like them to get out of his sight. At the start of interviews in alien territories, he will glance quickly around the room and demand of his bodyguards, "Whur's Curlee? Go get him and have him sit in here with us awhile." He needs to have them surround him as a kind of familiar and congenial weather, so that, in a sense, wherever he goes he takes his office with him; he is still in a Clio barbershop, the Clayton courthouse, a Montgomery café.

After Lurleen's election, he made one last official trip to attend an interim session of the national governor's conference at White Sulphur Springs, West Virginia, and for this excursion he was able to rummage up only Ralph Adams, his college boardinghouse companion whom he had appointed to preside over a state campus of his own. As the plane rose above the Montgomery airport, Wallace scurried from one side of the cabin to the other, plumping himself down in one seat to look out of its porthole for a long, silent moment and then scurrying across the aisle to gaze out that porthole, studying the earth below him. "Guess we're passin' over Putnam's Mountain now," he said. "They the first box to ever come in. Nothing but real sho-nuff mountain folk up there. They were sixteen to nothin' for us the last time." He reflected for a moment and then turned to Adams. "Make a note to invite those folks from Putnam's Mountain down to the inauguration."

Adams fumbled a pad out of his coat pocket, took out a ballpoint pen, and carefully transcribed that impulse. A small man, shaped something like a turnip, with a long lean neck, sun-chapped, protruding from collars that usually seem too large for it by the width of a finger, a lean slack face and a long nose, a sleepy tangle of gray hair, and narrow slightly hooded eyes, Adams rather resembles a snake-oil salesman. He has a way of talking with his head tilted back in mild suspicion, looking cunningly down the length of his nose and barely moving his taut thin lips. But he is, by nature, gentle and guileless and amicable, and becomes uneasily suspicious in the company of reporters and strangers only when he reminds himself that he should be. He does seem somewhat uncomfortable and even embarrassed in his position as a college president. He quickly explains, "You know, they want an administrator these days to run a college, they don't really want an academic man. I just leave all the professors alone down there, and that makes them happy enough." Wallace arranged for him to get an honorary Ph.D., but Adams nevertheless submits, "An honorary degree is a lot harder to get. They say anybody can go to school and study and get an academic degree, but you have to have already *achieved* something, *done* something to get an honorary degree—to be recognized like that. Least, I look at it that way." After his discharge, he tinkered around for a while in politics, then was recalled into the Air Force, serving for a while in the Pentagon. He was fetched back to Alabama by Wallace to head the state Selective Service system, and finally was appointed president of Troy State College. "Seems like I was in the Air Force one day and a college president the next," he muses. Wallace sometimes accompanied Adams to national conventions of college presidents, trips on which Adams is wont to take his luggage, merely a paper bag with one shirt in it, one change of underwear, and one change of socks. Riding to a hotel in a cab once, Wallace declared, "Adams, damnit, man, you a college president now, got to dress better than you do. You wear them fifteen-year-old suits and you don't shave. Ain't you ever gonna become anything? You just can't be takin' your clothes around with you in a paper sack anymore." One gets the impression that Wallace installed Adams in his exalted position in a moment of impishness, just as a prank to ruffle the academic community in general, to "take them down a peg or two," as he is fond of saying, by showing them someone like Adams was as capable of being a college president as any of them. There's no doubt he derived great glee from the horror among the academic community when he named Adams to his post. In any event, Adams dutifully has pages in the college's annuals devoted to pictures of Wallace and tributes to his statesmanship, and the school newspaper is strenuously forbidden to criticize the administration, a policy that created an untidy furor recently when a modest editorial of discontent was lopped whole out of the paper. Adams' professors also become periodically restive, but he endures all squalls with a serene imperturbability. Not surprisingly, he more or less concurs in Wallace's vague contempt for intellectuals, is of the opinion that professors spend too much time in the clouds, and happily supported Wallace's bill to ban subversive speakers from state campuses. For the most part, he also serenely endures Wallace's persistent tickled jests about his job. On the way to White Sulphur Springs Wallace sideswiped, his face bland, "Your wife figgered she was gonna marry herself a college presi-dent, didn't she, Adams? That's how come she picked you out, isn't that right?" Adams, smiling thinly, said, "That's right, guvnuh."

Then, when Wallace had disappeared into the flight cabin, Adams declared to a reporter on the plane, "Hell, I've seen political leaders all around the world. I flew the hump during World War II, I been all around the world, I've seen King Farouk, all of 'em, and I can tell you, he"—pointing toward the closed door of the pilot's cabin—"is a man of destiny. He's like Fiorello La Guardia." Later, in the limousine that picked up the party at the White Sulphur Springs airport, Adams began enthusing about Wallace again to the state patrolman who was driving them to the hotel, leaning forward with his nose almost touching the patrolman's ear, until Wallace reached out with one hand to gently pull him back. "Now, Ralph. Ralph. You gettin' carried away." But Adams continued reciting Wallace's statesmanlike qualities, until Wallace finally began talking to the patrolman himself, his voice several notches louder than Adams'.

Snow was scattered over the ground and under dark spruce and cedars, and the day was as bright and cold as crystal. Getting out before the Greenbrier Inn, a monumental white hotel with that particular wooden-lattice and potted-palm elegance of those huge resort hotels built during the twenties for the croquet-and-rocking-chair leisure of the very rich, Wallace immediately found himself enswarmed by a pack of reporters. Adams stood off to one side, smiling. It never fails to surprise and elate Wallace and his people to discover themselves the center of eager attention amid impressive surroundings, to draw such dizzying interest from strangers, and particularly the out-of-state press. They still don't seem quite able to believe it, and Wallace himself regards it all with a mild happy wonder, with an air of "Look at this, look what I done set off even here, and didn't even know it." Going on into the hotel, Wallace waved to a delegation of state troopers standing to one side of the glass doors, calling to them, "And I'm for the police, too." They all grinned and saluted him smartly. (One of them told him the next morning, after driving him back to his plane, "I'll be seeing you in Washington. . . .")

At that morning's executive session, Adams settled himself in a chair behind Wallace's place at the conference table and looked around at the collection of other governors. He then leaned toward a reporter beside him and murmured, "That man over there, now, he looks familiar. Who is he?" The reporter said, "That's Robert McNair of Carolina." Adams paused. "Carolina?" "Yeah," the reporter said. Adams paused again. "Is that North or South Carolina he's governor of?" "South," he was told. "Oh," he said. "That's right. I remember now." He slept through most of the session, slumped low in his chair, a small baggy dandruffy man with cheek propped on fist. Once he emitted a snore. He was awakened a few times by Wallace to go fetch a cigar. When a gavel ended the session, he abruptly stood up—perhaps a bit too quickly for whatever appearances he was guarding—and looked around blinking, his trousers drooping low under his paunch, a mild and almost sly little smile on his face. He then followed Wallace's party into the inn's spacious and chandeliered dining room, where Wallace, after he had seated himself, looked around him and pronounced, "You know, this is a real swan-é place." The waiter brought menus so large that Wallace immediately disappeared behind his, only his little hands visible at its edges. There was a long period of perusing the French and Italian dishes, and then Wallace's voice came from his menu, "Adams, you a college president now, you spose to be able to read this menu. What's it say?"

For the duration of the conference, Wallace kept pretty much to himself. Retreating back to his suite immediately after that afternoon's session, relaxed in his sitting room, he inquired of Adams—who had found a bowl of fruit and was now systematically ransacking it, perched on the edge of a chair with a newspaper spread on the rug at his feet to catch the orange peels and seeds (when the table was being cleared at lunch, he had lunged to retrieve an unfinished hunk of cornbread from his plate as it was being removed)—"Adams, what's everybody spose to do before supper? They got some kind of something goin' on down in the ballroom, don't they?" Adams spat a seed, hunched far over the newspaper with his elbows on his knees, and mumbled thickly, "Yeah, guvnuh, I think it's a honorary reception." "Well, what they gonna be doin', they not gonna be doin' anything but just standin' around and drinkin', are they? I don't see no need to go down there for that." Adams nodded, peeling off more orange peel with his pocket knife. "That's about all, guvnuh, I'd say—just standing around and talking." "Well," said Wallace, "I don't particularly care for that; we'll just wait up here till time for supper."

Presently there was a knock at the door, and a bodyguard admitted a radio reporter with a tape recorder, who knelt by Wallace's chair for a short interview. When it was over, Wallace told the reporter, motioning toward Adams, "Hell, this fella here just did finish the sixth grade, and I appointed him president of one of our colleges down there in Alabama. That just goes to show you, in Alabama we don't discriminate for any reason—race, creed, color, religion, *or* ignorance." When the reporter was gone, Adams muttered to Wallace, "Guvnuh, now you got to stop running me down in front of folks. You just got to quit talking about me that kinda way." Wallace grunted, "Aw, hell, Adams. You turnin' into one of them sensitive college presidents?"

They finally left the suite and headed for the dining room. In the elevator going down, a blonde glowing woman in a white stole, a jeweled necklace glimmering at her throat, reached forward after an exchange of greetings and brushed dandruff from Wallace's shoulders—he seems somehow to invoke such solicitude in most females, perhaps because of his boyishness. He thanked her warmly. Getting out of the elevator, he advised Adams, "You could use a few swipes there, too, Adams." Then, with his small party gathered around him in the hall, he plotted that they would simply stroll through the ballroom, where the reception was still under way, to get to the dining room. "I think we'll just walk on through here, boys," he murmured conspiratorially. When he entered the ballroom he was, of course, instantly waylaid—much to his delight. It was twenty minutes later before he finally settled himself at a table in the dining room, and he had collected three newsmen to have supper with him. He inquired of them, "Guess you fellas figger I'm a bad buggah, don't you?" They laughed. "Yeah, lots of folks think I'm a bad buggah. They think I'm a hate-monger. But I ain't no hate-monger—shit, life's too short for that. You can't waste it hatin' folks." After supper, while all the other governors were off in rooms talking together, Wallace lingered in the lobby with the newsmen, one hand hooked in his pants pocket by the thumb while a cigar smoldered between two stubby fingers, his other hand fingering his tie knot or running up and down his shirt under his coat lapel. "You boys shoulda been with us up there in Kenosha, Wisconsin, back yonder in sixty-four. That was the most rambunctious crowd I ever talked to. I never seen folks that much for us. I mean, you'd just open your mouth to try and say something, 'Ah—' and they'd be up outta those seats cheerin' and stompin'—"

He finally returned to his suite, sitting for a while in his shirtsleeves chatting with Adams. "Yeah, when we get to Washington, we gonna make Watson head of atomic energy. He's gonna look after atomic energy for us. . . ." He suddenly demanded of Adams, "You been in those sessions down there, I don't think any of those fellas sound more intelligent than I do, do they? That Romney, for instance—he don't sound all that intelligent. They all just ordinary men, like you and me. Hell. . . ."

The evening abruptly dissolved into yawns. Wallace started stripping off his tie and unfastening his cuffs, and the small party scattered to their separate bedrooms. Barely thirty seconds after closing the door to his own room, Adams was in bed, his shirt and trousers drooping from a chair, the covers pulled up under his chin—already beginning to snore.

The next morning Adams, attired in shorts and undershirt, ventured into Wallace's bedroom to wake him and managed to get no more than a muffled grumble. When breakfast was wheeled into Adams' room, Adams went back into Wallace's bedroom and said, "Guvnuh, they've brought in the breakfast—it's ready and waiting in there." There was a silence, and then a thick, querulous, "Ready in whur?" "In my room in there." "Adams, you didn't wake me up. You not doin' your job, Adams." Adams made a thin soft protest, "Guvnuh, I did, I did, I came in here at eight-thirty and woke you up, you just don't remember, you went on right back to sleep." There was another long silence. "You spose to see that I'm awake, Adams. What time is it?" Adams told him, and returned to the room where the breakfast tray was waiting. A minute or so later, Wallace clumped in from his bedroom, wearing his shoes under his rumpled pajamas, his hair askew and spiky and gluey. He tried to flatten it back with his hand as he sat down, and his first utterance after emerging from the transitory oblivion of sleep, even before he had tasted of his Spanish melon and coffee and toast and fried eggs, was, "Yessuh, sho sounded like a bunch of Southern guvnuhs down there yesterday, talkin' all about protectin' state sovereignty and all. I thought for a minute I was right back home. . . ."

His political isolation is virtually absolute. After Lester Maddox of Georgia—the only politician of any imaginable consequence who could have been considered a Wallace ally—began hinting he might stay within the Democratic fold in 1968, Wallace snorted, "Hell, he didn't even think he was gonna show over there in that guvnuh's race, didn't even have any idea he was even *close*. Then all of a sudden, he wakes up one mornin' and he's in the runoff, and he thinks, 'Why, goddamn! I could win this thing. I could actually be *guvnuh* of Georgia! So he gets all excited and starts tryin' to make everybody he can think of happy, snatchin' at anybody, makin' all these accommodations and stuff. Hell, it was funny. What's wrong with Lester, he just ain't got no *character*. . . ." Actually, he had already begun evidencing a particular aversion to any politician identifying with him too intimately; he tends now to lose respect for anyone who becomes too enraptured with him.

In fact, says one old friend, "It's almost got to where he don't trust anybody outside his own flesh." His deafness, a condition left from his war service, has been growing more serious, and this dimming of hearing, some speculate, will only deepen his fanaticism, his isolation, his estrangement from communication and all it involves—logic, compromise, the efficacy of words and the vitality of reason—and increase his reliance on passion and the visceral values.

After Lurleen delivered a speech in the spring of 1967 promising massive resistance to federal integration guide lines, Wallace toyed with the idea of assembling a kind of state-wide vigilante posse of some one hundred thousand volunteers, "so when the troops come, we'll have a few folks waitin' for 'em." This was a trifle raw even for his advisers, one of whom reports, "I told him, 'Guvnuh, I think it would be a mistake, you bound to draw in a few real hairy ones with a crowd of folks like that.' But then I told him it seemed like everything he'd done so far had turned out right no matter what everybody else had said at the time, that he always seemed to do the right thing. So I just didn't know what to advise him." There is a danger now that he will begin to entertain such notions about the genius of his instincts and perceptions—the final hubris of the demagogue.

At the same time, he seems now secretly to relish moving about among rumors of his own imminent martyrdom. For a long time, the only picture under the glass on Wallace's desk was a photograph taken of himself and President Kennedy, their arms around each other, when they met briefly at Huntsville before the University of Alabama crisis. When Kennedy was assassinated, according to a newsman close to Wallace, "it really bugged George. He sat there in his office and didn't move from in front of that television set through the whole thing. He kept wondering if he ought to go to the funeral, and he finally wound up flying to Washington to pay his respects to the family. But it kept bugging him. He started being conscious of the fact that he might go the same way." Now, he tells his friends, "If they gonna kill me, they gonna kill me." But it is not resignation; rather, it seems a kind of titillation at the prospect of assuming the ultimate heroic pose in not only his but the Southern sensibility: impalement, crucifixion.

He has come increasingly to crave the casual company of his old cronies—Ralph Adams, Oscar Harper, Glenn Curlee. When they are not available, he will seize upon anyone who is even remotely congenial and will listen to him. "He ain't gonna be alone," says Glenn Curlee. "He'll stay in that office till ten at night just to have folks around him to talk to. He ain't gonna be by himself till he dies, I reckon."

Not long after Lurleen's election, he kept a pair of out-of-state visitors in his office all through an afternoon and into dusk, with a hush gradually settling over the rest of the capitol, the coming of night outside marked merely by a subtle change in the light in the curtained room. Secretaries and aides looked in to tell him they were leaving for the day, but he barely glanced at them—he kept on talking to his visitors, occasionally standing to lift a silver water pitcher from a tray of glasses near him, gulping straight from the pitcher and wiping his mouth on his sleeve. About eight o'clock he said, "You fellas want to come and get a bite to eat with me?" Wrapping himself in his overcoat, he made a brief but clamorous stop in the bathroom just off his office, and then he and his two visitors stepped out into the sharp black winter night. "Let's go on down to Turk's," Wallace told his bodyguard. "I reckon he's still open." On the way, one of the visitors asked Wallace what he most wanted to do if he were elected President. "What would I do if I got elected? Goddamn, I haven't even thought about that. Wouldn't it be sumpum if I were to win this thing. . . ."

It was a bleak and dingily lit little café, nearly deserted, sitting in the somewhat seedier half of Montgomery's downtown, indistinguishable from the thousands of night diners one finds everywhere near bus stations and police stations. Wallace settled himself in a booth and ordered a hamburger steak, which, when it was presented to him, he promptly drowned in ketchup. The bodyguard sat by himself at a table over by the door, and when one of the visitors asked why the bodyguard was with them, Wallace muttered, "Don't worry, he's used to settin' alone." He quickly disposed of his steak and ordered coffee, which he drank with a spoon as he chatted on. "Yeah, when we went up to Washington for LBJ's inaugural parade, there were more folks to come by our booth out there along the street than came by the booth of any other governor. There was just a few at first, and then the folks really started swarmin' over when they saw everybody was shakin' hands with the bugguhman. A lot of folks found out I wasn't a bugguhman at all. I even had a request once from that Commie magazine out in California, *Ramparts*; they wanted to send somebody to see me. We told 'em no. They didn't want to write a story about anybody, they just wanted to be able to say they had interviewed that cat. . . ." While he was talking, a heavy man in a rayon jacket with a day's growth of beard on his sallow ashy face approached the booth and produced a "Wallace for President" bumper sticker, informing Wallace that orders for the stickers were coming in from all over the country to the newsstand he operated. Wallace, grinning and chewing on his napkin, fingered the sticker for a moment. It was black with red lettering, and Wallace chuckled, "You know, I just don't like anything that's got black in it." He took the bumper sticker anyway and told the man, "I'm gonna put it on my car. Might as well get this whole thing started, I guess."

He took his visitors on with him to the governor's mansion, sitting in the dark car talking to them for some twenty minutes. "No, I don't remember fightin' too much outside the ring. 'Bout the only time I guess I got in a fight was when I was in high school. I'd gone up to Birmingham for a boxin' tournament, and two or three of us were walking to the auditorium where we were gonna box that night when we saw two or three of these white boys pickin' on this little colored boy. We moved in. There was all kinda shovin' and pushin' and grabbin', and I sprained my hand. But we stopped them ruffians from pickin' on that li'l nigguh boy. I went on and boxed that night and broke my hand. I lost the fight to Aaron Franklin of Tuscaloosa. My thumb broke slap in two and my hand got as big as my head. They had to put it in a cast." He was waxing steadily warmer and more convivial. "Well, you boys come on in, heunh? It's a big ole house, but I'm livin' like I always have. I've always had about the same. I don't have any thousand-dollar chairs, but I don't feel sorry for myself."

The shelves in the downstairs rooms are spare of books, and those that are spotted around were mostly furnished by the state library. All the paintings on the walls are on loan from the state Archives and History Department.

Four years after the Wallaces moved in with only their clothes, the house still seemed as impersonal and anonymous as a hotel. Only in Wallace's bedroom were there signs of more than a tentative and fleeting occupancy: cigar boxes and humidors were scattered over tables and bureau tops and window ledges, and a stack of books sat on a table on Wallace's side of the bed—an odd assortment like the collection in his office: *Lee's Lieutenants* and *The Terrible Swift Sword, Vietnam Doctor,* something called *God and the Devil,* another tome entitled *As Lincoln Wanted It,* and a curious 1904 novel with yellowed crackly pages called *The Bondage of the Free,* which, according to its title page, is "a romance treating of the disenfranchisement of the Negro and including a scathing arraignment of the White House." For a long while there was also a crumpled-up "Wallace for President" bumper sticker on the bedside table. Hanging on the wall facing the bed, so that it is one of the first things Wallace saw when he sat up every morning, was a framed photograph of Wallace and President Johnson inscribed, "With warm regards, Lyndon B. Johnson," with Johnson looking down on Wallace and his huge hand engulfing Wallace's, Wallace himself looking away from the President with that faintly awkward and captured expression seen so often on the faces of those he clings to himself while not campaigning.

He sat in the back study downstairs with his visitors until almost midnight—his chair pulled over to the couch where they were sitting, his tiny feet propped up on the coffee table, and his hands shoved deep into his pockets, his coat tightly buttoned across his paunch, with ashes flaking over his lap from a cigarette pinched squintingly in the exact center of his mouth—and recounted with spasmodic, breathless, panting, delicious little snickers and sniggerings how during college and his Army service he had toyed with Yankees and innocent sophisticates by playing a dim-witted hillbilly. "We used to tell the girls in the sororities about how much whiskey we could drink, how we were just poor country folks. We took out these little girls from New Orleans once, and we had this pint jar filled with water with a corn-cob stopper we'd dipped in whiskey. We told 'em it was moonshine and let 'em smell the stopper. Then I turned the jar up and drank about half that water. It scared 'em to death. They couldn't get over how I could drink all that moonshine and still drive. When I was in the Army at Denver, I had this buddy from Mississippi, and we decided we'd give the girls out there some experience with some hillbillies. There was a bunch of girls workin' at the PX, and me and my buddy went in and asked 'em for a can of Brewton's snuff. They asked us what our fathers did, and I told 'em my daddy was in the penitentiary for makin' whiskey. They smiled and got all giggly—those gals had found 'em some real live hillbillies. I asked 'em, 'How'd you like to go sparkin'?' They agreed to go to a motion picture—a hundred thousand soldiers out there they wouldn't give a date to. They were so gullible. We walked in the theater, and I asked 'em, 'Where's the men's bathroom?' Like I couldn't read, you know. There was a Socialist League out there in Denver, had a girl with them named Kathryn Renfroe—a beautiful girl. She decided she'd make a study of us hillbillies. We let her study on us a little bit." He repeatedly tapped his cigarette in the general vicinity of an ashtray on the floor, a compulsive, quick, vigorous flicking, sometimes half-dislodging the coal so that sparks showered down over his coat when he stabbed it back in his mouth and he would have to pause for a moment of urgent slapping and whisking with one hand. "Those fellas in the barracks from New Yoke and Chicago, we'd been studyin' about the sun and heat and goin' up in airships, and these fellas were tryin' to tell me and my buddy how it was colder up on top of a mountain than in a valley. We'd say, 'Ain't the sun just a great big ball of fhar?' They'd say, 'Yes, but—' and we'd say, 'And the closer you get to a ball of fhar, the hotter it gets, ain't that right?' They'd get all mad and red in the face. 'Yes. I mean, no—' 'Don't tell me a mountain ain't closer to the sun than a valley,' I'd say. And they'd try to tell us about these elevated trains in Chicago, and we told 'em, 'Ain't no trains that run up over the ground. We ain't so country we don't know there ain't no trains runnin' along on tracks held up in the air with sticks. We ain't *that* country.' Man, their jewglur veins would pop out. They'd run out and get folks from Wyoming and Idaho and bring 'em in there to tell us about them trains. One fella told me, dammit, he was gonna send off and get a picture of those elevated trains to show me. I told him, 'Yeah. I know. A trick picture.' And they kept tryin' to explain to me about that sun business. A lot of those boys thought you were just ignorant 'cause you came from the South. Got to where they'd jump up outta their bunks every time me and this fella from Mississippi opened our mouths. All we had to do was just *start* to say something. We'd see how fast we could make a fella come up out of his bunk. 'By God, that ain't so!'—" He lowered his head and shook it like a baffled taunted bull, his arms waving, his fingers lashing. "They almost wanted to fight. Then, when I got that attack of meningitis and like to died, I heard folks talkin' about how meningitis could affect your mind. So after I got out, I'd pass these boys from New Yoke and Chicago in the hall, and 'bout the time I'd come up aside 'em, I'd do this little shuffle, you know, and kind of jerk my head at 'em. They'd jump clear over against the wall. We'd be eatin' in the dining hall, and I could feel them all watchin' me outta the corner of their eyes. So after a while I'd start talkin' crazy in a little low quiet voice, start sharpenin' this kitchen knife" —he made a slow steady motion like a barber stropping a razor "—and I'd tell 'em Roy Acuff was comin' to see me one of these nights. 'And if he don't come,' I'd say, 'I'm gonna come see a few of yawl when you're asleep.' I'd keep on sharpenin' that knife, lookin' at 'em, you know, and givin' a little jerk of my head ever once and a while—" He demonstrated, snapping his head sideways, like a Siamese dancer with a bad crick in the neck. "They'd give a little start, like somebody had goosed them under the table, but they'd keep on eatin'. Sometime, after we had all sat down at the table, I'd just start up singin' *Wabash Cannonball.* They'd wait a minute with their forks halfway to their mouths and stare at me, but I wouldn't look at any of 'em, I'd just rare back and cut loose with that *Wabash Cannonball,* so you could hear it all over the dining room. Then I'd stop and peer at them fellas down the table, all of 'em kinda leanin' over and lookin' at me, and I'd start sharpenin' that knife again and tell 'em, 'Ole Roy better get here tomorrow.' They finally hunted up the psychiatrist and told him about me. They had the guards watchin' me before long. The psychiatrist came down the hall one afternoon with one of those little rubber hammers, you know, that they use to tap you on the knee. He just walked real easy down the hall toward me, and then he kind of leaned against the wall and tapped that hammer in the palm of his hand and asked me, real casual-like, 'How you feelin'?' His voice was real light and high, you know—'How you feelin'? You havin' antagonisms?' So I told him"—Wallace ducked his head and whispered behind his hand—" 'Everything's fine, if Roy ever gets here.' He told me, 'Well, we put in a call for him, but—' I told him, 'Well, I sho appreciate that. You know, all these other fellas, they against me. They're crazy.' He said, 'Unh-hunh,' and nodded and walked off. After a while, I got to thinkin' about it, and realized things were gettin' a little serious. Folks were puttin' chairs up against their doors. I finally went to the psychiatrist and told him I'd just been foolin'. He just nodded and said, 'Unh-hunh' again, and then asked me if I was havin' antagonisms. It took me some time to convince him I'd just been playin'. . . ."

Close to midnight, the visitors finally stood and told Wallace they would have to be on their way. He instantly bobbed to his feet, and clinging to their hands, inquired, "Where yawl goin' now?" They told him they might drop by the Diplomat Lounge—a motel nightclub whose steam-driven go-go girls make it a favorite watering hole for state politicians in town. "Oh, yeah?" he said. He paused, taking a few shallow quick puffs on his cigarette, as if briefly pondering something, and then seemed to dismiss it, and escorted his visitors on through the kitchen to the back screen door. In the yard outside, several bodyguards were standing under a tree, smoking. "I'll have Dothard run yawl out there," Wallace said, and then added, almost furtively, "Whatcha gonna be doin' at the Diplomat?" His visitors told him they were only going to have a few drinks. "Well," said Wallace as he saw them out the door, "yawl look over that stuff out there, heunh?"

Of all the people in Wallace's life, probably no one, not even his grandfather, was closer to him than Billy Watson. As Watson explained it, "I was about fifteen years older than he was, and I guess he kinda looked on me as his father. He usually took my advice, and I could always talk to him and calm him down. . . ."

Watson always regarded Wallace with a gruff irreverence. One of Wallace's old friends from Barbour County remembers, "Billy always looked kinda like a political boss, big and right sporty, and whenever salesmen came through Clayton they'd usually come up to Billy to get information. Not long after George was elected judge, a salesman came through asking Billy where he could find Judge Wallace. 'I'm the man you want to see,' Billy told him. 'I run this place.' So the salesman showed Watson his wares, and Watson told him, 'You go on over there to the courthouse and tell Wallace that Watson said to buy this desk here. . . .' While George was judge, he stipulated there would be no smoking, no standing, and no hats worn in his courtroom, and he told the sheriff to enforce the rules. Well, Watson strolled into the back of the courtroom one morning with a bright yellow straw hat on his head, a cigarette in his mouth, and leaned up against the wall there in the back and stared at Wallace. Wallace called the sheriff and instructed him to inform Watson that he was no better than anyone else and that he'd be cited for contempt if he didn't take off his hat, put out his cigarette, and sit down. The sheriff walked to the back and told Watson what Wallace had said. Watson thought a moment, puffing on his cigarette, and then said, 'Sheriff, you go up there and tell that little pissant I put him in office and I can take him out. . . ." Watson's manner remained the same throughout Wallace's political ascent. During the second campaign for governor, Watson and Ralph Adams were riding in the car with Wallace, and the two of them, having bought beer at one stop, tossed the cans out the window on down the road. "Goddamn, Watson," piped Wallace, "here I am runnin' for guvnuh with yawl ridin' around with me breakin' the law, throwin' beer cans out of windows and everything—" Watson replied, "Wallace, the law's made for niggers and white trash, it's not made for me and Adams."

They both seemed to derive enormous amusement from each other. At a Junior Miss pageant once in Mobile, Wallace was forging his way through the contestants and their families exuberantly shaking hands, when Watson tapped him on the shoulder and said, "There's somebody here I want you to meet." Wallace whirled around, declares Watson, "and shook hands with a damn mannequin. That's right—a mannequin. And he kept right on goin'. I don't think he even noticed."

They frequently went to conventions together. On one trip, said Watson, "The best-lookin' woman on the plane was sitting right next to me, beside the window, and Wallace was sitting across the aisle from me. She didn't have her seat belt fastened, so I started fumbling around in her lap trying to help her. When George glanced over and saw what I was doing, he started kicking my leg, sniggering and carrying on and kicking my leg. 'Watson, stop 'at, Watson, watch out, here comes the stewardess. . . .' He came by to get me once to go to an American Legion convention with him—said, 'Watson, they gonna have all these pretty young gals there, you better come along.' He finally talked me into it, and turned out wadn't nothing but old bags wanting to grab you all the time. He sho thought that was funny."

On a rainy Sunday afternoon a few weeks after Lurleen's

election, Watson sat in the front parlor of his home in Clayton and recollected, "Back yonder when he wasn't getting along so good financially, he'd come into my store downtown and pick up something and walk out with it, and I'd call to him, 'Wallace, aren't you gettin' a little heavy on the books?' He'd answer back over his shoulder as he went out the door, 'I'm gonna pay you, Watson, don't worry.' And he would: two dollars at a time. Just enough to be better than one dollar a time. He owed as high as three hundred dollars, four hundred dollars sometimes. 'Course, he was such a bigshot and all, he was judge and everything then. . . ." Watson, wearing a brown sweater and a tie fastened to his shirt with a large gold Wallace tieclasp, was quiet for a long moment, his watery eyes blinking and his hands folded fragilely across his stomach as he reposed, barely seeming to breathe, in the solitary immediate glow of a table lamp. The French windows in the room were full of a watery gray light, dimly streaming, the afternoon dissolving away in them, while a coal-grate fire rustled in the stillness. " 'Course," Watson finally resumed, "he got so many votes in these last two campaigns, it's kinda gone to his head. He thinks everybody likes him now, and he don't even remember how many votes he got in some counties. Used to, he could tell you how many he got in every single county. Now, he's started forgetting exactly how many votes he got in each place. . . . He says he's gonna come back here one of these days to live, but I tell him, 'Naw, George, you too used to being around people now, traveling around. You too used to seeing things. You know you never gonna come back to Barbour County to live ever again." It was as if Watson—old now, his health fading, left behind in Clayton—was vaguely jealous of Wallace's extensions, felt that he had slipped irrevocably beyond him now and longed somehow to snatch him back to the old familiar custodial or at least paternal relationship. Watson grinned palely. "He called me up the other day after he'd been on this TV program, and he wanted to know if I had seen the show. I told him, no, I hadn't. So he hung up. . . ."

Nevertheless, Watson was on hand when Wallace returned to Clayton a few weeks later for the lighting of the Christmas tree on the square. The December night had a warm, damp flush in it, and as the townsfolk began to arrive from their supper tables and gather in front of the courthouse, a high-school band from nearby Eufala bleated out a thin and uncertainly assembled *Noel.* Then a piano whanged out *O Come, All Ye Faithful,* the choir on the courthouse steps following in sweet tinny unison. During the prayer by Wallace's hometown minister, a baby began crying at the far edge of the crowd in the hush, and a hound flowed between people's legs with silent and purposeful intentness, nose to the pavement. The mayor opened the cozy little holiday celebration with a dolorous sentence, "We'd ask you to look this evening to the gloom of Moscow—" the everlasting morbid preoccupation with the Red Peril touching even this gentle Christmastime occasion on this little town square in southern Alabama. Wallace's own speech was an improbable alchemistic blend of religion and patriotism. While he delivered it, his bodyguards stood at the edge of the courthouse porch scanning the crowd, indulging in what has become for them the fine are of female-thigh-spotting, perfected over countless public speeches over the years. "See sittin' over there next to that fella in the—no, on the right of him, that other one; now watch her, she's about to cross her legs like she did a minute ago. . . ." After Wallace's address, one of the town's rare Republicans stood at the microphone with his wife, the two of them dressed in maroon choir robes, and "rendered a vocal duet" while the antic shadows of children who were dancing before spotlights in the grass swooped and wheeled across the white brick wall of a store beside the courthouse. Wallace's smallest daughter, Lee, concluded the service with a speech of her own which began, "We are the littlest angel . . ." the rest being pretty much unintelligible, and after she finished, the mayor rushed up to the mike and boomed, "Now, how about that! Lee did a wonderful job, didn't she?"

After the lighting of the tree at the square, there was a private dinner at the newly remodeled Victorian home of a young Clayton lawyer and his bright young wife—a young man highly regarded by the elders for the restraint he had shown in not running for the legislature yet. "He's just too young," said one lady, "and I thought he was so smart to wait. He has plenty of time to get up there. Next time would be so much better." The gathering was small; reports rippled among the guests of people who had been offended because they hadn't been invited. Watson arrived and began grumbling because no liquor was being served. Looking at the host, Watson murmured, "He's a good Methodist, he don't believe in it." The house was soon filled with quiet, gay voices. The men were mostly standing, the women mostly sitting. Then Wallace appeared, announcing with a snicker as soon as he came through the door, "Watson's mad because we let that Republican get up there and sing," and Watson replied impassively, "That's right, we shouldn't of even let his ass come." Wallace went on off into the crowd, still saying "Yeah, Watson's mad now. We let that Republican get up there and sing, and he's mad now."

It was an ample buffet: turkey and ham and dressing and green-bean casserole and various garnishments, arrayed on the dining-room table in the soft glow of candles. Wallace, his plate filled, somehow strayed, slipped out of his usual pocket of attention, and sat for a few moments alone at one end of the table in the living room, stranded before the white expanse of tablecloth under the bright ceiling lights—looking momentarily like a small boy, forsaken, vulnerable, strangely touching. The first person to sit down at the table seemed to startle and bewilder him briefly, but then, as others began settling around him, he revived. "What I'm gonna do, I'm gonna run on a platform where I'll move the nation's capital out of all that muggin' and so on, move it to some place safer nearer the center of the country. And I'm gonna stop *all* foreign aid for a year, and tell those countries tradin' with our enemies they ain't gettin' theirs back until they stop it. Even

Britain, yessuh." He went on to speculate, "Let me tell you, you let a couple million people get out of work in this country, you gonna have a little ole revolution on your hands. There's gonna be some burnin' and shootin' sho nuff. Some folks gonna get killed. Only reason that hadn't happened before now is the high rate of employment in the country. . . ." He then received, by asking for it directly, a common assent around the table that there had never been a governor in Alabama's history popular enough when his term was over to be reelected. He was asked if his wife's candidacy, then, had not violated the spirit if not the letter of the constitution, and he snapped, "There's one thing more powerful than the constitution, than any constitution, and that's the will of the people. What is a constitution anyway? They're the products of the people, the people are the first source of power, and the people can abolish a constitution if they want to. . . ." His heat and aggressiveness in answering the question caused a slight flutter of nervousness around the table. The host began talking about football, and Wallace fell to eating in silence for a moment, listening to him.

It was, on the whole, a nice evening, a nice supper, and just as soon as everyone had finished eating, they rose from the table, got their wraps, found their mates, and departed. The house seemed to empty just as abruptly as it had filled. They had come to eat supper there, and as soon as they got that done, they left.

Wallace drove to Watson's house to watch a high-school football playoff game on Watson's color television in a tiny back sitting room with green-painted board walls and starched white organdy curtains. Wallace watched the game in silence for a while, smoking a cigar in the lamplight, his legs crossed and one small foot in its little-boy's shoe twitching. Presently he noticed Watson's dog idly chewing at something on the rug, and he turned to Watson. "Say, you got fleas in the house, Watson?" He sniggered, but Watson kept silent, watching the television. It seemed almost as if he were sulking

—that faint helpless peevishness of old men who have lost the skill for aggressive banter, who find themselves betrayed by the almost feminine sensitivity of their childhood again, but who can not bring themselves to show it in the company of younger men who do not realize yet the change in them. During an airline commercial, Watson ventured an observation about a stewardess shown smartly clacking down a terminal corridor, "She's fixin' to go fly now." Wallace said, "Say what, Watson?" Watson, his voice a little flatter, repeated it. Wallace asked him again, "Say she's fixin' to do what, Watson?" This time Watson didn't answer; he merely gazed fixedly at the television. Wallace tried once more, "Say you reckon she's fixin' to go fly now, Watson?" and then leaned back and gave a brief snuffling snicker. After a moment he began kneading his side with his fist. "Believe I got a little indigestion." Watson's wife—a small, taut, brisk, assertive woman with a gruffly kind face resembling the Indian on the old nickel, who seems also to take a certain private delight in Wallace, her eyes twinkling when Watson the Sunday before had recounted how Wallace once broke his arm "over some woman"—went next door and shortly returned, the screen slapping behind her, with a bottle of Pepto-Bismol. Wallace sat up and leaned slightly forward in his chair, his hands lying passively and submissively on his knees, and, his face uplifted like a newly hatched bird, dutifully took one large pink spoonful, which left a trace of a crescent at the edge of his mouth, he wiping it off with the back of his hand as he leaned back again.

A month or so later Watson appeared in the basement cafeteria of the state capitol, where Wallace was sitting with a table of out-of-state visitors. With slow, fragile care, he made his way down the cafeteria line, Oscar Harper at his elbow to steady him, passing right by Wallace's table. Wallace didn't speak to him; Watson didn't speak to Wallace. He emerged from the line with only a glass of water and sat down with Harper at a table only a few feet away from Wallace. While Wallace talked to the visitors, Watson watched him vacantly, one hand wrapped around his glass of water, lifting it only now and then for a careful token sip. But Wallace, when he was through with the visitors, did not turn to greet him, though Watson's rheumy blank eyes stayed on him; he merely waved at a few people in the back of the room and was gone. Watson sat for a little longer at the table with his glass of water. Then Harper helped him get to his feet, and they made their way up to Wallace's reception room. Watson settled himself in a chair along a far wall, quiet and inert, with a dim little smile on his face, looking superfluous and isolated as people milled thickly past him. Wallace appeared in the room once but then vanished back into his office, apparently without having noticed Watson. After about an hour, Watson left.

Only a few weeks later, flying north on one of the first forays of his 1967 presidential mission, Wallace abruptly announced to an Alabama reporter sitting across from him on the plane, "Billy's in the hospital, you know." He gazed out his porthole a moment, his cigar stuffed in the side of his mouth, his hands folded between his knees. "Yeah, Billy's dyin'. He's about to die. . . ."

Lurleen sat up with him through his last night. While Wallace was greeting visitors from far corners of the country at the capitol the next morning, he received the call that Watson was dead. He stayed on at the capitol until late that afternoon, though one of his secretaries reported, "He's feelin' pretty low today. He just doesn't feel like doin' much. It hit him mighty hard. . . ."

Not long after Watson's death, it was discovered that Lurleen had suffered a recurrence of cancer. The word around the capitol and in the editorial offices of the Montgomery newspapers was ominous. Wallace, talking to a reporter in his office a few days after the news was announced, admitted, "Yeah, well, we were awfully shocked." His face had a grave and almost reverent expression. "It a terrible thing, sho is. She's mighty sick, hurtin' awful bad and all. . . ." With cigar in hand, he leaned back in his chair and described an earlier operation in which "she slung a blood clot. It was just a little ole bittly thing, 'bout like 'at"—his forefinger measured a small distance on his thumb—"but it got hung up in her heart here." He pulled back his coat and began tapping, thunking his torso. "We had to bring her to Montgomery unconscious on a stretcher. She's sho had a lot of sickness in her life." He described a gallstone operation she had also survived. "They had to cut her whole side here—" He pulled his coat even farther back, hitching it all the way back to his hip pocket, and twisting in his seat, traced a long arc along his shirt. When the reporter suggested that the spring and fall campaigns had been rather vigorous for someone who had just undergone massive surgery, Wallace quickly protested, " 'Course, that wadn't what caused this thing now, you know. The doctors said it was a *tonic* for her. Said it was *salubrious*. Actually, it was a lot more rigorous on me than it was on her. But before we ever got into it, I went out to the mansion one night and told her, 'Honey, I don't think we should do it,' and she said, 'Well, I'll be mighty disappointed if we don't.' And anyway, we had already gone so far and all. . . . But it didn't cause this thing now. 'Course, me, I just don't want to ever believe anything's there until I have to, but—uh, from what the doctors say—I mean, it sounds awfully serious. 'Course, Lurleen would want me to continue in this movement no matter what. That's always been her feeling all through. Oh, yes, I don't have any doubt she'd want me to go on. But I don't know. We'll just have to wait and see. . . ."

He got up from behind his desk and leaned on the conference table, pausing a moment to refire his cigar. "You shoulda seen that crowd we got up in Ohio the other day. Whole football field, and they were stretched back all the way past the goal lines. I'm tellin' you, folks in this country—now, all the others, they think they gonna switch around now and start talkin' like I do. You know, I was kinda a pathfinder. Well, I'm not gonna let 'em switch. All I got to do is tell the folks,

'Here's a fella who said this back yonder, and now he's sayin' this because he sees that's how the people feel. Well, I'm tired of all this switchin' back and forth, I'm tired of all these folks who're one thing today and sumpum else tomorrow!' Let 'em try it. I hope they do." He was now as animated and ferocious as ever, one hand chopping in his open palm, light glinting off the lens of his glasses as he chewed savagely on his cigar. "That Ronald Reagan, he ain't nothin' but a sissy actor anyway. They say he's got a computer out there and all these punch cards, and he don't make a move unless that computer and them punch cards say move. Every statement, every single thing he does, they run it through that computer first. He just don't have much on the ball, you know." He measured a space between his thumb and forefinger about the size of a B-B, daintily rolling his two fingers. "I watched him at that governors conference up at the White House awhile back. He was at a table with Volpe, Herndon, a few others. Everybody else was talkin', but he didn't say a thing. He just sat there watchin' everybody else talk. He didn't know what was comin' off. I sat there and watched him real close for a long time, I just wanted to see what he was like. He ain't much. Hell, I'd make him get off all those generalities of his, I'd make him come down to specifics. I'd make him say whether he was gonna turn folks' schools back to them or not. Johnson, now, he's the kind you could really be for. If he just believed some different things, boy, you could really be for him." He swung his fist emphatically.

Before the reporter left, Wallace touched his arm and said, "Right here, wait a minute, I want to show you—" and plucked from his shirt pocket that fat, well-thumbed pack-rat's wad of odd cards he usually carries. "I got folks in here all the way from Montana, Ohio, New York, writing me. I mean local officials, too." He shuffled through the pack a moment, as if to make sure no one had gotten lost. "Yessuh. Oregon, Idaho, Missouri, Texas, Michigan, Wisconsin—Iowa, Indiana—New Hampshire." He cradled the cards in one palm and extended it slightly. "I got lots of folks in there. . . ."

Three months after Lurleen's inauguration—on a bleary wet morning in late April—George set out on an expedition into New York, Pennsylvania, Ohio, and Indiana, beginning his great national adventure. He was somewhat grave and subdued when he boarded the plane and did not wander from his seat much during the flight. Occasionally he would stroll down the aisle to the restroom in the back, winking at the newsmen he passed and proposing, with a rather extravagant sense of his own displacement, "I'm gonna unbalance the plane here. . . ." If caught somewhere in the aisle during moments of bumpiness, he would scuttle back up front to his seat, clap his seatbelt together, and hang on with his hands gripping the armrests like two small claws, looking steadily out the window even while someone was talking to him.

There was a brief refueling stop in Greensboro, N.C.—the weather was still drizzling and messy, and reporters huddled in the small terminal building, eating cheese crackers and drinking Cokes, as Wallace, wearing a black raincoat and flourishing a White Owl cigar with a well-gnawed plastic filter, chatted happily with airport employees. "Yeah, I was through this country back yonder before the war, sellin' magazines. Yeah, I love North Carolina. . . ." He was swigging a Coke himself as he talked, tilting it up high and quick, one elbow leaning on a counter. He motioned toward the reporters gathered around him and told the airport employees, "See all these fellas? We got the national press with us today—they came along on a distortion mission." His face remained bland as the reporters laughed. "Well, fellas," he said, "we gonna give you a good show, I hope."

He arrived in Syracuse late in the afternoon, and at twilight his cavalcade left his motel and journeyed to the Syracuse University campus, pulling up before a fraternity house where Wallace was to eat supper before his address in the Syracuse Coliseum. Students were gathered along the sidewalk outside, some of them attired in sheets. They hooted as Wallace's party made its way through them. Forging up the steps, Wallace glanced back cheerfully at the reporters and cameras tumbling up after him, vibrant with that same buoyant schoolyard spirit of adventure with which he had promised them, back in the airport in North Carolina, "Well, fellas, we gonna give you a good show"—it was now as if he were asking them, "Well, fellas, how's this so far?"

But once inside the fraternity house—old and dim and sparsely furnished with genteel but slightly sleazy Victorian furniture—Wallace seemed a bit uncomfortable among the clean-faced, dapper students with their Kennedy coiffures. (He asked a reporter once, in a low, earnest voice, "How come you reckon Bobby Kennedy wants to wear all that hair? I mean, I been wondering about it. You reckon that's why he's so big with all these college kids?" And unconsciously, he touched his own limp, oil-combed streaks with the heel of his hand, as if he were fleetingly considering whether he himself could muster a mane.) Running his finger around under his collar, he kept calling Glenn Curlee and Seymore Trammell to his side, addressing most of his remarks to them while the fraternity members crowded around him. "See those folks out there, Curlee?" he said. "I didn't know they had the Klan up here, did you?" When sirens pulsed faintly outside, he stepped over to a window, stooped, and peered out. Turning back to the room, he said, "What we done started out there?" and gave his short little gasping boyish snigger.

Later in the trip, his plane passed over Washington, and the pilot called back to the passengers over the intercom, "As you look over the real estate, you might see something you'd like around 1968." There were cheers and clapping. Wallace stopped in Richmond for a hotel session with his campaign workers there, and wound up spending the night. A cabdriver taking him to his plane the next morning chirped, "Now, I want to see you in D.C. in 1968." Wallace said nothing then, but later, standing on the airport runway waiting for the plane to be fueled, he took a reporter aside and remarked in a low and earnest voice, "You hear what that cabdriver said? Lot of folks, you know, tell you stuff like that and have faith in you, but—" He was quite grave, quite pensive. "You know, that's an awfully big job, being President. You really wonder what you'd do. I don't think any man's big enough for that job until he gets there." The congenial remarks of cabdrivers inspire him now to such lonely speculation, and the increasingly palpable possibility that he might, by some convolution of fate, wind up in the White House seems to leave him thoughtful and even vaguely philosophical. It's as if he were already trying to evolve, within himself, a profundity and soberness to meet the image he entertains of the office he has decided he wants most.

He made one stop in Pittsburgh to address an evening convocation of "The Amen Club," a fraternal assembly of Pittsburgh's industrial and social barons—described by one member of the group as "local products of excellent vintage." The club represented the missing element so far in the coalition he hopes to strike, and as he drove into Pittsburgh from the airport to solicit their goodwill, the element of the coalition which is already his—workmen along the side of the road—saluted him as he went by.

Outside the hotel where he was to speak, a massive stream of pickets circled the block in the cold late afternoon, marching with the quiet, steady deliberation of the children of Israel tramping around the walls of Jericho. A five-o'clock proliferation of junior executives was caught up in the current; faces studiously empty, they gingerly but briskly threaded their way with their attaché cases through the flow of Negroes, priests, young white students. Waiters came out from one of the hotel's restaurants to watch, standing on the sidewalk in eighteenth-century livery, white napkins across their arms. The land now seems full of such curious scenes. The quiet shuffling march continued on through dusk.

Wallace, meanwhile, was up on the sixteenth floor of the hotel at a cocktail reception given by the club's executive board. His bodyguards, standing along the hall outside the suite, watched the tuxedoed club members file past with their expensive wives, and those coming out, leaving the reception a little flushed and unsteady—one lady, being irritably hustled back down the hall by her husband, grazing the wall at times and then wobbily negotiating the turn at the end of the corridor. "I guess this is the upper crust," one bodyguard loudly observed to his companion. "You know what the upper crust is?" As another couple tottered past, his companion called back, "No, what's the upper crust?" The first bodyguard announced, "A few crumbs held together by a lot of dough."

At the party inside, Wallace too was wearing a tuxedo, but his temporary transition from old Folsom Populist to ally of the Big Mules was not quite total—the glass in his hand contained Royal Crown Cola. While the people there did not seem quite to know what to make of him, they were undeniably beguiled and even delighted by him (and later, during his speech, cheered him boisterously). One of the club's officers wandered over and, introducing himself, happened to mention that he had been born in Germany. Wallace quickly said, "Yeah, you know they maneuvered us into fighting the enemies of communism back during World War II. The Germans and the Japanese were a mighty brave people, they were mighty brave soldiers. All these organizations that are against our being in Vietnam now, some of them are the same organizations that were all for war back there in 1940. It just so happens that the war today involves Communists. I'm sorry it was necessary for us to fight against those anti-Communist nations. I thought that back then. Hell, we should have been in those trenches with the Germans, with yawl, fightin' them Bolsheviks. . . ."

Presently Wallace went to a window to see if he could see the marchers on the sidewalk down below. The windows were partly opened, letting in a chill breeze from the cold twilight outside, with the long white smokelike curtains tossing, milling, with a kind of soundless soft demented fitfulness, along the walls—and suddenly it seemed a certain wildness, a certain madness, was blowing through the room in the lamplight, marked only by the ghostly thrashing of the curtains. Like figures in some dream, the heavy, graying, flushed, bluff millionaires in their tuxedoes moved quietly about with their glimmering groomed ladies, their conversation muted, unfinished glasses of Scotch and bourbon standing on the marble tables, amber and pale gold and glinting delicately under the lamps. No sound whatever rose up from the march still circling below in the gathering night—but there was an uncanny sense of forboding in that room, and Wallace, still at the window, all alone, leaning forward slightly with his Royal Crown Cola in his hand, was engulfed in the blowing curtains. They flowed and seethed around him in the night wind, and he seemed lost, captured in their midst, a vague, dark, dwarfish figure absorbed in the single changeless meditation of his life since its beginning, thinking, *Well, now, I got something. But maybe I can get more. Maybe I can do a little better, maybe I am going to be able to do even better. . . .*